WOMEN AND
TEXAS HISTORY

Women and Texas History

SELECTED ESSAYS

Edited by Fane Downs and
Nancy Baker Jones

with a keynote essay
by Elizabeth Fox-Genovese

Texas State Historical Association
Austin

Copyright © 1993 by the Texas State Historical Association. All rights
reserved. Printed in the United States of America.

Library of Congress Cataloging-in-Publication Data

Women and Texas History : selected essays / edited by Fane Downs and
    Nancy Baker Jones : with a keynote essay by Elizabeth Fox-Genovese.
        p.   cm.
    Includes bibliographical references
    ISBN 0-87611-119-3 (acid-free paper)
    1. Women—Texas—Biography. 2. Women—Texas—History.
    3. Texas—History. 1. Downs, Fane. 11. Jones, Nancy Baker. 111. Title:
    Women and Texas history.
    HQ1438.T4W62   1993
    305.4´09764—dc20   93-7188
                                                                  CIP

10 9 8 7 6 5 4 3 2 1

Published by the Texas State Historical Association in Cooperation with the
Center for Studies in Texas History at the University of Texas at Austin.

The paper used in this book meets the minimum requirements of the
American National Standard for Permanence of Paper for Printed Library
Materials, Z39.48-1984.

Front cover: Minnie Fisher Cunningham (right), and two unidentified
supporters, during her 1926 campaign for the United States Senate.
Photograph courtesy Austin History Center, Austin Public Library.
Photo ID # PICA 16817. Design by David Timmons.

Contents

Foreword

NANCY BAKER JONES*

THE PUBLICATION HERE OF THIRTEEN PAPERS originally presented in October 1990 at "Women and Texas History: A Conference" is the happy result of the collaboration by many people over a number of years to turn a hunch into a reality. The hunch was that there were enough people trained to research and write about the history of women in Texas that one might accurately state that a scholarly field of inquiry existed, and that enough research had been conducted to support an entire conference of papers devoted to the field.

"Women and Texas History" would not have been possible in 1980. That it became a reality in 1990 is the result, in large part, of a remarkable decade of renewed interest in—one might call it devotion to—recovering the history of women from obscurity.

The work accomplished during this decade was built on a long, if spotty, connection between women and Texas history. The first known history of Texas in English was written by a woman, Mary Austin Holley, and published in 1836. By 1888 Anna Pennybacker's history of the state had become a standard text. The study of women in Texas history, however, began more recently. Annie Doom Pickrell's 1929 book, *Pioneer Women of Texas*, was one of the earliest attempts to record women's experiences. Scholars conducted research about women in Texas as early as the 1930s, and in 1936 the Women's Collection at Texas Woman's University, the nation's oldest and largest resource collection about women, was created. Not until the 1980s, however, did a statewide surge of interest occur.

---

* Nancy Baker Jones earned the Ph.D. in American civilization from the University of Texas at Austin. In her capacity as associate editor for the *Handbook of Texas* revision project, she coordinated the conference "Women and Texas History."

In 1980 the Texas Women's History Project of the Texas Foundation for Women's Resources, with assistance from the Texas Committee for the Humanities, among others, published the *Texas Women's History Project Bibliography*, a description of primary and secondary sources on women in Texas. In 1981, using the resources uncovered in the bibliography, the Texas Women's History Project, with assistance from the TCH, the RGK Foundation, and others, produced a project unique not only in the state, but also in the nation, by creating a landmark exhibit entitled Texas Women: A Celebration of History. The exhibit traveled throughout the state to wide acclaim and is now on permanent display at TWU. As another result of this large undertaking, an archive about Texas women is now part of TWU's Woman's Collection.

In 1984 the Texas Foundation for Women's Resources, TWU, and the Temple family (through the Katherine Sage Temple Fellowship) funded a research assistantship in women's history for the Texas State Historical Association's mammoth *Handbook of Texas* revision project, which enabled the Association to conduct much-needed research into the lives of women for the *Handbook*, the standard reference work in Texas history. In 1985 the TSHA cosponsored a conference, "Women and Texas," designed to identify and discuss topics about women that should be covered in the revised *Handbook*. In 1987, in response to congressional designation of March as National Women's History Month, the Texas Historical Commission began to coordinate the celebration of the event throughout Texas.

The 1980s also witnessed the emergence of a growing number of graduate students and new Ph.D.s in Texas women's history, and the consequent publication of more scholarly articles, monographs, and books than had previously been possible—enough, for example, to warrant a revision of the *Texas Women's History Project Bibliography* by TWU. Interest in women's history in general had grown so significantly that by 1986 historian Fane Downs could write that the study of the history of women had evolved "from the historiographical stage of 'oh look! oh look!' which catalogued women and affirmed their presence, to works of synthesis and interpretation, which are attempting to describe the larger issues in women's history. . . ."[1] And by 1988

---

[1] Fane Downs, "'Tryels and Trubbles': Women in Early Nineteenth-Century Texas," *Southwestern Historical Quarterly*, XC (July, 1986), 36.

the field in Texas could support the compilation of Ann Patton Malone's bibliographic essay "Women in Texas History," which appeared in *A Guide to the History of Texas* (Greenwood Press).

As a result of this progress, it could be said that there existed a scholarly field identifiable as the history of women in Texas, in which important new work was being conducted; that there was an identifiable group of practitioners in this field; and that an audience existed for their work.

In March 1989, during the annual meeting of the TSHA in blizzard-struck Lubbock, McMurry University's Fane Downs, University of Texas graduate student Judith McArthur, TWU's Dorothy DeMoss, and I discussed this growth, as did many others in the late 1980s. We noted what others were saying as well: that there finally existed a body of knowledge great enough to support an entire conference on the history of women in Texas.

Armed with these convictions and the support of TSHA director Ron Tyler, I became the coordinator of the effort to transform resolve into reality. The result was "Women and Texas History," held from October 4 to October 6, 1990.

This conference was both a culmination and a beginning, during which we could at once look back at the growth that had made it possible and ahead to the discoveries that the work of its participants portended. In addition to the obvious purpose of sharing what we knew, its goals were to acknowledge the progress of the past, discuss the impact of recent scholarship on the historical study of women in Texas, and generate a research agenda.

Twelve cosponsors made the conference possible by donating time, staff, equipment, and financial support. An advisory committee of thirteen provided advice, labor, and ceaseless commitment. A planning group of five and a volunteer support staff of ten anticipated and then transformed the innumerable details of conference planning and production into a virtually flawless three-day performance.

The conference consisted of thirty-two sessions; a book exhibit; an evening panel in which journalist Liz Carpenter, former gubernatorial candidate Sissy Farenthold, presidential campaign advisor Hazel Obey, and Houston mayor Kathy Whitmire discussed Texas women and politics; a reception at the LBJ Library and Museum that included excerpts from the musical based on Ruthe Winegarten's book, *I Am Annie Mae*; a reception for and opening of the exhibit Mosaic: Women's

History Resources at the Eugene C. Barker Texas History Center at the University of Texas at Austin; and a keynote address by historian Elizabeth Fox-Genovese. In addition, the results of a preconference survey of the holdings in Texas libraries and archives related to women were published as *Women and Texas History: An Archival Bibliography*. The Barker Texas History Center now houses the conference archives.

A sample of some of the best papers presented at that conference is published here, to offer what can only be, within the limits of a book, a suggestion of the breadth and depth of research in progress in the 1990s.

The research results presented here and at "Women and Texas History" reveal that the field is not only healthy but also vigorous; we are growing a significant number of historians in the state who want to study the state. Despite these positive signs, we are still merely scratching the surface of what is left to know about women in Texas.

Perhaps because Texas is one of the most mythologized states in the nation, and because its mythology has so often stood for the nation itself, the weight of Texas history is overwhelming at times. Like the Sitting Ghost described by Maxine Hong Kingston, it is always with us, awake or asleep, and remains a tough customer with which to wrestle. When we consider the history of women, we begin to come to terms with our own Sitting Ghost. When we incorporate ideas and issues about gender and move the study of women from periphery to center, we rearrange old stories and redefine familiar terms.

Toward that end, the work presented here is a beginning.

Introduction

FANE DOWNS*

THE HISTORY OF PUBLISHING is marked by hundreds of publications claiming to be "milestones"; without embarrassment, we claim that designation for this collection. These essays are the best works of scholarship submitted for publication from "Women and Texas History: A Conference," itself a milestone, described in the Foreword. They represent the emerging maturity of the field of Texas women's history; moreover, they add significantly to our knowledge of the complex and diverse history of Texas.

Women's historical scholarship has moved through several stages: "compensatory history," which catalogued "worthy" women and affirmed their presence; "contribution history," which described women's participation in various political and social movements; "feminist history," which documented women's oppression by male institutions and values (patriarchy); and "less value-laden monographs," which illuminate the experiences of individuals or groups.[1] The present volume is representative of the latter stage. As Elizabeth Fox-Genovese observes in her essay in this volume, women's history must depend on the accumulation of information about women. As scholars produce

---

* Fane Downs is associate pastor of First Presbyterian Church in Dallas and an advisory editor for women's history for the *Handbook of Texas* revision project. She is a former chair of the Department of History at McMurry University and a former member of the Executive Council of the Texas State Historical Association and the Editorial Advisory Board of the *Southwestern Historical Quarterly*. She holds B.A., M.A., and Ph.D. degrees from Texas Tech University and an M.Div. degree from the Austin Presbyterian Theological Seminary.

[1] Gerda Lerner, "Placing Women in History: Definitions and Challenges," *Feminist Studies*, III (Fall, 1975), 5–7; Ann Patton Malone, "Women in Texas History," *A Guide to the History of Texas,* eds. Light Cummins and Alvin Baily, Jr. (New York: Greenwood Press, 1988), 123–125.

more works of this nature and quality, others will have the data and foundation on which to advance synthesis and interpretation, not just for women's history, but for *human* history.

Taken together, the papers presented at "Women and Texas History" comprise a body of scholarship which might be considered *sui generis*, a genre unto itself. These presentations included "standard" works of history using the discipline and method of historical inquiry; reflections on women's experiences using women's literature; case studies using an individual or group as paradigm; illustrated lectures showing women's contributions to the arts or other fields; analyses of literature by or about women; panel discussions on Texas women's experiences in politics and war; and descriptions of the material culture of women's lives. Thus the conference generated more than history papers; it advanced women's studies, historical and otherwise. More than one scholar has observed that women's historical study must be multicultural and interdisciplinary, using the insights of anthropology, linguistics, archeology, psychoanalytic theory, and sociology.[2] While many of the presentations of the genre of women's studies were compelling and illuminating, we decided that this anthology should represent the best of the historical scholarship from the conference. Thus these essays are works of history, with the exception of the final four, two of which are works of literary history, one a work of theory, and the final one a challenge for the future.

This might appear to be an idiosyncratic collection. Since these essays were originally presented in conference sessions, each of which had a particular goal and emphasis, they do not naturally form a coherent collection; that is, they do not address a particular issue, group, period, or movement. These papers document, illuminate, and analyze the history of some Texas women; therein lies their coherence.

We have made no attempt to provide a balanced collection, either chronologically or ethnically. Most of these papers deal with the twentieth century, a fact that should not be disturbing, because works on the nineteenth century have long been more numerous. The greater concern is that most of the articles are about white middle-class

---

[2] Carol Ruth Berkin, "Clio in Search of Her Daughters/Women in Search of Their Past." *Liberal Education,* LXXI (Fall, 1985), 208; Joan Jensen and Darlis Miller, "The Gentle Tamers Revisited: New Approaches to the History of Women in the American West," *Pacific Historical Review,* II (May, 1980), 212–213.

women. The dominance of Anglo women's history probably has to do with the plethora of available sources and the fact that most graduate students and university professors are Anglos. An active group of scholars is researching Hispanic women's history; we have included two of their works. For reasons not entirely clear, no corresponding group of scholars is working in either Native American or African American Texas women's history, both of which beg for thoughtful treatment.[3] Taken together and individually, these works show that scholars and teachers ignore the experiences of Texas women at their peril. Without intelligent and sensitive integration of the history of *all* Texans in Texas history, our understanding of the past is at best incomplete and at worst distorted.

In "Texas Women and the Writing of Women's History," which also served as the conference's keynote address, Elizabeth Fox-Genovese reflects on the writing of women's history in the intellectual environment of competing theoretical constructs of that history. She notes that some historians emphasize the diversity of women's experiences and thereby avoid generalizations entirely, while others identify, document, and describe a "women's culture" common to all women. She suggests that both these positions "inadvertently end in a denial of history" and argues that "History constitutes the essence of women's experience and values, the very structure of their lives and their minds." She calls for a "massive increase" in knowledge about women's historical experience because no theory of women's history can be sustained without adequate data as to similarities and differences between women. She concludes:

> But until we can write with confidence of the experience of different groups of women, we will not be able to reason intelligently about women's participation. Until we can write with confidence of the experience of different groups of women, we will not even know how the groups should be defined. Somewhere between the multiplicity of individual women

---

[3] For a survey of Texas women's historiography see Fane Downs, "Texas Women: History at the Edges," in *Texas Through Time: Evolving Interpretations,* eds. Walter Buenger and Robert A. Calvert (College Station: Texas A&M University Press, 1991), 81–101; Malone, "Women in Texas History," 123–136.

and the culture of all women lies the history of how women have historically related to each other, to men, and to the American past.

Barbara J. Rozek, in "The Entry of Mexican Women into Urban-Based Industries: The Experience in Texas During the Twentieth Century," surveys the literature of labor history, government documents, and specialized studies to show that Mexicanas have participated significantly in the urban workforce in this century. Rozek makes no attempt to differentiate between more numerous legal immigrants and undocumented workers; for the purposes of her study this distinction is not particularly helpful. Because of the concentration of Hispanic population and availability of sources, Rozek focuses on San Antonio, Corpus Christi, and El Paso. This paper raises interesting questions about patterns of Texas women's work and differences among these patterns for Hispanic, African American, and Anglo women of various classes.

Another work dealing with Hispanic women surveys much of the same period, but with a very different focus. Elizabeth C. Ramírez treats the importance of actresses and theatrical companies in her "Hispanic and Mexican American Women on the Texas Stage, 1875–1990." She documents the careers of two actresses, Concepción Hernandez and Virginia Fábregas, as representative of the Mexican theater, which contributed so much to the cultural life of Hispanic Texans in the late nineteenth and early twentieth centuries. She observes that Mexican American theater declined during the Depression and experienced a renaissance in the 1960s as part of the Chicano movement for cultural identity and civil rights. This paper, along with the author's other published works, invites inquiry about the power of popular entertainment in shaping cultural identity and, in the case of Mexican Texans, reinforcing ties to their Mexican heritage.

That this anthology contains four papers on women during the Progressive era should not be surprising, as women's participation in this complex political and social movement is relatively obvious and easy to document. "Pauline Periwinkle: Prodding Dallas into the Progressive Era," by Jacquelyn McElhaney, describes the two-decade career of the first woman's editor of the Dallas *Morning News.* Sara Isadore Miner adopted her *nom de plume* in 1896 and soon became well-known in Dallas and around the state. She publicized and promoted a variety of women's and children's reform efforts on the Progressive agenda, including education, juvenile courts, libraries, and pure food laws. She did more than write; she helped organize several influential local and statewide women's organizations. Her career as a "mainstream" or moderate Progressive suggests consideration of the limits of that reform agenda.

Two papers deal with women's leadership of and participation in political crusades of the day. Judith N. McArthur on child labor and Paul Lucko on prison reform document women's effectiveness in state politics. In "Saving the Children: The Women's Crusade Against Child Labor, 1902–1918," McArthur traces the efforts of the Texas Federation of Women's Clubs and the Texas Congress of Mothers in child labor reform. Working alone and in coalition with other organizations, women learned and practiced effective organizational and persuasive techniques, ultimately adding their newly-won power at the ballot box to accomplish their legislative goal of enforceable child labor laws.

Paul Lucko describes the ambitious and ultimately unsuccessful drive for prison reform in "The 'Next "Big Job"': Women Prison Reformers in Texas, 1918–1930." The Texas Federation of Women's Clubs, the Texas League of Women Voters, and the Committee on Prisons and Prison Reform were three of the organizations which attempted to educate and influence legislation to reform Texas's brutal prison system by instituting a more humane, rehabilitative penology. Lucko sees women's involvement in this movement as illustrative of social feminism, which sought to transfer women's moral guardianship from the home to society at large. Child labor reform likewise derived from social feminism. Using these two articles, readers might consider the strengths and weaknesses of social feminism as a reform ideology.

The most influential Texas woman educator of the early twentieth century was Annie Webb Blanton, elected state superintendent of public instruction in 1918 and a long-time professor at the University of Texas. Debbie Cottrell chronicles Blanton's contributions to the professionalization of teaching in "Professional, Feminine, and Feminist: Annie Webb Blanton and the Founding of Delta Kappa Gamma." Believing that "merit, not gender, should determine leadership roles in education, that cooperative efforts could be very positive, and that the potential of feminine leadership was unlimited," Blanton founded Delta Kappa Gamma in 1929 and served as its moving spirit until her death in 1945. Cottrell concludes that Blanton's leadership and non-doctrinaire agenda shaped the organization and accounted for its success in advancing professionalism among Texas women teachers. This essay might raise comparisons with other individual and cooperative efforts to improve the working conditions and status of women. Moreover, the story of Delta Kappa Gamma invites discussion of the role of moderate reform organizations, including women's clubs, in bringing about social change.

Patricia Cunningham describes an episode of women's political activity in "Bonnet in the Ring: Minnie Fisher Cunningham's Campaign for Governor of Texas in 1944." Because of the conservative Democrats' plan to oppose Franklin Roosevelt's reelection in 1944, "Minnie Fish," as she was known, ran against Gov. Coke Stevenson in that year's Democratic primary. Although her candidacy posed no serious threat to Stevenson, she succeeded in raising the issue of party loyalty to the national candidate. Traditional women's issues seem to have counted for little in the election; Minnie Fish's campaign reflects intraparty squabbles rather than feminist consciousness. The question arises whether this election had any significance in the political history of Texas women.

Two papers consider the impact of the ideology of domesticity on Texas women. Diana Davids Oliens, in "Domesticity and the Texas Oil Fields: Dimensions of Women's Experience, 1920–1950," argues that in oil field communities, both the "ragtowns" and camps, women accepted traditional roles and in fact "oil field living conditions, for the most part apparently incompatible with conventional domesticity, ended in enhancing its appeal and its strength." The paper invites comparison to the experiences of women in other environments inhospitable to domesticity.

Sylvia Hunt, on the other hand, finds that teachers were not particularly bound by the ideology of domesticity. Hunt analyzes one of the time-honored myths of nineteenth-century women—that schoolteachers were single and quit teaching when they married—and finds it wanting. In "To Wed and To Teach: The Myth of the Single Teacher," she identifies forty-nine married teachers for whom she found personal history documents (memoirs, reminiscences, and poetry) in the period from about 1850 through 1930. She asked of her sources, "Did Texas teachers uphold, exemplify, or believe in domesticity, and was separate sphere a reality for them?" Hunt concludes that the Texas educators of her sample were not captives of domesticity; they taught to supplement family income and successfully combined career and family. Hunt's work suggests a closer resemblance between contemporary women educators and the pioneers in the field than we might have imagined. This paper continues the conversation on the usefulness of the domesticity paradigm as descriptive and prescriptive for women's experiences.

That women and men are influenced by the popular press is axiomatic; how the portrayals of women in that press shape reality is more elusive. Sherilyn Brandenstein analyzes the images of women in a Texas African American magazine of the early 1950s in "*Sepia Record* as a Forum for Negotiating Women's Roles." *Sepia Record* presented a variety of models for black women——career, civic leadership, marriage——consistent with those presented in magazines aimed at white readers of the 1950s. Questions of the influence of popular culture in shaping popular attitudes spring to mind; in today's mass culture the role of the regional press may be minimal.

Lou Rodenberger considers another facet of cultural history in "Women as Literary Participants in Contemporary Events." Beginning with Mary Austin Holley, she surveys women writers of fiction and nonfiction, and concludes that "These writers represent the world from a female perspective, often reexamining myths of the past, many of which glorify masculine accomplishment and ignore feminine contributions in both frontier and modern society." Students of women's history will ask how works of fiction by women illuminate the historical experience of Texas women, and how these works might be used as *historical* sources.

Sylvia Grider continues this discussion on the desirability of conversation between the disciplines of literature and history in "Women's Literature and History in Texas: A Confluence of Traditions." She suggests that our ignorance of the literary history of Texas women has seriously limited our understanding of the roles and experiences of Texas women, and urges that we "eschew the artificial distinctions of academe" in order to recover a fuller knowledge of the past. Grider and Rodenberger remind us that women's studies must be conducted across conventional disciplinary boundaries. "Women and Texas History" demonstrated the value of this interdisciplinary enterprise.

In the Afterword, Elizabeth York Enstam raises provocative questions about the direction of future research in Texas women's history, noting the need for monographs and syntheses, cross-cultural and comparative studies, and statistical and gender analyses. Competent, imaginative, and committed scholars statewide are engaged in the significant work of recovering women's history; they are accumulating, analyzing, and interpreting information in order that human history may be more fully comprehended. It is for this purpose that "Women and Texas History: A Conference" was conducted, and to this end that this volume is dedicated.

WOMEN AND
TEXAS HISTORY

Texas Women and the Writing of Women's History

ELIZABETH FOX-GENOVESE[*]

LOOKING AT THE RICHNESS AND VARIETY of Texas women's experience, it is tempting to say that all the world is Texas. Yet, notwithstanding the extraordinary flowering of women's history during the past three decades, the history of Texas women remains comparatively unexplored. Happily, some important recent dissertations, like the papers in this volume, are beginning to fill the gaps. And as new work begins to appear, it is becoming clearer than ever that any attempt to write Texas women's history necessarily intersects with the most pressing issues of theory and method in women's history in general.

As a growing body of work in women's history has taken shape, the attention of scholars has increasingly moved from the accumulation of (previously neglected) information to the consideration of theory. It has become a cheerful commonplace that we have transcended our own recent naive projects to recover women worthies and to restore women to the existing (male) models of history, primarily understood as the history of political power. Women's history, many proudly proclaim, has its own logic and dynamic, its own "dialectic," which challenges the most entrenched assumptions about how history should be written and interpreted. Thus, for growing numbers of scholars, women's history has become feminist history, although differences about the meaning of "feminist" persist.

* Elizabeth Fox-Genovese teaches history at Emory University, where she is the
Eleonore Raoul Professor of the Humanities. Her most recent books include *Within
the Plantation Household: Black and White Women of the Old South* (1988) and *Feminism
Without Illusions: A Critique of Individualism* (1991).

This extraordinary transformation has occurred as women's historians, in step with a variety of other critics of Western culture and its fundamental presuppositions, have discovered pluralism, diversity, and multiculturalism. Having begun with the assumption that the recovery of women's experience required the restoration of woman to man's self serving accounts, women's historians are now acknowledging that any simple model of woman itself denies the complexity of the experience of women in all their diversity. Gender, race, and class have, in the process, emerged as the signposts of any women's history that claims to attend to the differences among women.

The discovery of diversity has, in some respects, moved women's history in healthy new directions. No longer is it safe to assume that the experience and values of white, middle-class, normally northeastern women are an acceptable proxy for the experience and values of women of different classes, races, and ethnicities throughout the country, much less the world. It is no longer even safe to assume that the ideology of separate spheres, which had long been taken to articulate the experience and values of white, middle-class women, faithfully captured the reality of any women's lives. Many, perhaps most, American women never enjoyed the luxury of remaining at home to raise their children amidst sparkling cleanliness and an ample store of provisions. With a few privileged exceptions, American women have known not leisure, but long hours, days, and lives of strenuous labor. As slaves, sharecroppers, migrant farm laborers, factory workers, domestic servants, laundresses, and even teachers, librarians, nurses, and clerical workers, most American women have combined their domestic responsibilities with labor outside the home. And many of those who have been able to remain within their homes have combined domestic labor with labor for others than their own families, taking in laundry, piecework, or boarders.

As with experience, so with values. It is now widely recognized that not all women internalized the values of the cult of domesticity with its implicit white, middle-class biases. Working-class women frequently defied even the most benevolent and well-intentioned efforts to remake them closer to the middle-class norm of propriety. African American women, in slavery times and since, have learned to practice a form of dissemblance that masks their innermost thoughts and feelings, protecting them from potentially demeaning or destructive white incursions on their privacy. Women of all ethnic groups have frequently cherished and preserved the values and traditions of their own people. Today, attention to the differences among women by race and class is rivaling attention to the similarities that unite women as members of a sex.

However welcome, this new attention to the diversity of women's experience and values harbors some potential dangers. For in essential respects, attention to diversity has simply discredited the universal claims of previous theories without reconstructing them. Confusion has resulted. Many of those who most enthusiastically champion the claims of diversity have, in effect, openly repudiated the ideal of a general theory, or even a general narrative, of women's history. At least for the moment, it is said, we can at best hope to know only "partial truths."[1] Since our primary responsibility remains to recapture the voices of discrete women and groups of women with as much immediacy as possible, we should do better to avoid generalizations entirely. Yet others, who are no less interested in the differences among women, cling to some notion of a women's culture—to the sense that women are, in important and historically significant respects, different from men. The problems with both positions are legion, but do usefully highlight the most pressing challenges in women's history.

Significantly, those who focus most explicitly on the irreducible diversity of women's experience are also focusing on women's subjective assessment of their own experience. Such scholars, especially when explicitly influenced by postmodernist literary theory, are quick to dismiss any attempt to generalize beyond women's immediate experience as an illegitimate exercise of power. For, they reason, the generalizations that our culture has produced have invariably promoted binary oppositions, such as black and white, male and female, self and other, that have legitimated women's oppression. Freedom for women, in this view, must begin with an attack on these most crippling and deeply entrenched forms of oppression. Women, above all, should understand that the time-honored opposition between male and female has regularly resulted in women's being cast as "the other," and

[1] Jacqueline Dowd Hall, "Partial Truths: Writing Southern Women's History," in *Southern Women: Histories and Identities,* eds. Virginia Bernhard, Betty Brandon, Elizabeth Fox-Genovese, and Theda Purdue (Columbia: University of Missouri Press, 1992).

in the denial of women's independent claims to subjective authority.[2] And if the problem is acute for women in general, how much more acute must it be for women of disadvantaged class, ethnic, and racial groups. Would it not be ultimately presumptuous for white women to impose their own categories upon the experience of African American women, who have suffered unique forms of oppression from which white women have frequently benefitted? If African American women's experience and values have demonstrably not conformed to white, middle-class paradigms, must we not reject those paradigms and, more ominously, reject any paradigms that do not emerge directly from African American women's own lives?[3] The same questions, obviously, arise for Native American, Hispanic American, and other women.

This position, at the extreme, holds that the only possible legitimate knowledge must arise from unmediated consideration of the specific features of specific women's lives. In this respect, the position privileges the social and cultural history of everyday life, which alone can hope to capture ordinary women's experience—their actual behavior and, to the extent we can determine, their actual thoughts. Pursuit of these goals has resulted in newly rich and evocative pictures of the lives of people whom historians had too frequently dismissed as lost to historical knowledge. But such history, notwithstanding its considerable appeal and value, does make generalization, not to mention narrative or a sense of historical development, notoriously difficult.

Postmodernists would counter that their purpose is precisely to complicate, deconstruct, and even sabotage the possibility of a comprehensive narrative. Arguing that power resides in language, they insist upon the necessity for each to reclaim her own voice and, above all, to refuse being encoded in the dehumanizing language of others. The very idea of difference, notably the difference between male and female, they proclaim, must be recognized as an artifact of language,

---

[2] The best known formulation of the problem of women as other to male consciousness is Simone de Beauvoir, *The Second Sex,* trans. H. M. Parshley (New York: Knopf, 1952). For a thoughtful recent discussion of the problem, see Nancy K. Miller, *Subject to Change: Reading Feminist Writing* (New York: Columbia University Press, 1988).

[3] See, for example, Patricia Hill Collins, *Black Feminist Thought: Knowledge, Consciousness, and the Politics of Empowerment* (London: HarperCollinsAcademic, 1990).

as a manifestation of illegitimate power.[4] Men, who have monopolized cultural as well as social, political, and economic power, have cast women as different in order to subordinate them. So long as difference persists, so will hierarchy.

Difference in this sense apparently means binary difference, or the notion of difference in the abstract. For those who most enthusiastically repudiate difference as an organizational paradigm no less enthusiastically celebrate the multiplicity of differences that distinguish all human beings from one another. It takes little imagination to grasp that the concept of difference, specifically sexual difference, has served to disadvantage women. But that very difference which has so effectively helped to limit women to subordinate roles and ambitions also affords the primary justification for women's history as a subject. How, in other words, does the abolition of difference as an overarching category not result in the abolition of women as an historical subject? The emphasis on diversity at the expense of difference would seem to open the possibility that more divides women among themselves than divides women as a group from men. Under these conditions, the common experience and values of those individuals who are able to bear and suckle children evaporates under the weight of the various aspects of their condition that divide them.

To be sure, some of those who emphasize the social, economic, and political divisions among women nonetheless remain loyal to the notion of a women's culture. As the psychologist Carol Tavris has argued, the notion of a distinct, much less uniform women's culture raises other problems.[5] Any notion of a women's culture must rest on some assumptions about experiences or values that women share independent of class, race, ethnicity, nationality, or historical epoch. Intuitively most of us accept that women, or most women, do in fact tend to behave more like each other than like men. But most of our intuitions derive from our own experience. The women we know tend to behave more like each other than like the men we know: women are more likely to prefer shopping to a boxing match; or, in the more popular example, women are more likely to cherish children and hate war.

[4] See, for example, Joan Wallach Scott, *Gender and the Politics of History* (New York: Columbia University Press, 1988).

[5] Carol Tavris, *The Mismeasure of Woman* (New York: Simon and Schuster, 1992).

Cross-cultural comparisons have, nonetheless, taught us to be suspicious of easy generalizations on these matters. There are cultures in which men delight in shopping. The association of women with the nurture of children and men with warfare is more pervasive across cultural boundaries, but even that association may be modified in particular cases. Should we therefore conclude that all differences between women and men result from culture and are, accordingly, subject to modification or even abolition? If not, should we assume that physiological characteristics, which women do share across cultural boundaries, determine women's culture? And, if so, does history not offer grim lessons? How, in short, do women's historians propose to separate women's culture from women's subordination?

The dilemma starkly exposes the greatest challenges that confront women's history as a coherent discipline. In effect, as theories, both the postmodernist and the women's culture positions inadvertently end in a denial of history. In practice, however, both can be understood to underscore the centrality of history to any serious interpretation of women's experience and values. As Ramon Saldivar has argued for the Chicano narrative, *"history* is the subtext we must recover because history itself is the subject of its discourse."[6] In the case of women, to cast history simply as the background or context of experience and values is to radically divorce women from history rather than understand that, divorced from history, women become either biological beings or abstractions. History constitutes the essence of women's experience and values, the very structure of their lives and their minds. This insistence upon the historical contingency of all human experience should not be taken as a repudiation of physiological differences between women and men or even of abiding values; it does, however, focus attention upon the social consequences that different peoples in different eras attribute to those differences, and to the salient political, social, economic, and cultural relations within which they are elaborated.

There is no easy way of writing a satisfying women's history and no ready-made grand theory to encompass the entire corpus of women's experience. Any adequate theory of women's history must simultaneously attend to similarity and difference, always asking similar to

---

[6] Ramon Saldivar, *Chicano Narrative: The Dialectics of Difference* (Madison: University of Wisconsin Press, 1990), 5.

and different from whom, and in which ways. The task is all the more complicated since all of us, willy-nilly, write from within the Western tradition in general and the American tradition in particular. However much we may protest the injustices, oppressions, and exclusions of that tradition, our deepest assumptions, beginning with our attitudes towards women, derive from it. Thus even if we successfully expose the operation of the ideology of separate spheres as misleading and oppressive, every time we speak of women as a group—or as individuals— we betray our complicity with it.

The complicity is not, in my judgment, especially dangerous, provided we retain our critical vigilance. For the very tradition that so successfully propounded the universal ideology of spheres also propounded the universal ideology of individual freedom and individual rights that has proven our strongest basis for criticizing it. It is, in short, our history, the fabric of our identity. No determination to repudiate difference as inherently hierarchical can eradicate a past in which most women experienced their difference from men as central to their sense of self and to the rhythm of their lives. No enthusiasm for women's culture can transform a past in which most women found their difference from women of other groups as important as their difference from the men of their own group.

In this perspective, the most important task that women's historians confront remains a vast increase in information about women. Perhaps the most daunting feature of women's history lies in the interrelated tasks of distinguishing among and appropriately grouping together women. For most of human history and, more to the point, most of American history (however defined), most women have spent most, if not all, of their lives as daughters, sisters, wives, and mothers within rural households. From the perspective of the women themselves those lives have been as varied as the human species. The food women have eaten, the shelters in which they have lived, the languages in which they have spoken, the ways in which they have worshipped, the clothing they have worn, the goods they have been able to barter or to trade, the ways in which they have raised their children, and their relations with their kin and neighbors. Like snowflakes, no two women are alike. But then neither are any two men.

From the perspective of generalization or analysis, however, the similarities are no less decisive. Throughout rural societies, women's lives have followed the patterns of the seasons and their own life-cycles just as they have fallen into predictable patterns of work. Throughout rural societies, women have traditionally assumed responsibility for the preservation and preparation of food, the rearing of children, the making and repairing of clothing, the care of the sick and the elderly, the carrying of water, and frequently the smoothing and sustaining of relations among generations and kin. It would be possible, with no gross violations of accuracy, to use the same words to describe the lives of rural women in early modern Europe, precolonial West Africa, the antebellum South, and late-nineteenth-century Texas. With no greater violation of accuracy it is also possible to use the same words to describe the lives of African slave women, Hispanic women, Anglo women, Italian peasant women, Serbian Jewish women, and Swedish women in Minnesota.

Somewhere between the diversity and the similarity lies the substance of women's history. To make sense of that history we need, in the first instance, enough information to generalize. For example, we learn little, if anything, from repeated pronouncements about the oppression of African American and Hispanic women in Texas. We learn a great deal from Julia Kirk Blackwelder's discussion of the employment experience of different groups of women in San Antonio during the depression.[7] Suddenly, oppression acquires a specific content: as the economy worsened, women of socially advantaged ethnic groups displaced those less advantaged. Anglo women took jobs previously held by Hispanic women who, in turn, took jobs previously held by African American women, who were pushed back into domestic service and laundry work, if they could secure employment at all. To talk seriously of the experience of different groups of women, we need innumerable other studies of this kind. Otherwise we will only be able to persist in our tiresome groaning about oppression or to relate detailed personal stories of individual women, which may or may not be typical of anything.

We also need enough knowledge to assign women to the appropriate groups. We now have ample evidence that, in general, Hispanic women fared less well in Texas than Anglo women. But that generalization obscures significant variations. As Jane Dysart has demon-

[7] Julia Kirk Blackwelder, *Women of the Depression: Caste and Culture in San Antonio, 1929–1939* (College Station: Texas A&M University Press, 1984).

strated, during the early American period some Hispanic women in San Antonio married well-placed Anglo men.[8] As a rule, those who did tended to be of light skin and of politically powerful, wealthy families. These women brought their husbands important political connections and frequently substantial economic assets as well, largely because Mexican law prescribed equal inheritance for daughters and sons. As married women, moreover, they continued to participate in many aspects of their own culture. Even when their husbands were Protestant, they raised their children as Catholics, maintained strong ties to their own kin, and gave their children Hispanic *compadres,* or godparents. In the end, however, they paid what many might view as a stiff price for their membership in the political and social elite, for most of their children came to identify with their fathers' culture. And, tellingly, Anglo and Hispanic culture, notwithstanding pronounced differences in customs and manners, shared a strong emphasis on male authority and values. It is surely significant that during the same period San Antonio witnessed almost no marriages between Anglo women and Hispanic men.

Studies such as this one provide the essential building blocks for any comprehensive theory of women's history. The experience of these women encapsulates in microcosm some of the many complexities that bedevil women's history. Not unlike the free women of color of the Gulf Coast during the antebellum period, they rank as an anomalous minority. Yet their anomalous status illuminates much about women's roles in mediating between racial and ethnic groups, just as it illuminates the dangers in arbitrarily codifying women by their gender, race, or ethnicity with no attention to class. It is hard to imagine that these women did not employ Hispanic servants, and hard to imagine that they did not regard those servants as socially inferior to themselves. To be sure, they may have employed Irish or German servants, or even owned African American slaves. Whatever the case, as upper-class women they surely did have servants and surely did, in part, define themselves in relation to them.

How they defined themselves in relation to their husbands and redefined themselves through their husbands in relation to the ethnic community into which they were born constitutes a separate and no

---

[8] Jane Dysart, "Mexican Women in San Antonio, 1830–1860: The Assimilation Process," *Western Historical Quarterly,* XVII (Oct., 1986), 365–376.

less interesting problem. From an anthropological perspective, they can easily be recognized as objects of exchange, pawns in the consolidation of a new elite. Whether they saw themselves in that way remains unknown. There is no evidence to suggest that the free women of color of the Gulf Coast identified with slave women, and abundant evidence to suggest that they fiercely defended their free status. However deep these Hispanic women's religious, cultural, and personal ties to their communities of origin, their marriages represented a limited kind of upward mobility and perhaps the realization of personal ambition. Since we know that men may experience the conflicting claims of ambition and cultural roots, on what grounds can we assume that women may not?

My plea for a massive increase in what we know about women should not be confused with a commitment to Rankean empiricism. To the contrary, information about women's lives and values is always more difficult to come by than comparable information for men. Thus even the questions and hypotheses that lead us to seek certain kinds of information represent preliminary contributions to any serious theory. More important, however, only substantial and comparable data about the specific features of women's lives could permit us to ascertain how to appreciate women's historical roles. We have, for example, become reasonably sophisticated in our understanding that, at least from the early decades of the nineteenth century in the United States, women have tended to become church members in larger numbers than men. Elizabeth Turner, drawing upon the work of Ann Boylan, has even argued convincingly that the kinds of churches to which women belonged tended to play a role in their attitudes towards benevolence and reform. But, to take only the case of Texas, we know a good deal less about the social attitudes and activities of practicing Catholic women than their Protestant counterparts.

The issues are not trivial. There is good reason to believe that church membership, and beyond it faith, simultaneously empowered and restricted women. Church activities introduced women to new roles and responsibilities outside their immediate families, frequently encouraged them in a sense of social responsibility, and frequently encouraged them to work with other women. Faith frequently endowed women with a sense of righteousness and of serving a cause with which man had no right to interfere. But the ministers, priests, and texts of faith normally reminded women of their own secondary status and not infrequently imbued them with the conviction of their own sinfulness. If faith, in other words, offered many women a purpose and even a structure for their self-representations, it also constantly reminded them that they were women in a world dominated by men.[9] But in communities rent by social inequality and ethnic difference, the observance of faith in specific denominations probably did not lead all women into the belief that they shared a culture with all other women. Indeed, to the extent that women have experienced religion as central to their culture, many may have drawn upon it to define and differentiate other groups of women.[10]

That class position, like ethnicity and race, divided women no longer comes as a surprise to scholars in women's history. And many have taken the recognition of these divisions as evidence that the general ideologies of womanhood do not apply to the experiences of all women. The concept of separate spheres, as most of us now acknowledge, was a myth. We have further learned that innumerable women rejected the myth as an adequate description of their own lives and, especially, their ambitions. But as Megan Seaholm has demonstrated, elite women devised ways of turning the myth to their advantage. Seaholm's elegant dissertation on club women in Texas argues, among other things, that Texas club women drew upon the myth of separate spheres to claim aspects of the public sphere as peculiarly and appropriately their own.[11] In so doing, they were simultaneously strengthening their own roles as women within the white elite and drawing attention to the needs of other women who were divided from them by class, ethnicity, and race. We do not need, naively and inaccurately, to assume that such women felt bound in sisterhood to women less fortunate than they in order to accept that they did believe

[9] See Elizabeth Fox-Genovese, "Religion in the Lives of the Slaveholding Women of the Antebellum South," in *That Gentle Strength: Historical Perspectives on Women in Christianity,* eds. Lynda L. Coon, Katherine J. Haldane, and Elisabeth W. Sommer (Charlottesville: University Press of Virginia, 1990), and Jean E. Friedman, *The Enclosed Garden: Women and Community in the Evangelical South, 1830–1900* (Chapel Hill: University of North Carolina Press, 1985).

[10] Elizabeth Fox-Genovese, *Within the Plantation Household: Black and White Women of the Old South* (Chapel Hill: University of North Carolina Press, 1988).

[11] Megan Seaholm, "Earnest Women: The White Women's Club Movement in Progressive Era Texas, 1880–1920" (Ph.D. diss., Rice University, 1988).

that women's position in society required active defense and even improvement. Nor do we need, just as naively and inaccurately, to believe that less fortunate women were deluded by the invocation of women's sphere into believing that privileged women fully understood or defended their needs. But we might begin by acknowledging that women of very different conditions could, for their own reasons, draw upon an ideology of separate spheres to pursue specific, and frequently divergent, goals.

In this perspective we can, again, recognize Texas as all the world. For the extraordinary complexity of Texas, with its multiple nationalities, its slaveholding, farming, ranching, and urbanizing sectors, its religious and cultural diversity, and its indomitable sense of its own destiny and power, offers a microcosm of the complexity of the United States as a whole. If we can begin to understand the place of women in the Texas which has recently given us Ann Richards, Sarah Weddington, Barbara Jordan, and Sissy Farenthold, we might begin to piece together a theory adequate to understanding the history of women in the United States and the world.

In the end, any theory of women's history depends upon our ability to accumulate information that permits us to identify the similarities and differences in women's lives. In this quest, no presuppositions will serve. Women have always shared much as women; women have always been divided by much as historical, which is to say social and political, beings. The history of men, as written by men, cannot be dismissed as alien to women's experience and values, for women have always participated in it. But until we can write with confidence of the experience of different groups of women, we will not be able to reason intelligently about women's participation. Until we can write with confidence of the experience of different groups of women, we will not even know how the groups should be defined. Somewhere between the multiplicity of individual women and the culture of all women lies the history of how women have historically related to each other, to men, and to the American past.

The Entry of Mexican Women into Urban Based Industries:

Experiences in Texas During the Twentieth Century

BARBARA J. ROZEK*

THE DOMINANT THEME IN LABOR HISTORY is that of the strong, virile male worker on a farm or in an urban factory. Labor history has frequently ignored the unorganized (non-unionized) worker, has often not noticed the female worker, and has routinely discounted the uniqueness of the labor experience for Mexicans in the United States. This paper attempts to help remedy these omissions as it focuses on the shift during the twentieth century of female Mexican workers in Texas from rural agricultural employment to urban based industrial employment. During this ninety-year time span, varying terminology has been used to identify the person of Mexican descent whose primary language is Spanish. While Chicana may have been the preferred term during the 1960s when discussing politically assertive women, the most appropriate term to cover the entire twentieth century is Mexicana or Mexican American. I make no attempt to distinguish legal immigrants from Mexico, living and working in Texas, from undocumented workers. It should be pointed out, however, that the majority of Mexicans in Texas fit the first category.

* Barbara J. Rozek is a doctoral candidate studying Southern history at Rice University. Her research interests include immigration into Texas since 1865. She received a B.A. degree from Valparaiso University in 1967 and an M.A. degree from Southern Methodist University in 1986 and has taught American history at the high school and community college levels.

The belief that Mexicans have only recently left the agricultural work force and moved to the cities is inaccurate. Research documents Mexicana participation in urban based industries since the 1930s. A minor theme, recurring throughout this research on working women, is the sense of women as a subset of a whole. It has been commonly assumed that they do not stand on their own but rather labor as part of a family unit. Their experiences are overlooked or downplayed because of this preconception, both by the women themselves and by observers.[1] Since the women are often not viewed as complete and discrete entities apart from their families or husbands, trying to weave the fabric of their story often becomes an effort at pulling threads out of the general Mexican male-focused historical records. Since solid primary historical resources on the Mexican population are few in number, the problem becomes doubly difficult. This paper endeavors to weave such a story through a chronological portrayal of Mexican women's participation in the Texas labor market.

Historians face a multitude of problems in identifying the exact degree of participation of women in the work force. Many questions are left unanswered. Did women work full-time or part-time, and what number of hours helps render precisely that designation? When women worked outside the home, were they adding to the family income or serving as the primary wage earner? How do we deal with the lack of consistent terms to identify the general Spanish-speaking population through such sources as the census records? And how can we compare one decade to another when the terminology varies and seems imprecise?[2] The careful work of several authors suggests that we

[1] The following sources contained little or no information on the Mexicana in the labor force, despite their titles: Joseph A. Hill, *Women in Gainful Occupations, 1870 to 1920: A Study of the Trend of Recent Changes . . .* (Westport, Conn.: Greenwood Press, 1978); John Chala Elac, *The Employment of Mexican Workers in U.S. Agriculture, 1900–1960: A Binational Economic Analysis* (San Francisco: R and E Research Associates, 1972); Charles Carr Winn, "Mexican-Americans in the Texas Labor Movement" (Ph.D. diss. Texas Christian University, 1972); and Roden Fuller, "Occupations of the Mexican Born Population of Texas, New Mexico, and Arizona, 1900–1920," *Journal of the American Statistical Association*, XXIII (Mar., 1928), 64–67. In 1934 Emory S. Bogardus wrote, "We may now consider briefly the labor conditions of Mexican girls and women." He then wrote six short paragraphs identifying females in citrus packing, walnut picking, domestic service, and clerking. Emory S. Bogardus, *The Mexican in the United States* (Los Angeles: University of Southern California Press, 1934), 43.

[2] Lyle Saunders wrote in 1949 that "The United States Census has never done

need to be cautious.[3] In discussing Mexican women in the urban labor markets of Texas, a variety of experiences appear. Documents dealing with San Antonio, which sustains the largest Spanish-speaking population in Texas, provide the bulk of the historical sources that identify and describe the urban labor force. Some sources recording the experiences of Mexicanas in El Paso and Corpus Christi supplement that primary material.

Victor Clark's classic work documents the way many women from Mexico gained entry into Texas during the first decade of the twentieth century. He suggests that the majority of Mexicans were transient laborers first "pulled" into this country through the railway lines which offered work opportunities.[4] A common pattern evolved. Men came first by themselves. finding work plentiful, they then returned to Mexico and brought their entire family to the United States. Clark quotes a railroad official to document this experience.

> Ten years ago our Mexican immigrants were chiefly men. It was rare to see a woman among those who came through here for any distance down the line. About 1900, men who had been in the United States and returned to Mexico began to bring back their families with them. Usually they were also accompanied by a number of single men, or married men without their families, who had never before been in this country. Most of the men who had families with them did not go back the following season, but the men without their families did, and some of them in turn came back the next

a satisfactory job is [*sic*] isolating data concerning Spanish-name people." His work struggles with the kinds of questions we are asking today. Lyle Saunders, *The Spanish-Speaking Population of Texas* (Austin: University of Texas Press, 1949; reprinted in Lyle Saunders et al., *The Mexican Experience in Texas* [New York: Arno Press, 1976]).

[3] For example, Mario Garcia, using the manuscript census of 1900, interprets statistics from El Paso to suggest that "almost one fifth (17.11 percent) of Mexican households contained a working woman." He cautions the reader to put this in the appropriate context, pointing out emphatically that in "no case in the sample did a woman with an employed husband have a job." Mario Garcia, *Desert Immigrants: The Mexicans of El Paso, 1880–1920* (New Haven: Yale University Press, 1981), 75. More detailed analysis is necessary to refine the interpretive meaning from the statistics.

[4] Victor Clark, *Mexican Labor in the United States,* Department of Commerce and Labor, Bureau of Labor Bulletin no. 78 (1908; reprint, New York: Arno Press, 1974), 466, 474.

year with their families to remain permanently. So the process goes on, with, I believe, a larger proportion of women and children among the immigrants each year, and a larger proportion remaining in this country.[5]

El Paso, a Texas border town, frequently served to funnel Mexican families into the southern regions of the state.

In addition, during these early years of the twentieth century, El Paso generally gave Mexican women their first experience of life in the urban environment. While Mexican immigrant women often came to Texas cities such as El Paso, they were seldom employed in urban based industries. In 1908, for example, Clark wrote that

> Mexican women and children do not usually work in factories in the United States. This is partly because husbands and fathers oppose it, having a peasant prejudice to their women leaving home, and it is partly because these women lack the foundations of industrial training.[6]

Over a period of many years, some of these culturally based hesitancies melted away. In addition, as the years passed, the Texas economy developed some manufacturing and industrial jobs that pulled unskilled women into the ranks of the employed.

The Dillingham Commission of 1911 also documented the early immigrant experience of Mexican women. The commission's report noted that 58.2 percent of the railroad workers entered the United States accompanied by their wives.[7] Once here in the states, few women worked outside the home. Nevertheless, females discovered numerous ways to earn money, primarily supplementing the family income. In the border town of El Paso many women took in boarders or washed clothes for others. While mothers in families did not often seek outside employment, their daughters more and more frequently did so, especially in formal laundry businesses and through domestic

[5] Ibid., 520–521.
[6] Ibid., 495.
[7] Mario T. Garcia, "The Chicana in American History: The Mexican Women of El Paso, 1880–1920—A Case Study," *Pacific Historical Review*, XLIX (May, 1980), 316–317.

service.[8] By 1920 opportunities in the urban areas included working in the garment and cigar factories, serving as clerks and sales personnel in downtown stores, or laboring as cooks and dishwashers. Typically, a dual wage system clearly favored Anglo workers, who received an average of $16.55 a week while the Mexican woman averaged $6.00 a week in 1919.[9]

Although the first jobs for Mexican men often involved constructing and maintaining railroad lines, large numbers of the men moved from this work into agriculture. The prospects of obtaining employment for more family members no doubt encouraged this shift to agricultural work. Clark made this observation when he witnessed entire family units working by the piece rate picking cotton in the fields.[10] Young and old, children and adults, male and female, worked at planting and harvesting Texas crops. Manuel Gamio gained a number of reflective insights from his conversations with Mexicans in the United States, including several examples of family solidarity. Concepción Laguna de Castro spoke to him of the jobs her daughters held in the pecan shelling factories in San Antonio. When the family needed more money, they searched for additional sources. Seasonal agricultural work provided that opportunity, so "All of the family went. . . . In order to go the girls had to leave the factory, but they kept the little house they had, for it is hard to get a house when coming back from the harvest."[11] Sra. Castro's comments indicate that the migrant workers were beginning to develop "ties" to the city. Since pecan shelling was predominantly winter work, the majority of the family's income must have come from migrant agricultural work in the summer and fall.

The majority of the conversations recorded by Gamio were with male Mexican workers. As a result there is a paucity of documentation

[8] Rosalinda M. Gonzales suggests in reference to El Paso that the "entrance of an increasing number of Anglo women into the work force was subsidized with the labor of Mexican servant women." Rosalinda M. Gonzales, "Chicanas and Mexican Immigrant Families, 1920–1940: Women's Subordination and Family Exploitation," in *Decades of Discontent: The Women's Movement, 1920–1940*, eds. Lois Scharf and Joan Jensen (Westport, Conn.: Greenwood Press, 1983), 68.

[9] Garcia, "The Chicana in American History," 325, 329, 335.

[10] Clark, *Mexican Labor in the United States*, 482.

[11] Manuel Gamio, *The Mexican Immigrant, His Life-Story* (Chicago: University of Chicago Press, 1931), 76.

of women in the paid work force. Considering the amount and depth of Gamio's work, it is disappointing that he did not conduct more conversations with women, whether they were part-time or full-time workers.

John Bodnar in *The Transplanted: A History of Immigrants in Urban America* provides one interpretive insight which deserves application to the Mexican worker in Texas. While Bodnar addresses primarily the large urban populations of the Northeast and Midwest, he points to the centrality of the "family" experience. He claims that the primary goal of immigrants was "to secure the welfare and well-being of their familial or household base."[12] As family members came into contact with the capitalistic system in the United States, they made their choices of work, play, purchases, and dwelling place not as individuals but as members of a family unit.

This "transplanting," rather than "uprooting," of familial concerns stresses the continuity of the move. Such a theory applies particularly well to the Mexican immigrants since they most frequently move across a flexible and porous border to "arrive" in the United States. The application of Bodnar's concept to Mexicans fits neatly, partly because Bodnar's work crosses religious and ethnic lines. He believes that immigrants as a group were primarily motivated by family concerns, whether or not that family came from a Roman Catholic background, came from a tradition of "protecting" their women, or expected to return to their native land.[13]

Changes on the national scene affected the Mexican worker in Texas. The expansion of the cotton industry in the early twentieth century, in addition to the revolutionary rumblings in Mexico in 1910, propelled more Mexicans into the Texas labor force.[14] United States

[12] John Bodnar, *The Transplanted: A History of Immigrants in Urban America* (Bloomington: University of Indiana Press, 1985), xvii.

[13] Manuel Garcia supports this emphasis on the family when he writes that "the Mexican family seems to have remained strong and retained its native character rather than being weakened by the immigration process." Garcia, "The Chicana in American History," 317. Richard Griswold Del Castillo, in *La Familia: Chicano Families in the Urban Southwest, 1848 to the Present* (Notre Dame, Ind.: University of Notre Dame Press, 1984), speaks also of the importance of family ties to the Mexican community.

[14] Carey McWilliams, *Ill Fares the Land: Migrants and Migratory Labor in the United States* (Boston: Little, Brown and Co., 1944), 170; Lamar B. Jones, "Mexican-American Labor Problems in Texas" (Ph.D. diss., University of Texas, 1965), 3.

involvement in World War I resulted in labor shortages and campaigns by Herbert Hoover and the New Food Administration to increase food production in 1917. Women were actively recruited as farm workers.[15] The Immigration Act of 1917, with its literacy requirement and $8.00 head tax, began to have an impact upon the movement of people into this country. One source reported that "Even El Paso housewives felt the effect of the restrictions because the law barred Mexican servants who could neither read nor write from employment, forcing many housewives to do their own work."[16] As the restrictions tightened, efforts to use more effectively the immigrant labor already in this country intensified and thus, as the economy expanded, more Mexican women were recruited for work.[17] Changes in production patterns also took place. American people increased their consumption of fruits and vegetables, which influenced Texas agriculture. Production of fresh produce expanded in the lower Rio Grande Valley of Texas and in areas of California. Migrant Mexican workers—men, women, and children—were gradually pulled into those jobs.[18]

Paul Taylor's work on laborers in Nueces County documents the availability of a variety of jobs in Corpus Christi for men and women. Mexican males often worked in the railroad industry. Others were employed in the building trades, or worked on streets and highways. Many served as attendants in garages and gas stations. Mexican men were also active in the fishing industry, in which many women found related employment on shore. In 1934, according to Taylor, approximately 150 Mexicans were involved in "the boating side of the industry, and twice that number of Mexican women are engaged in the work of cleaning fish, peeling shrimp, canning, etc." Corpus Christi Mexicanas also worked as clerks, dressmakers, laundresses, and domestic workers.[19]

---

[15] Mark Reisler, *By the Sweat of Their Brow: Mexican Immigrant Labor in the United States, 1900–1940* (Westport, Conn.: Greenwood Press, 1976), 25.

[16] Garcia, *Desert Immigrants*, 46.

[17] This recruitment intensified during the "fear years" immediately after passage of the literacy law. With fear that a sufficient number of workers would not be available, employers became more ingenious. In the Southwest, however, the continued flow of undocumented Mexicans soon obviated the need for such ingenuity.

[18] Reisler, *By the Sweat of Their Brow,* 77.

[19] Paul Schuster Taylor, *An American Mexican Frontier: Nueces County, Texas* (Chapel Hill: University of North Carolina Press, 1934), 159–160, 161.

Frequently the only work available for women in Corpus Christi, El Paso, or San Antonio was "part-time." This meant that women often worked only when jobs were available or when they could spare time from bearing children and raising little ones. In many instances this part-time work was also accomplished in the home, while the mother additionally performed household duties. A study undertaken in San Antonio in the 1920s surveyed 1,550 homes and 9,000 Mexicans. In 5 percent of the cases both the father and the mother worked. "Yet, it was found that a large part of the work done by the mothers, was piece work from garment factories or was pecan shelling for candy factories, all of which could be done in the home."[20] There was a tendency to minimize the value of women's work since it "could be done in the home." Again, the sense of women as only a part of an economic whole is pervasive. While the study reported that working women of Mexican descent received much less in wages than the men, i.e., $6.70 compared to $15.71, it also declared that in "one-sixth of the Mexican families, there is no support from a father."[21] The automatic assumption that a woman worker was part of a larger economic unit with a co-supporter critically hampered efforts of those women who were the sole supports of their families. Women in San Antonio performed industrial-type work in cigar factories, garment firms, and pecan shelling enterprises. Females struggled to feed themselves and their families on wages earned in the urban environment.

While some Mexicanas began to enter the industrial workplace, others still toiled in the fields in Texas. Ruth Allen studied these "Mexican Peon Women," as she called them. According to Allen, the women had no separate identity in the agricultural system: "even when the woman becomes a hired laborer she has no individual economic existence. Her husband, father, or brother handles the financial affairs. . . . The wage paid is a family wage and the family is distinctly patriarchal in its organization." When Allen speculated on the future of the young Mexican woman moving into the town and receiving at least some "definite remuneration," she reported that "Barriers of racial prejudice will hem her in. . . . it is rather staggering to think of

---

[20] William John Knox, "The Economic Status of the Mexican Immigrant in San Antonio, Texas" (M.A. thesis, University of Texas, 1927), 14.

[21] Ibid., 20, 23, 38.

her helplessness in a world of individualistic competition. . . . she will have weight to drag with her all women and all men who work for wages in the industrial life which she touches."[22]

Elsewhere Allen wrote about Anglo, Mexican, and Negro women working in the cotton fields. She hinted at the coming shift to urban work when she reported that her study group "comprises approximately one-fourth of the population of a state which is in a period of rather rapid transition from an economy that is largely rural to one which is urban." She predicted that from "the women and girls here considered the factories will draw largely their labor supply."[23] Concerned with the effect of woman's work in the fields on the whole economic picture, Allen repeatedly pointed out that the women were "unpaid laborers" toiling in the field and that their agricultural work outside the home was rarely recognized independent of the family.[24]

A telling reflection of early 1930s thought appears in a 1931 article by Paul S. Taylor. Entitling his article "The Mexicans North of the Rio Grande," he wrote of the trickle of Mexican immigration before World War I which developed into a stream during the 1920s and then shrank back to a trickle. He boldly asserted that "The epoch of Mexican mass migration to the United States is now closed."[25] Taylor seemed to be attempting to reassure the American population that the "migration from south of the Rio Grande is predominately rural; the Mexican laborers live on the whole, as a class apart, maintaining a separate domicile and culture."[26]

Observers like Taylor judged Mexicans to be permanently rural beings and encouraged Anglos not to see them as a threat to white urban populations. These writers were apparently oblivious to the drift of Mexicans into the cities, already evident in the early part of the twentieth century. San Antonio is the best example of a Texas city heavily populated by Mexicans. In 1930 San Antonio was "an urban

---

[22] Ruth Allen, "Mexican Peon Women in Texas," *Sociology and Social Research*, XVI (Nov.–Dec., 1931), 137, 141–142.

[23] Ruth Allen, *The Labor of Women in the Production of Cotton*, University of Texas Bulletin no. 3134 (Austin: University of Texas Press, 1931), 13–14.

[24] Ibid., 145, 147, 169.

[25] Paul S. Taylor, "Mexicans North of the Rio Grande," *Survey*, LXVI (May 1, 1931), 135, 205.

[26] Ibid., 136, 202.

center of about 230,000," of which at least 83,000 were of Mexican descent.[27] These Mexicans, both men and women, performed a variety of industrial jobs.

The Works Progress Administration of the 1930s conducted a study among the Mexican Americans who labored in the pecan shelling industry of San Antonio. The WPA report took an in-depth look at the process by which technology displaced large numbers of Mexicans during the most difficult years at the end of the 1930s. The agency surveyed a representative group of 512 Mexican families. With an average annual family income of $251 (based on a median family size of 4.6 people), these workers were "one of the lowest-paid groups of industrial workers in the United States."[28] Oddly enough, though women constituted at least 80 percent of the workers in this industry,[29] of the 512 workers interviewed in the study "a majority were men." This statistic reflects the continuing expectation of the surveyors that women's participation was not as important as male participation. The study's authors explained their rationale as follows:

> Among the pecan workers in the families interviewed, men outnumbered women by nearly 2 to 1. This ratio is probably much higher than would obtain in the industry as a whole, since the selection of families with incomes mainly from pecans eliminated many women part-time workers and earners of supplementary wages.[30]

Other studies of the pecan shellers of San Antonio have also omitted the story of the women.[31]

---

[27] Julia Kirk Blackwelder, *Women of the Depression: Caste and Culture in San Antonio, 1929–1939* (College Station: Texas A&M University Press, 1984), 1.

[28] Sheldon C. Menefee and Orin Cassmore, *Pecan Shellers of San Antonio* (Washington, D.C.: Works Progress Administration, 1940), xvii.

[29] Martha P. Cotera, *Diosa y Hembra: The History and Heritage of Chicanas in the United States* (Austin: Statehouse Printing, 1976), 88.

[30] Menefee and Cassmore, *Pecan Shellers of San Antonio*, 5.

[31] See, for example, Harold A. Shapiro, "The Pecan Shellers of San Antonio, Texas," *Southwestern Social Science Quarterly*, XXXII (Mar., 1952), 229–244, and Kenneth P. Walker, "The Pecan Shellers of San Antonio and Mechanization," *Southwestern Historical Quarterly*, LXIX (July, 1965), 44–58.

The pecan shelling industry had existed for many years in the San Antonio region. The hand shelling was done in a variety of environments: large warehouse-type rooms, smaller rooms set up by contractors, and in the homes of the workers. "Home-work" in the pecan shelling industry was extremely common[32] and fit neatly into the pattern of Mexican female workers who routinely did not work outside the home if married or if married with small children. It also fit neatly the Mexican tendency to keep their daughters cloistered and "protected," for they, too, could work at pecan shelling or garment construction in the home environment.[33] Although the work was done in the home, it must be viewed as part of the industrial base of San Antonio.

These urban workers regarded the city as their home base, renting houses year-round or owning their own dwellings. Information suggests that almost 96 percent "paid rent on their San Antonio houses during the entire year, even when they were working in the cotton or beet fields, or (as was true in a considerable minority of cases) owned their homes there."[34] They were residentially segregated in certain barrios, with that on the west side of town being close to the factories in which the women worked. The location of the factories made it possible for the women to walk to the workplace rather than having to travel long distances at an expense that would have made their meager paychecks worth even less.[35] Of course this also tended to segregate these industries, effectively excluding blacks and Anglos.

In San Antonio women frequently worked on erratic schedules because work was not always available. Their tasks as bearers of children and homemakers also competed for the time needed to earn a wage outside the home. The WPA report stated that "Women would

[32] Robert Garland Landolt, *The Mexican-American Workers of San Antonio, Texas* (Ph.D. diss., University of Texas, 1965; reprint, New York: Arno Press, 1976), 226–227.

[33] Julia Kirk Blackwelder, "Women in the Work Force: Atlanta, New Orleans, and San Antonio, 1930 to 1940," *Journal of Urban History* XIV (May, 1978), 339.

[34] Menefee and Cassmore, *Pecan Shellers of San Antonio*, 53.

[35] Blackwelder, *Women of the Depression*, 84, 99. Blackwelder's book reflects extensive work with quantitative methods. The appendix is full of charts and tables documenting the extent to which women worked in San Antonio during the depression years. She also develops her theory that caste can explain the experiences of Mexicanas in San Antonio. The inflexibility of the job market was a reflection of the city's acceptance and rigid enforcement of caste structure in the labor force.

come to work for a few hours while their children were in school, returning home to prepare lunch and dinner for their families."[36] The document shared some "typical" cases of pecan shellers: "His wife and their 18-year-old daughter also worked in the shelling plants, but altogether they could earn only about $6 a week." "His wife also worked in the shelling plants when she could get away from the children."[37] The tendency has been to discount the importance of this part-time work, yet it was often critical to the survival of the Mexican family.

While the pecan shelling industry is an excellent example of women's participation in urban-based industries, San Antonio had a number of other opportunities for Mexicanas. Garment making factories existed, although most frequently these plants served as a pickup spot for home work done by family members. Adequate statistics on the extent of this participation are difficult to obtain because frequently one person would pick up and return the finished pieces, although many in the family would have been responsible for the sewing.[38] Some writers are beginning to use terms like the "invisible work force" for such laborers, mostly women, who are not employed full-time at an industrial location, yet are doing work supportive of that industry. They also label this "informal work," meaning it has not been given formal recognition or documentation by the business bureaus, census department, or government offices.[39] The words "invisible" and "informal" fit all too well the perceived image of female workers in the economy.

Women also worked in laundries around the city, a large cigar factory, a chili powder factory, cement plants, and several meat packing houses. Some worked as domestic servants or as salesladies.[40] Other studies of immigrant groups suggest that immigrant family homes often served as boarding houses for other workers. In this way the woman's work in the home also contributed needed earning to the family. According to one historian of San Antonio, however, this was not a common practice among the Mexicanas.[41]

[36] Menefee and Cassmore, *Pecan Shellers of San Antonio*, 9.
[37] Ibid., 24–25.
[38] Blackwelder, *Women of the Depression*, 67.
[39] Beverly Lozano, *The Invisible Work Force* (New York: The Free Press, 1989).
[40] Menefee and Cassmore, *Pecan Shellers of San Antonio*, 31.
[41] Blackwelder, *Women of the Depression*, 35, 77.

That women were active in the labor force in San Antonio is also verified by the extent of their participation in union strikes. Women were instrumental in the development of the International Ladies Garment Workers Union locals in San Antonio and in the big strikes of 1936.[42] One feminist writer goes so far as to say that "The development of the International Ladies Garment Workers Union in Texas is largely due to the bodies and dues which Chicanas provided for strikes, and salaries for organizers."[43] Houston and Laredo were also sites of active Mexicana involvement in the ILGWU.

The concept of living in the city part-time and working in the country part-time is also incorporated in the story of the San Antonio pecan shellers. The WPA study suggested that about 25 percent of the pecan shellers worked in agricultural pursuits some time during the year.[44] Generally the Mexican residents of San Antonio who worked in this industry had been in the community for many years, probably a part of the tripling of the Mexican population in the United States from 1910 to 1930.[45] San Antonio provided flexibility for the Mexican family. The city sustained small urban based industries and served as a depot for agricultural workers. Julia Blackwelder suggests that sometimes women remained in San Antonio, working in such industries as garment making, while their men left for seasonal agricultural work. By the late 1930s this might have been one of the few choices available for Mexicana workers. Additionally, as the mother maintained a home base with her young children, a certain family stability could evolve. Census records indicate high numbers of family units in which women were the recorded heads. Such statistics might reflect the "possibility that many males followed the crops and were not recorded as workers in the city."[46]

The 1930s mark a shift in the story of Mexican workers in Texas. Mexicanas moved from participation in the rural work force to city living and industrial-based employment. Using census data, Mario Barrera developed some interesting statistics for Mexicana participation in the various occupational categories in Texas. The percentage of

[42] George W. Green, "The ILGWU in Texas, 1930–1970," *Journal of Mexican American History*, I (1971), 145–146.

[43] Cotera, *Diosa y Hembra*, 86.

[44] Menefee and Cassmore, *Pecan Shellers of San Antonio*, xvii.

[45] Ibid., 2.

[46] Blackwelder, *Women of the Depression*, 71–72.

women working as farm laborers statewide dropped from 25.9 percent in 1930 to 8.1 percent in 1950 and 2.3 percent in 1970. The figures for Mexican women in clerical and sales positions also changed dramatically, from 8.7 percent in 1930 to 23.5 percent in 1950 and 33 percent in 1970. Those in the operatives-semiskilled category remained fairly constant, at 16.4 percent in 1930 and 19.7 percent in 1970.[47] While the semi-skilled category does not show much increase over the forty-year period, the other categories underwent a radical transformation. By 1970 Mexican women in Texas were working primarily in cities. A population shift from rural to urban areas was taking place in the United States as a whole. In Texas, specifically, Barrera shows Mexican male and female participation in this overall trend.

The conclusion that large numbers of women were living in cities is also borne out by Jet Winters, a professor of home economics at the University of Texas. He examined home life in San Antonio and Austin and published his conclusions in 1931 as *A Report on the Health and Nutrition of Mexicans Living in Texas*. That enough Mexican families lived in these two cities to conduct the survey suggests the heavy influx of Mexicans into urban areas.

A more recent author suggests one reason that the census of 1930 did not list an even higher number of Mexicana workers in San Antonio. Since much of the garment industry's work was done by married women in the home, as was much pecan shelling, those toiling in these industries were not commonly counted when census workers tried to identify the working population.[48] Again we come up against the problem of locating adequate statistics to verify women's active participation in the labor market.

Today it is commonly believed in the United States that the movement of Mexican men and women into the cities is a fairly recent phenomenon. Yet a historical view of the information from the late 1920s and 1930s clearly testifies to a constant flow of these laborers into urban areas during this period.[49] As Reisler wrote, "By 1930 the Census Bureau classified slightly more than half the Mexican population in the

[47] Mario Barrera, *Race and Class in the Southwest: A Theory of Racial Inequality* (Notre Dame, Ind.: University of Notre Dame Press, 1979), 132.

[48] Blackwelder, "Women in the Work Force," 351.

[49] Reisler, *By the Sweat of Their Brow,* 96–126.

United States as urban."[50] Other sources using the same census statistics describe the cities as "magnets" drawing workers to them.[51]

Rosalinda M. Gonzales goes one step further to point out that the "Mexican-Origin" population in the United States had "a greater number of Mexican women than men living in urban areas." As she interprets the statistics, 120,008 females lived in cities in 1940, as opposed to 117,977 men.[52] Even though most of these were newly arrived immigrants, the statistics reflect the contemporary urban shift. In a 1948 study reinforcing this information, Lyle Saunders wrote that

> The total Spanish-speaking population of Texas is probably between 1,100,000 and 1,300,000, plus an undetermined number of illegal aliens which may include as many as several hundred thousand persons. The Spanish-speaking group are increasingly becoming an urban population. They are particularly concentrating in the larger cities of the state.[53]

The 1940s introduced a variety of other factors that influenced rural-urban mobility. The World War II military effort and the increasing development of national defense industries began to drain available workers. The draft also pulled large numbers of men off the farms at a time when the nation was trying to increase its agricultural production for the Allies.[54] These forces had a push/pull effect upon Mexicans within the labor market. In Texas, the Farm Labor Office targeted Mexican workers, male and female, asking for help in producing crops. Government intervention and advertising reflected the relatively small supply of Mexicans in rural areas.[55]

---

[50] Ibid., 267.

[51] Richard Griswold Del Castillo, *La Familia: Chicano Families in the Urban Southwest, 1848 to the Present* (Notre Dame, Ind.: University of Notre Dame Press, 1984), 94–95.

[52] Gonzales, "Chicanas and Mexican Immigrant Families, 1920–1940," 71.

[53] Saunders, *The Spanish-Speaking Population of Texas*, 14–15.

[54] McWilliams, *Ill Fares the Land*, 344–347.

[55] Pauline R. Kibbe, *Latin Americans in Texas* (Albuquerque: University of New Mexico Press, 1946), 187–188; George O. Coalson, *The Development of the Migratory Farm Labor System in Texas: 1900–1954* (San Francisco: R and E Research Associates, 1977), 72–73.

Pauline Kibbe's *Latin Americans in Texas*, published for the Good Neighbor Commission in 1946, helped to define life for the Mexican in Texas during the Forties. She wrote in detail about federal housing projects in Dallas ("Little Mexico Village") and San Antonio (the "Alazan-Apache Courts"). She also pointed to improvements in working opportunities when she reported that "one of the leading Fort Worth hotels employed Latin American girls as elevator operators" and that other hotels followed suit.[56] While her optimism must be understood as a public relations effort on the part of the state, it also echoes changes supporting the shift from rural to urban.

The move to urban areas continued in the years following World War II. Mexican Americans participated fully in the increasing urbanization of America. While a few writers still clung to the image of Mexican people as only rural and agriculturally oriented,[57] the statistics paint a different picture.[58] The works available from 1960 to the present continue to document the involvement of the Mexicana in the paid labor force in Texas and around the country.[59]

[56]   Kibbe, *Latin Americans in Texas*, 163.

[57]   John R. Scotford, *Within These Borders* (New York: Friendship Press, 1953; reprinted in *Aspects of the Mexican-American Experience* [New York: Arno Press, 1976]).

[58]   Rosemary Santana Cooney, "The Mexican American Female in the Labor Force," in *Cuantos Somos: A Demographic Study of the Mexican American Population*, eds. Charles H. Teller et al. (Austin: University of Texas Press, 1977), 177–195; Robert H. Talbert, *Spanish-Name People in the Southwest and West: Socioeconomic Characteristics of White Persons of Spanish Surname in Texas, Arizona, California, Colorado, and New Mexico* (Fort Worth: Texas Christian University Press, 1955), 23.

[59]   See, for example, Laura E. Arroyo, "Industrial and Occupational Distribution of Chicana Workers," *Aztlan*, IV (Fall, 1973), 343–382; Walter Fogel, *Mexican Americans in Southwest Labor Markets*, Mexican-American Study Project, Division of Research, Graduate School of Business Administration, Advance Report no. 10 (Los Angeles: University of California Press, 1967); Charles Carr Winn, "Mexican-Americans in the Texas Labor Movement"; Mary L. Cothran, "Occupational Patterns of Rural and Urban Spanish-Americans in Two South Texas Counties" (M.A. thesis, Texas A&M University, 1966); Robert Landolt, "The Mexican-American Workers of San Antonio, Texas"; Vilma Ortiz and Rosemary Santana Cooney, "Sex-Role Attitudes and Labor Force Participation Among Young Hispanic Females and Non-Hispanic White Females," in *The Mexican American Experience: An Interdisciplinary Anthology*, eds. Rodolfo O. de la Garza et al. (Austin: University of Texas Press, 1985). Albert Camarillo, *Chicanos in a Changing Society: From Mexican Pueblos to American Barrios in Santa Barbara and Southern California, 1848–1930* (Cambridge, Mass.: Harvard University Press, 1979) is an example of excellent research done on California.

The increasing participation of Mexicanas in the labor force also mirrors the greater involvement of women in the work force as a whole throughout the United States.[60] Robert Landolt's study of San Antonio and its Spanish speaking population in the early 1960s has ample statistics to point to the degree of labor involvement by women. He suggests and documents the opening of a wider range of opportunities for the Mexicana. Some women were moving into the nursing field, while quite a few were already helping birth babies as midwives. Women worked for a large insurance company, a refrigerator and air conditioner manufacturer, and an electrical equipment manufacturer, as well as in the more traditional laundry, garment construction, pecan shelling, and clerical and sales tasks.[61] Landolt, in viewing the Mexican labor force in San Antonio, gives the women high marks for their union activities. He writes:

> It is interesting to note that in each of the three industries in which union memberships and strike participation in San Antonio have been predominately Mexican-American—cigar manufacturing, pecan shelling, and garment making—the great majority of workers and strikers have been women.[62]

Yet another fascinating look at the Mexicana involved in the labor market was a study undertaken by Belden Associates, a Dallas firm specializing in survey techniques. They attempted to identify the Mexican American market in the United States. Their target area included Arizona, California, Colorado, New Mexico, and Texas. They interviewed 500 "housewives" in April 1962. These interviews were held in "all urban places (as defined by the Census) which in 1960 had a projected Mexican-American population of at least 40,000."[63] They were conducted in Spanish by bilingual Mexican-American interviewers. Interviewers traveled to Phoenix, Los Angeles, San

---

[60] Landolt, *Mexican-American Workers*, 60.

[61] Ibid., 202–203, 206–207, 247, 250–252, 258.

[62] Ibid., 172–173.

[63] Belden Associates, *The Mexican American Market in the United States: Market Characteristics from a Personal-Interview Survey in Spanish, City and County Populations from the U.S. Census* (Dallas: Belden Associates, 1962; reprinted in *Aspects of the Mexican-American Experience* [New York: Arno Press, 1976]), iii.

Diego, the San Francisco Bay Area, and Denver as well as six urban areas in Texas. The women said that 72 percent of the men and 19 percent of the women worked full-time, while 9 percent of the men and 8 percent of the women worked part-time. Eleven percent of the women said someone in their family had left the city during the previous twelve months to work temporarily somewhere else, while 87 percent said no one in their families had done so.[64] These significant findings verify the urban base of the Mexican population.

As each year passes and more Mexican American women work outside the home, research on employment by Mexicanas documents their continued participation in the labor market.[65] An excellent study of contemporary industries in Ciudad Juarez and El Paso points to the internationalization of capital investments and the shift of American money to just south of the border. These businesses primarily employ female workers in garment assembly or the electric-electronics industry, and see women as part of a whole family or labor package.[66] The failure to see the women as individuals works the harshest effects upon the women who are the sole support of their households.[67] In-depth research points to the racial discrimination faced by the Mexicana and how much that discrimination costs the female workers.[68] Texas's Mexicanas in the garment industry played a prominent role in the strike against Farah Slacks from 1972 to 1974; in fact, "The Farah strikers were virtually all Chicanas." With the backing of the union,

[64] Ibid., A-6, A-12.

[65] Fred E. Romero, *Chicano Workers: Their Utilization and Development* (Los Angeles: University of California Press, 1979); Cotera, *Diosa y Hembra*, 120.

[66] Maria Patricia Fernandez-Kelly, *For We Are Sold, I and My People: Women and Industry in Mexico's Frontier* (Albany: State University of New York Press, 1983).

[67] Rosaura Sanchez and Rosa Martinez Cruz (eds.), *Essays on La Mujer*, Chicano Studies Research Center Publications anthology no. 1 (Los Angeles: University of California Press, 1977), 6–9; Alfredo Mirande and Evangellina Enriquez, *La Chicana: The Mexican-American Woman* (Chicago: University of Chicago Press, 1979), 130–131; Elizabeth Waldman, "Profile of the Chicana: A Statistical Fact Sheet," in Magdalena Mora and Adelaida R. del Castillo, *Mexican Women in the United States: Struggles Past and Present*, Chicano Studies Research Center Occasional Paper no. 2 (Los Angeles: University of California Press, 1980), 195–204.

[68] Tetcho Mindola, "The Cost of Being a Mexican Female Worker in the 1970 Houston Labor Market," *Aztlan*, XI (Fall, 1980), 231–247.

a national boycott, and their own tenacity, these women stated clearly the meaning of their participation in the labor market.[69]

The effort to document Mexicana activity in the labor force continued through the 1980s. It pointed to the continued heavy involvement of such workers in urban areas of Texas and the U.S.[70] One study in 1973 recorded oral histories of twenty-six older women of Mexican descent. Many of these women reminisced about their participation in the paid work force.[71] Such efforts may help us to recapture the fuller experience of Mexican women working in the cities of Texas. Much work still needs to be done in this area of Hispanic studies. Hidden or sleeping documents about Mexicans in Texas and in the Southwest can, one hopes, be uncovered. Researchers must approach the Mexican community individually and encourage it to share oral or written information. Hopefully this will lead various government bodies to recognize how long Mexicans have been in cities and to stop ignoring their presence, their problems, and their contributions. The existing documents justify the basic thesis that Mexicanas have been an active part of the Texas work force for much of the twentieth century; that they have concentrated geographically in the cities, having found paid work there; and that the shift to the cities was clearly underway by the 1930s.

---

[69] Lauri Coyle, Gail Hershatter, and Emily Honig, "Women at Farah: An Unfinished Story," in Joan Jensen and Sue Davison, *A Needle, A Bobbin, A Strike: Women Needleworkers in America* (Philadelphia: Temple University Press, 1984), 227–277.

[70] Margarita B. Melville (ed.), *Mexicana at Work in the United States*, Mexican American Studies Program Monograph no. 5 (Houston: University of Houston, 1986); Vicki L. Ruiz and Susan Tiano, *Women on the U.S.-Mexico Border: Responses to Change* (Boston: Allen and Urwin, 1987); Lillian Schlissel et al., *Western Women: Their Land, Their Lives* (Albuquerque: University of New Mexico Press, 1988).

[71] Arleen Stewart, "Las Mujeres de Aztlan: A Consultation with Elderly Mexican-American Women in a Socio-Historical Perspective" (Ph.D. diss., California School of Professional Psychology, 1973).

Hispanic and Mexican American Women on the Texas Stage, 1875–1990

Elizabeth C. Ramírez*

SEVERAL STUDIES dealing with theatrical activities in Texas prior to 1900 show that they were an important and vibrant part of the cultural life developing in the state. The Anglo American theater, however, was dominated by the large touring companies traveling from the East Coast and abroad, generally giving only short-run performances. In Texas, only the Mexican American community had resident professional theater on a regular basis.[1]

Information regarding the development of the Spanish-language professional theater in the United States is sadly lacking. We know, however, that during the twentieth century, and even earlier, professional acting companies from Mexico established a lasting tradition in

* Elizabeth C. Ramírez received her Ph.D. from the University of Texas at Austin. She has published a book, *Footlights Across the Border: A History of Spanish-Language Professional Theatre on the Texas Stage, 1875–1935,* and numerous articles and reviews on Hispanic American theatre. She has taught at the University of Arizona and Harvard University and currently teaches at the University of Oregon.

[1] Joe Manry, "A History of the Theatre in Austin: 1839–1905" (Ph.D. diss., University of Texas at Austin, 1979), 1–33, 171–228; Charles Bennet Myler, "A History of the English-Speaking Theatre in San Antonio Before 1900" (Ph.D. diss., University of Texas at Austin, 1968), 1–13, 346–355; Jack H. Yoacum, "A History of Theatre in Houston, 1836–1954" (Ph.D. diss., University of Wisconsin at Madison, 1955), 140; Donald V. Brady, "The Theater in Early El Paso, 1881–1905," *Southwestern Studies,* IV (1966), 25–39; Ann Taylor Reeves, "Nineteenth Century Theater in Northeast Texas" (M.F.A. thesis, University of Texas at Austin, 1962), 40–92, 177–246; Christa Carvajal, "German Theater in Central Texas" (Ph.D. diss., University of Texas at Austin, 1977), 3, 35–36, 57–60, 65–66.

Texas and the United States. This theatrical heritage stemmed from a long history of both amateur and professional Spanish-language activity originating in Spain. Few scholars have emphasized that the Golden Age of Spain coincides with the great entry of Spain into the territory of what is now the United States. The conquistadores not only brought a great interest in theater to New Spain, but more significantly they provided the first dramatic performance on American soil.[2]

My book, *Footlights Across the Border,* details professional Mexican American theater in the state of Texas from its beginnings in 1875 to its demise in 1935. This study shows that, along with an amateur theater, professional companies appeared regularly from Mexico; that there was a development of culture and taste of Mexican Americans evident through detailed analyses of representative plays produced by the dramatic companies; that three types of companies appeared between 1875 and 1935, namely touring, resident, and combination "star" companies, each with distinct organization, operations, and contributions; and that the theater, through its language and cultural themes, created a cohesive force for Mexican Americans that supported their identification with the mother country and provided an experience in which the entire family could participate.[3]

The attention given to production elements in newspaper reviews and accounts of performances, while scant, indicates a focus on the actor. The first quarter of the twentieth century brought a great many Spanish-language actors to Texas. Reviews of their performances also reveal the value that critics placed on the plays themselves. Accounts of the performances emphasized the plays, especially their didactic and moralistic merits. The performers were generally noted for their ability to convey the full meaning of the play. The performers not only acquainted audiences with traditional and innovative drama, but they often set standards in language, customs, manners, and fashion.

This essay examines the unique contributions of the actress. I must include Hispanic actresses along with Mexican American ac-

[2] Elizabeth C. Ramírez, "A History of Mexican American Professional Theatre in Texas Prior to 1900," *Theatre Survey* (May and November, 1983), 99–116; John W. Brokaw, "A Mexican American Acting Company, 1849–1924," *Educational Theatre Journal,* XXVII (1975), 23–27; George C. D. Odell, *Annals of the New York Stage.*

[3] Elizabeth C. Ramírez, *Footlights Across the Border: A History of Spanish-Language Professional Theatre on the Texas Stage* (New York: Peter Lang Publishing, 1990).

tresses because of their major role on the American stage, although they did not remain permanently in Texas. My research has been drawn primarily from rare collections of plays, playbills, and memorabilia of the Mexican American Project in the Benson Latin American Collection; the extensive Spanish-language newspaper collection at the Eugene C. Barker Texas History Center; and private collections and accounts.

The most numerous accounts of an actress performing prior to 1900 are about Antonia Pineda de Hernández (?–ca. 1927). At the age of eighteen she married Encarnación Hernández, whom she met when he was performing with a company in Colima, Mexico. Without a theatrical background, she was trained as an actress by Hernández. She eventually became the leading actress of the company organized by Encarnación, the Compañía Hernández. Her responsibilities were great. Upon her husband's death, around 1888, she assumed the management of the company until her retirement in 1904, when her son-in-law, Carlos Villalongín, took over. She also continued as leading actress to Villalongín. Her children included one son, Luis, who acted with the company, and two daughters who became actresses in the Hernández-Villalongín company and later in the Compañía Villalongín. Herlinda, who generally performed in second-line parts, married Carlos Villalongín, and Concepción assumed the leading roles when she could fill the parts and as her mother took on fewer or smaller roles and eventually retired. Antonio Pineda de Hernández was best known for her roles in romantic tragedies and melodramas. Her last known performance was as the leading actress in *La Campa de la Mudaña* (the title appears to be slang for "The Camp of the Mute") for a benefit at Beethoven Hall in San Antonio in 1917.

The peak of her career as an actress was before 1900.[4] The twentieth century brought many more performers and performances to Texas. The tastes and demands of the Mexican American community influenced the policy and practice of the acting troupes which soon appeared in large numbers. Three actresses stand out as particularly powerful figures on the Mexican American stage in Texas: Magdalena Solórzano, Margarita Fernández, and Concepción Hernández. Since

---

[4] Ramírez, "A History of Mexican American Professional Theatre in Texas," 99–116.

these three women performed in more or less the same style, it is possible to select one as representative.[5]

Concepción Hernández is an excellent example of the type of leading actress commonly found in the Mexican touring companies that appeared in Texas. She is also important because she is representative of the actress who remained in Texas to continue the theatrical tradition through the resident company.

The features most often noted by newspaper critics were an actress's intelligence, ability to comprehend her part, and skill in presenting a well-studied role with clarity in diction, all of which Hernández displayed. Her principal strength, however, was a unique vocal range. A vivid description remains of her most memorable role, as Marta in *Tierra Baja* (The Lowlands); Carlos Villalongín included in his memoirs a newspaper review of the performance of February 20, 1910, in Matamoros, Mexico. This review is important because it provides an account of a production that the Compañía Villalongín also presented in San Antonio. The review says that Concepción Hernández was "truly inspired. . . . Her potent voice ranged from a ferocious roar of injured dignity; to the soft cooing and billing of a dove, sweet and harmonious, as a murmur of breezes from the fjords, when, for the first time, she felt the beating in her heart of the sweet sensations of true love." She used that voice with great skill in conveying emotion: "All her inflections imprinted a stamp of truth to the different sensations of hate, indignation, dignity, contempt, passion and tenderness with which the difficult role of Marta is filled; in all of those transitions, this singular artist knew how to triumph, receiving for it merited ovations."[6]

Tradition required that the declamatory actress perform in moral and instructive dramas suitable for the entire family. The fact that Concepción Hernández was performing in a family enterprise, always accompanied by her mother, sisters, and other relatives, probably enhanced the image of wholesome entertainment that the Compañía Villalongín provided.

[5] Elizabeth C. Ramírez, "Compañía Juan B. Padilla," "Compañía Teatro Solórzano," and "Compañía Villalongín," in *American Theatre Companies, 1888–1930*, ed. Weldon Durham (Westport, Conn.: Greenwood Press, 1986), 353–358, 413–416, 449–453.

[6] "Memoirs of Carlos Villalongín," in possession of María Luisa Villalongín de Santos, San Antonio, 96, 108, 123.

Her training began in childhood and she grew into the parts she played. Her parents were actors and managers of the Compañía Hernández prior to its merger with the Compañía Villalongín. In later years Concepción would have had to share roles with her sister, Herlinda, but upon her marriage Herlinda turned her attention to other matters, such as bearing and taking care of nine children. Thus Concepción was almost exclusively the leading lady of the company. Among her principal roles, besides Marta in *Tierra Baja,* were *María Antonietta, La Llorona* (The Weeping Woman), and Doña Ines in *Don Juan Tenorio.*

Concepción Hernández received many gifts from people offering tokens of admiration and friendship. Some of these are in the Villalongín Collection in the Benson Library, including cards and photographs from admirers, generally wishing her success in benefit performances. In one poem we get a glimpse of her unique qualities: "The inspiration of your creations is born in your soul; and you lovingly make it [the melodrama] live in the hearts of everyone. You create a reality of both suffering and feeling. Your modesty is . . . [a] gift of art! . . . you move everyone's soul. . . ." Not long after these words were written the actress moved permanently to San Antonio, where the company performed at the Teatro Aurora.[7]

The Mexican Revolution caused Carlos Villalongín, his family, and some other actors to remain in Texas instead of returning to Coahuila, where the company held temporary residence. Thus, the Mexican Revolution enabled the tradition of Spanish-language drama to continue on the American stage through resident companies. Carlos Villalongín's children were the first Spanish-language performers born in the United States. María Luisa Villalongín de Santos, who still resides in San Antonio,, was among them.[8]

Combination companies, that is, companies traveling with a star and full company, were less frequently seen on the Mexican American stage than other kinds of companies; nevertheless, they had a considerable impact on the practice and policies of the others. Combination companies generally featured female stars, and generally arrived from

[7] Fidencio M. Chinauya [spelling unclear], Sabinas Hidalgo, Apr. 9, 1911, in ibid., 100.

[8] Ramírez, *American Theatre Companies.*

the Mexican stage, although some Spanish companies also appeared. The Compañía Virginia Fábregas is an excellent example of this type.

Virginia Fábregas probably best represents the "modern" actress, although there are other examples, such as Mercedes Navarro, Rosita Arriaga, and María Guerrero, the major Spanish actress of the modern period, who appeared in San Antonio in 1927. Many of these actresses were significant for their new styles of acting and introduction of new roles. Although none resided permanently in Texas or the United States, their contributions were important.

No individual star had a greater influence than Virginia Fábregas, both on the Mexican stage and the Mexican American stage in Texas. Mexican American actors and actresses often drew directly from her company's organization and practice. According to Rodolfo Usigli, "She is the first actress with vision, not of what the theatre was then [in the last decade of the nineteenth century] but of what it would be later, and consequently, she is the first modern actress of Mexico." Probably her most outstanding attribute was her ability to convey emotion in a thoroughly natural and believable manner.[9]

She was internationally acclaimed in *La Mujer X* (Madame X) and her portrayal of Angelica in *La Hija del Rey* (The Daughter of the King) was significant in the revival of romanticism in Mexico. She later turned with much enthusiasm to plays by modern dramatists, believing that presenting drama with universal appeal, capable of reaching the widest possible audience, was the greatest accomplishment of any performer. Fábregas sought constantly to provide for her public a "new repertory, new decorations, and new actors and actresses." She was said to "possess the unique ability among leading actresses and actors of sensing the need of updating the repertory with the latest works of world theatre." She introduced San Antonio audiences to such works by Pirandello and Oscar Wilde as *All for the Best* and *Lady Windemere's Fan,* and set the standard of performance by which other combination companies were judged.[10]

---

[9] Rodolfo Usigli, *Mexico in the Theatre,* trans. Wilder E. Scott (University of Mississippi Romance Monographs, 1975), 110; *La Prensa* (San Antonio), Apr. 4, 1923, Nov. 25, Nov. 28, 1926, May 2, 1928; Manuel Mañon, *Historia del Teatro Principal de México* (Editorial Cultura, 1932), 152.

[10] Elizabeth C. Ramírez, "Spanish-Language Combination Companies on the

Several individual performers and performances made important contributions to American theater. The professional Spanish-language companies were instrumental in introducing and popularizing new ideas and practices, and women made distinct contributions as actresses, managers, and part of the family nucleus that comprised these companies.

Nicholas Kanellos's book *A History of Hispanic Theatre in the United States: Origins to 1940* reveals the problems theater historians often encounter in trying to assess the contributions of women: his discussion of activity in San Antonio seems to dismiss completely the leading actress and her place in history. Kanellos's study is disappointing primarily because it lacks a clear methodological approach and fails to place an important movement within the context of American and world theater. Nevertheless, the contributions of women to Texas history emerge as significant even if some writers fail to assess them properly.

Mexican American theater thrived for a long time in Texas. It died down during the Depression and arose again in the 1960s with the Chicano theater movement. Luis Valdez, the director of El Teatro Campesino, has been credited with using his art to relate the cultural tradition of Mexicans living in the United States to society as a whole. Valdez and other Chicano dramatists have looked to pre-Columbian rituals and ceremonies along with the amateur dramatic tradition as the primary sources of Spanish-language theater.

Contemporary Chicano theater companies in Texas, always in search of plays drawn from their own experience and background, can draw from this source of plays and performance tradition and attempt to reinterpret these works for contemporary audiences, as many resident companies throughout the country are attempting to do with the classics of world drama. The Guadalupe Cultural Center in San Antonio, for example, houses a theater company with notable actresses, but often relies on art exhibits, film festivals, and other media, as well as out-of-town dramatists and productions, for its fare because of the lack of available native drama. Roberto Pomo's experimental Chicano theater group, first at the University of Texas at El Paso and

---

American Stage: Organization and Practice in Texas, 1915–1935," *Theatre History Studies*, IX (1989), 77–91.

now at Texas A&M University, and Joe Rosenberg's Teatro Bilingue in Kingsville have often drawn from a Latin American tradition in their search for new plays. These groups and others can clearly benefit from the knowledge of a dramatic heritage that was once prominent in Texas. More importantly, it is time to challenge what Oscar G. Brockett describes as the "consensus" point of view in history, the preoccupation with tracing the development of the mainstream English-language stage. We must broaden the scope of historical inquiry, as Brockett suggests, by including such traditions as those provided by women on the Texas stage to reveal the multicultural richness of our past. We cannot afford to omit, disregard, or misinterpret the significance of women in theater history.[11]

[11] Oscar G. Brockett, *History of the Theatre* (5th ed.; Boston: Allyn and Bacon, 1987), 733–734.

Pauline Periwinkle:

Prodding Dallas into the Progressive Era

Jacquelyn McElhaney*

PAULINE PERIWINKLE—such a Victorian-sounding *nom de plume* evokes the image of a prim and proper writer of nineteenth-century courtship advice or romantic novels. The remarkable woman who used this pen name, however, did something quite different. To the clubwomen of Dallas and to readers of the Dallas *Morning News* and Galveston *News* throughout the state of Texas from 1893 to 1916, she was a driving force in bringing about numerous improvements which occurred during the Progressive Era in Texas. She recognized the power of the press and used her position as woman's editor of the Dallas *Morning News* as a forum from which she educated her readers about some of the pressing social needs of Dallas and the rest of the state. While she educated Texas women, she also publicized the activities of the women's clubs which were making efforts to correct the abuses or deficiencies she had reported.

Although active in many of the organizations she wrote about, she felt her greatest contribution could be made through her column, noting in 1900 that "printer's ink judicially applied to the club idea is a great lubricator and will make it run further and smoother than anything I know."[1] She was willing to apply that ink, as she wrote in

---

* Jacquelyn McElhaney received her B.A. and M.A. degrees in history from Southern Methodist University. As a historical consultant, she has assisted, among others, the SMU Archaeology Program, the Sixth Floor Exhibit, and the Dallas County Historical Commission. She has written a history of the efforts to make the Trinity River a navigable waterway and edited the diary of Dallasite Frances Killen Smith for the quarterly *Legacies,* of which she is a contributing editor.

[1] Dallas *Morning News,* June 4, 1900 (hereafter cited as *DMN*).

1909 to the president of the Texas Federation of Women's Clubs: "I will do anything in my line, such as giving publicity and such little pen influence I wield to any good cause you wish furthered." She later remarked that she felt she was more effective "as a sort of silent partner, though not silent when it came to boosting . . . plans and measures."[2]

Where did this extraordinary woman come from, and how was she able to effect so many changes in Dallas? The answers begin in Battle Creek, Michigan, where she was born Sara Isadore Sutherland in 1863. Her father died from injuries sustained in the Civil War and her mother remarried a short time later. Because her stepfather was, as she described it, "rather inconvenient . . . indeed so much so that I have never lived at home with any peace," she moved in with her "Auntie Rose," who lived in nearby St. Clair, Michigan.[3] She graduated from high school in St. Clair in 1881, and by 1883 had found work in Battle Creek. She was hired by the Seventh Day Adventist Publishing Association, which was closely allied with the famous Battle Creek Sanitarium established by Dr. John Harvey Kellogg. His brother founded the Kellogg Cereal Company.

Her writing for the *Review and Herald* naturally focused on health matters, as did her later work for the monthly magazine *Good Health* which was printed at the Sanitarium. The forward-looking people with whom she worked had a decided influence on Sara Isadore Sutherland, who married a fellow employee, James Miner, in 1884. Her associations with other women on the staff left their imprint: such women as Dr. Kate Lindsay, said to have been the first registered woman physician in the first sanitarium in the world, and Mrs. Eva Giles, an early editor at *Good Health* magazine who later edited the monthly publication of the Michigan Federation of Women's Clubs.[4]

By 1890, having risen to the position of an editor, "S.I.M.," as she signed her articles, had taken up progressive causes and was suggesting "what the wage-earning women of our land have most need of is not

---

[2] Letters in TFWC Papers (uncatalogued at this time), TWU. My thanks to Judith McArthur, whose forays into this uncatalogued source produced these two letters which she shared with me.

[3] S. Isadore Miner to Probate Judge of Calhoun County, Michigan, Oct. 8, 1877, Calhoun County, Michigan, Probate files. Copy in author's possession.

[4] Unattributed clippings dated June 24, 1913, and Feb. 27, 1932, in Ross Coller Collection, Willard Library, Battle Creek, Michigan.

money aid, but sympathy and help in securing their rights." She penned articles on such topics as "Objectionable Advertising" and "Cooperative Housekeeping," which foreshadowed the style her Dallas columns would take.[5]

The failure of her marriage prompted Mrs. Miner to take a position in Toledo, Ohio, with the Toledo *Commercial* in March, 1891. This job lasted only two years, for she was hired by the Dallas *Morning News* and moved to Dallas to start work on January 1, 1893. Her reasons for going to Dallas are unclear, although her mother and stepfather, from whom she had been estranged, were living there at the time, as well as the daughter of a friend from Toledo. Perhaps the forward-looking reputation of the Dallas *Morning News* and its then-business manager G. B. Dealey, as well as the career opportunities in a city which had become the largest in Texas by 1890, influenced her decision.

Her arrival in Dallas was unheralded, but she soon began to make her presence known. Five months after going to work, she helped establish the Texas Woman's Press Association, by drafting the constitution and bylaws of the organization.[6] In October of that same year she addressed a session of the inaugural meeting of the Woman's Congress held during the Texas State Fair, informing them of "The Vocations Open to Women."[7] Her role as a newspaperwoman who created interest in women's affairs in Texas began to emerge with the founding of the Woman's Congress, for as one woman attending the Congress reported: "The [*Morning*] *News* . . . was a potent factor in keeping them posted on matters of importance constantly arising and many said that all they knew of the movement was what was eagerly looked for in the *News*."[8]

She continued to make speeches, addressing the Texas Equal Rights Association meeting in June 1894 on the need for "School Suffrage for Women." But Mrs. Miner's speechmaking was not confined to women's groups. (Her profession of journalism had accepted women writers reluctantly, a shortcoming which had been responsible for the founding of Sorosis, an organization of women writers in New York

[5] *Good Health,* Feb.–Mar., 1890.
[6] *DMN,* Aug. 21, 1916.
[7] Ibid., Oct. 24, 1893.
[8] Ibid., Oct. 30, 1893.

City in 1868.[9]) In Texas the male journalists extended an invitation to her to speak to their Texas Press Association that same June (1894), making her the first woman "to sit in the presidential chair of an assembly composed exclusively of men." She offered the newsmen her views on "What Can Be Done to Improve the Average Woman's and Children's Departments in Newspapers?"[10]

Her ideas on improving the women's and children's departments of the Dallas *Morning News* obviously pleased her superiors, as she was made the first woman's editor of the paper in 1896 and given a page titled "The Woman's Century" to fill once a week. Her first column on April 15, 1896, was signed "Pauline Periwinkle," a *nom de plume* that would become a household word in Dallas and Texas for the next twenty years.

She made it clear from the outset that her readers would no longer be fed a diet of only social events and fashion advice. Instead, she wrote, "I am a firm believer that good accrues from woman's familiarizing herself with affairs that affect her immediate community first, her state next, and her country ultimately—good both to the woman and to the object of her inquiry."[11] She offered a very timely view for 1896 when she observed that "One of the most alluring of the many phases presented by the new woman movement is the promise it holds in store for the middle-aged woman of the future. . . . It remains for this latter day trend of thought to disprove what has long been held, that when a woman marries she incapacitates herself for any future usefulness outside the home. . . ." She urged her reader to cultivate her mind and body while her children were at home so that she would have "laid a foundation for good work to be done when her family no longer requires her constant care."[12] This acknowledgment of the "new woman" movement clearly aligned her with Progressive thinking at the time, and it was obviously her intention to convey the currents of the movement to her readers.

---

[9] Karen J. Blair, *The Clubwoman as Feminist: True Womanhood Redefined, 1868–1914* (New York: Holmes & Meier, 1980), 20.

[10] Elizabeth Brooks, *Prominent Women of Texas* (Akron, Oh.: Werner Co., 1896), 127–128; Ferdinand B. Baillio, *A History of the Texas Press Association, from Its Organization in Houston in 1880 . . .* (Dallas: Southwestern Printing Co., 1916), 170.

[11] *DMN*, Oct. 14, 1896.

[12] Ibid., July 5, 1896.

Pauline Periwinkle viewed the woman's club as an ideal vehicle for the "good work to be done" as well as for cultivating the minds of her readers. She lost no time in promoting a project for Dallas women: a new public library. The city had a library, stuck away in a room in a municipal building, but earlier efforts to gain support for a new library building had foundered. In March 1898 she wrote, "if anything is timely it is a general stirring up and educating up of the public to the need of a library in every town. . . . Surely no better field for practical demonstration of the value of organized effort among club women could be afforded." She added fuel to her efforts by publishing letters from her women readers, including one which snorted: "A city claiming 50,000 inhabitants with not a vestige of a library! Surely we should boast no more."[13]

Dallas clubwomen, newly organized into the Dallas Federation of Women's Clubs, adopted a public library as their first objective in 1899, following the lead of the state Federation of Women's Literary Clubs, which had made public libraries their state-wide project. The women contacted Andrew Carnegie's organization and secured a commitment that would supply funds for a library if the City of Dallas could come up with the land for a building and agree to provide $4,000 for yearly maintenance of the facility. Pauline Periwinkle was elected secretary of the Dallas Public Library Association, which was formed to help raise funds, and went to work, writing more than one hundred local businessmen to ask for their support. She then published some of their endorsements of the idea, thereby laying the groundwork for public acceptance and financial support. The library fund drive raised over $10,000 in two months and Dallas opened its Carnegie Library on October 30, 1901.[14]

In addition to libraries, the columnist was an outspoken advocate of education, from free kindergartens to college education for women. Of college she wrote: "four of the best and most susceptible years of one's life spent in the company of noble thoughts and high ideals can not fail to leave their impress, and a generous education should be the birthright of every daughter of the Republic, as well as of every

---

[13] Ibid., Mar. 28, 1898.
[14] Heidi G. Stein, "Dallas Public Library's Association with Andrew Carnegie's Library Philanthropy" (graduate school independent study paper, North Texas State University, 1987).

son. . . ."[15] While her position seems unassailable from our vantage point, there were nationally-known educators, such as one Professor Thorndike of Columbia, who claimed that because a larger proportion of university-bred women did not marry, the "university both unfits a woman for domesticity and inoculates her positively against the wiles of matrimony." Pauline Periwinkle saw an ulterior motive in the professor's protest, observing that

> the wise ones among us have been anticipating something ever since the issue of the annual post-graduation statistics showing that during the last year out of every twenty-five honors in co-educational institutions sixteen were won by the young women. This injudicious activity on the part of college girls was bound to be heard from, even if it took the form of opposing any kind of education for women. Opposition to women's education is of much the same caliber as opposition to women's voting. Man would let her vote if she promised not to hold office and he would acquiesce to her presence in college if she would agree not to win any of the honors.

Then she noted, with tongue in cheek: "Unless our girls learn discretion with their other studies, our co-educational system is doomed."[16]

But she found little humor in the lack of kindergartens in the public school system. Pointing to the success of the Dallas Free Kindergarten Association, a private group supporting three kindergartens, she told her readers that "if that larger general public was alert to the full meaning of this work . . . it could see to it that . . . [it] was a paid-up part of that public spirit that is building a newer, better Dallas." She viewed kindergartens as a "social and moral force . . . conceded to be indispensable to the healthful growth of the city."[17] The women's clubs, meanwhile, provided support to the private kindergartens in the city through various fund raisers, including the 1905 publication of a small book, *The Legal Status of Women in Texas*, by Lawrence Neff, which found a ready market among women's clubs.

[15] *DMN*, June 7, 1896.
[16] Ibid., Oct. 7, 1901.
[17] Ibid., Jan. 5, 1903, Jan. 18, 1904.

The Dallas clubs, unfortunately, were not successful in convincing the public school system to take over the kindergartens, for it was so overburdened that it could not afford to fund them until 1922.

Pauline's concern for children, however, was not simply limited to their schooling. She was appalled at the jailing of two six-year-olds in a nearby city, with the possibility of their being sent to a reformatory, for stealing thread. She wrote in 1903 that "little children do not need reformatories; what they need is a home, in the highest and best sense of the word." That column began her crusade for Dallas and Texas to establish juvenile courts, secure police matrons and detention homes, and even playgrounds where children could expend their energy in innocent activities.[18] She peppered her readers with information about what was happening in New York, Chicago, Boston, and Denver with the creation of special schools, play parks, and juvenile courts. The Dallas Federation took up the cause, sending a representative to visit Denver's famed Judge Ben Lindsay, who had established the first juvenile courts in the U.S., and to bring home detailed plans of how they operated. The clubwomen paid a call on the police commissioner and jail to discuss hiring a police matron in Dallas. They were successful in this venture, and agreed to pay the salary of the police matron for the first few months on the job, until the city acknowledged her usefulness and made her a city employee.[19]

The juvenile court system was not as easy to implement. It required an act of the Texas Legislature to establish such courts, and this meant convincing a group of men that, in Pauline Periwinkle's words, "It is wiser and less expensive to save children than to punish criminals."[20] Despite the concerted efforts of women's clubs, working with police chiefs and mayors of numerous towns, and the facts and figures marshaled by the editor of the Woman's Century page of the *Morning News* for more than two years, the Twenty-ninth Legislature failed to pass the juvenile courts bill. When this happened, she let the gentlemen know, in print for distribution throughout the state, just what she thought of their inaction.

Incensed that relief had been "denied for treating . . . the boy on any middle ground between innocence and crime," she observed with

18 Ibid., Feb. 2, 1903.
19 Ibid., Jan. 4, Jan. 11, 1904, Oct. 1, 1935.
20 Ibid., Jan. 4, 1904.

disgust that "the very house that killed the bill framed to protect the boy passed one to protect goats and squirrels." "Texas is away behind the procession of States that have cast aside the hide-bound, medieval method of treating wayward children as criminals," she wrote. "We boast of our empire of wealth, of the fact that it outclasses all other sections in the variety and quantity of its productions and, content with material prosperity, we give little if any concern to the more important development—that of character and good citizenship. . . . Until we direct the prosperity of the State to the upbuilding of its people, we have little of which to boast."[21]

Undaunted, the women's clubs continued work with the mayors, judges, and police chiefs who supported the concept, pressing their case until the juvenile courts bill was passed in 1907.[22] The clubwomen had obviously taken to heart the observation about crusading women made ten years earlier by their fearless spokeswoman: "The progressive woman can always console herself with the knowledge that people have opposed everything new from time immemorial. The inventor of the umbrella was stigmatized for interrupting the designs of Providence, for when showers fell it was evident God intended man should get wet."[23]

Another idea which required an uphill battle to gain acceptance was the need for play parks. Strange as it may seem, one hundred years ago most parks were designed with no thought of children. Formal drives, flower beds, and gazebos for band concerts comprised the layout of most parks. Not a swing set, see-saw, or jungle gym could be found. "Keep off the grass" and "no fishing" signs were common. As far as a child was concerned, there might as well have been a large "no having fun" sign. Pauline Periwinkle, reflecting her awareness of progressive trends elsewhere, shared the belief that play parks could provide a means of reducing the incidents of young boys getting into trouble, and told her readers why: "The movement for playgrounds in cities means far more than the question of a little fresh air. It means hearty, healthy outdoor play for a class of boys who ought to be thoroughly tired out when night comes, ready to go to bed instead of ready to prowl the street in search of excitement. The majority of the

---

[21] Ibid., Apr. 2, 1905.
[22] Ibid., Dec. 17, 1906.
[23] Ibid., Nov. 22, 1897.

misdemeanors committed by young boys are the result of misplaced energy."[24]

She pressed her case in subsequent columns when she reminded her readers that "To no other form of preventing juvenile delinquency is so much attention being paid at present as to the child's recreation. 'Where does the child put in his idle hours? Where does the man put in his idle hours? The answer to either of these queries will give the key to the character of child or adult."[25] She went on to point out how the women's clubs of Pittsburgh and Philadelphia were helping establish playgrounds. In contrast, she observed, "Hot weather, in Texas or elsewhere, calls for fresh air and thirst quenching. . . . It is safe to assert that there is not a city in the state that has enough of either [public parks or public drinking fountains] to meet the necessities of man or beast."[26] She was not above trying to shame Dallas city fathers into supporting play parks, using as her example the city of San Francisco, which was still recovering from the devastating earthquake of 1906: "If stricken San Francisco can set aside $65,000 yearly to be used for playgrounds in the scheme of the city's regeneration," she observed, "it would seem as if cities that have experienced no calamities or financial backsets might do proportionately as much."[27]

The efforts of Pauline Periwinkle and the City Federation of Women's Clubs succeeded, and Dallas's first "play park" was dedicated on Thanksgiving Day, 1909.[28] Trinity Park, as it was called, was the culmination of a two year fund-raising effort, spearheaded by the clubwomen of Dallas, who instituted a "Tag Day" on the last day of February. On that day, the downtown was overrun by women selling badges which noted the wearer supported efforts to help the children of the city. The city, with help from the Tag Day proceeds, purchased the site and installed equipment, while the Women's Federation paid the first few months' salary of a playground supervisor, as it had done with the police matron.[29]

It was evident to anyone recalling the ten years preceding the opening of the play park that the women's clubs of Dallas had under-

[24] Ibid., Feb. 2, 1903.
[25] Ibid., Feb. 17, 1908.
[26] Ibid., July 29, 1907.
[27] Ibid., May 10, 1909.
[28] Ibid., Nov. 21, 1909.
[29] Ibid., Feb. 29, 1908, Feb. 23, Nov. 26, 1909.

gone a remarkable transformation. From a narrow focus on social and literary matters, they had widened the scope of their interest to civic improvements, or as Pauline Periwinkle phrased it, from "eatables and wearables" to "thinkables and doables." The Federation of Women's Clubs had, in her words, "awakened to the fact that the progress of the world does not depend on the acquirement of a little more culture on the part of a limited number of fairly well-educated women, but on the amount of leavening those women are enabled to impart to the masses."[30]

As a newswoman, Pauline Periwinkle was constantly providing the ingredients for the leavening. Her columns on the need for a pure food law for the city of Dallas were masterpieces of the art of persuasion. Comparing local citizens who did not object to the condition of their food and water to the peasants of Italy who lived in the shadow of a smoking Vesuvius, she concluded with a dramatic flourish: "Let us not deplore the foolhardiness of those who choose the perils of fire and water while we supinely await the ravages of disease because we are too indolent and miserly to keep clean. Better perish on the volcano's slope than die on top of a dunghill."[31]

Pointing out the lack of success of "those who have been working for pure food laws in Texas," she observed that they had "evidently overlooked the mighty factor of the sensitive stomach in the anxious search for a possible heart." She then proceeded to describe in great detail the appalling extent of food and milk adulteration taking place in Texas.[32] Her efforts were rewarded when the city of Dallas, pressured by local women's clubs, passed the first pure food law in the state in 1906.

Even with the passage of the state's first pure food law, she did not relax. She is credited with convincing Dr. J. S. Abbott to apply for the position as head of the Dairy and Food Commission, instead of letting politicians choose a chairman who would not enforce the law as stringently as the women might wish. Yet she saw clearly that the law lacked sufficient appropriations.

To overcome the shortcomings, she publicized the Texas Federation's creation of subcommittees of women all over the state to make the law

---

[30] Ibid., Jan. 28, 1904.
[31] Ibid., June 9, 1902.
[32] Ibid., July 31, 1905.

work. She reported on the work of these committees, which made inspections, collected samples of suspected foods, and publicized the requirements of the new law in their communities. She published examples of the loopholes that existed in the new law, and urged clubwomen to pressure their legislators to close them. The women's efforts paid off when an improved pure food law was passed in 1909.[33]

By 1909, it was clear that Pauline Periwinkle was one of the most effective weapons that progressive women in Texas had. Thanks to the wide readership of the Dallas *Morning News* and its sister publication the Galveston *News*, she was a household word in the state. Were her successes duplicated elsewhere? Were there other journalists doing work similar to Pauline Periwinkle? Texas had a few newspaper women, such as Kate Friend of the Waco *Times Herald* and, a few years later, Harriot Russell of the Houston *Post*, who wrote of the need for city improvement, but not with the regularity or following of Pauline Periwinkle.[34] The Woman's Century editor, however, did have counterparts in other areas of the country.

The New Orleans *Picayune* had actually been edited by a woman, Eliza Nicholson, from 1875 to 1896. Although she didn't write a weekly column, she editorially supported civic improvements such as draining the swamps to prevent epidemics, developing an artesian water system, and electrifying the city's lighting system, as well as better pay and tenure for women school teachers and a police matron.[35]

At the Atlanta *Constitution* Ismay Dooly headed the women's department, which backed measures involving the welfare and advancement of women and children. Much like Pauline Periwinkle, she had been instrumental in the founding of the Atlanta City Federation of Women's Clubs and Georgia Federation of Women's Clubs. In the Midwest, the Cleveland *Press* had Winona Wilcox Payne, whose column was filled with progressive ideas, noted for putting "punch and irony into the woman's page at a time when it was still smothered in lavender and old lace."[36]

[33] Ibid., May 11, 1908, Feb. 1, June 17, 1909.
[34] Kate Harrison Friend papers, Texas Collection, Baylor University; Hallie Flint papers, Woodson Research Center, Rice University.
[35] B. H. Gilley, "A Woman for Women: Eliza Nicholson, Publisher of the New Orleans *Daily Picayune,*" *Louisiana History,* XXX (Summer, 1989), 236, 241, 246.
[36] Ishbel Ross, *Ladies of the Press: The Story of Women in Journalism by an Insider* (New York: Harper & Brothers, 1936), 553, 594–595.

In New York City, Rheta Childe Dorr wrote for the *Evening Post* from 1902 to 1906, focusing on women's clubs and charitable activities. She was appointed chairman of the General Federation of Women's Clubs' committee on the industrial conditions of women and children, and her committee was instrumental in persuading Congress in 1905 to authorize the Bureau of Labor to conduct the first official investigation into the condition of working women in the United States. Another female journalist, Sophie Loeb, wrote for the New York *Evening World* about the need for child welfare boards and state support for destitute widows with children, penny school lunches, cheaper and safer taxis, and public play streets.[37]

With these talented women writing in major metropolitan newspapers, it is particularly notable that Pauline Periwinkle was asked to represent women in journalism by speaking at the "Women in the Professions" program at the 1906 biennial meeting of the General Federation of Women's Clubs in St. Paul. Following her success in getting the juvenile courts bill passed by the Texas Legislature, she was asked to represent the state of Texas at the Conference on Childsaving sponsored by the National Conference of Charities and Corrections.[38]

Growing national recognition did not lessen her involvement in Dallas. She was one of two women appointed to the city plan committee, which in 1910 adopted the Kessler Plan, calling for an orderly rearrangement of the city's thoroughfares. She served as a vice president of the Dallas Equal Suffrage Association in 1913. She kept up the demanding schedule of her weekly column, as well as making a home for her husband, W. A. Callaway, whom she had married in 1900, and two orphaned nieces she had taken in shortly after her marriage.

This dark-haired woman of boundless energy and intellect was dedicated to improving the quality of life in Dallas, especially that of women and children. Her columns provide a textbook example of the power of the press to shape public opinion. Granted, she had a strong ally in publisher George B. Dealey, who proved himself a strong advocate of improving the city of Dallas in a myriad of ways. Not the least of these was the encouragement and support he gave his women's

---

[37] Edward T. James, ed., *Notable American Women, 1607–1950: A Biographical Dictionary* (3 vols.; Cambridge: Belknap Press of Harvard University Press, 1971), I, 503, II, 416–417.

[38] *DMN*, Mar. 5, 1906.

editor. There appears to have been no censorship of Pauline Periwinkle's views, many of which were certainly outspoken. The list of causes for which she rallied the citizens of Dallas does not end with the ones just described. Her woman suffrage columns are extraordinary examples of clarity and logic.[39] Even Minnie Fisher Cunningham, president of the Texas Equal Suffrage Association from 1915 to 1920, wrote to her that "Most of my best arguments for Suffrage were gleaned from [your] column."[40] Sadly, Pauline Periwinkle did not live to see woman suffrage, a cause for which she had worked so long, become a reality for the women of Texas. She died in 1916, at the relatively young age of fifty-two. Tributes poured into the *Morning News*, conveying just how powerfully this woman journalist had affected her readers.

Dr. Henry Curtis, a noted child welfare expert, termed her one of the four outstanding women in America, along with Jane Addams, Dr. Anna Howard Shaw, and Carrie Chapman Catt.[41] An old friend who had also been a newspaper woman observed that "Her heart's inclination was to help; her head's requirement to help intelligently; and her long journalistic training disposed her to get at the root of fact." Other friends offered a more personal view: "How are we going to get along without her? There is not a woman in Dallas who would be missed so much." "It has been said that there is no place in the world that cannot be filled. Commercially, this may be true, but in the hearts of her friends there will never grow another flower so straight and true and brilliant as 'Pauline Periwinkle.'"[42]

Although she claimed only the ability to publicize the work of others, she was in reality a driving force behind the establishment of the Women's Congress, the Dallas Federation of Women's Clubs, the Equal Suffrage Club of Dallas, the Dallas Women's Forum, and the Texas Woman's Press Association.[43] As a long-time acquaintance de-

[39] Ibid., Mar. 30, 1903, Feb. 11, May 6, 1907, Jan. 23, Sept. 11, 1911, Feb. 12, Mar. 18, Aug. 19, 1912, Mar. 10, 1913, Feb. 2, June 22, Aug. 3, Nov. 16, 1914, Feb. 1, 1915.

[40] Letter, Sept. 16, 1915, Minnie Fisher Cunningham papers, Houston Metropolitan Research Center (now Texas and Local History Department), Houston, Texas. My thanks to Elizabeth York Enstam, who discovered this letter, as well as many other helpful items which she has generously shared.

[41] *DMN*, Apr. 11, 1942.

[42] Ibid., Aug. 21, 1916.

[43] Texas Federation of Women's Clubs, *Who's Who of the Womanhood of Texas*, I, 1923–1924 (Fort Worth: The Federation, 1924), 33.

scribed her, "she was so modest and unassuming about it all. . . . It mattered not how hard she worked for a result, she never claimed the credit. She planned and organized and worked, and then, when the hardest of the fight was over, she stepped aside to allow others to fill the offices while she stood behind them with encouragement and advice."[44]

This 1916 observation might explain why some who have researched and studied Texas women's history have not heard of Pauline Periwinkle before now. Fortunately, she left a paper trail: her organizational abilities were matched by her writing talent, as seen in her weekly column on the Woman's Century page. She was quite skillful at describing Dallas's needs and problems, pointing out what other communities in the nation were doing about similar situations, then suggesting solutions. Her sense of humor, straightforward style, and frank appeal to the civic pride of citizens helped garner support for a wide range of public improvements, including the first Carnegie Library, juvenile courts, a police matron, play parks for children, and pure food ordinances. Working in tandem with the Federation of Women's Clubs, she helped make Dallas a much healthier, more humane and livable city.

From our late twentieth-century perspective we can see limitations in her vision for a better Dallas. But many of her views, such as regarding charity for the "needy poor" only, the position that "children of negative heredity and training should early be taught obedience and self-control [since] children born of rebellion and lawlessness are anarchists at birth," and the unsuitability of the latest literature and motion pictures, which she characterized as "trashy," reflected the current thinking of many social reformers throughout the nation.[45] Her pseudoscientific characterizations of the Chinese and Negro races, however, and particularly her support for denying the admission of colored clubs to the General Federation of Women's Clubs despite the efforts of Jane Addams of Hull House, were especially unfortunate. Her views of "the Negro" were Southern and stereotypical ("predominance of emotion in make-up, indifferent to reason") and she wrote of

[44] *DMN*, Aug. 21, 1916.
[45] Ibid., Nov. 13, 1899, Oct. 14, Nov. 18, 1901, Apr. 11, 1904, Jan. 20, 1908, Nov. 22, 1909.

African Americans so infrequently that it was obvious that their social problems were not the focus of her attention.[46] She was no doubt ahead of her time in Texas, but not without a myopia regarding the minority community.

Another revealing aspect of her reform impulse can be found in her views about women's rights. While an early supporter of woman suffrage, Pauline Periwinkle was also a vigorous advocate of women who worked. She decried the wage discrimination experienced by women that was an accepted tenet of the economy, as well as the obstacles to advancement created by social conventions. Despite the difficulties faced by working women, she urged her women readers to recognize that divorce or death could change their comfortable existence, and that they might find it necessary to take care of themselves and their families. She wanted all women to be prepared to be financially independent and supported those measures that would make such independence possible.[47] What her readers could not have known was that Pauline Periwinkle was writing from personal experience. She never revealed publicly that she had been divorced from her husband in Battle Creek after he abandoned her. Instead, she listed herself as a widow in the 1897 and 1898 Dallas city directories. Her decision to do so suggests that she realized that social acceptance of her outspoken views would be easier if she were known as a widow, not a divorcee. She bowed to the social conventions of the day to appear "respectable," yet worked to change those conventions which placed women at such a disadvantage. Even though her reform spirit had blind spots and at one time she apparently felt constrained by the need for social acceptance, she was still a remarkable presence among Texas women.

[46] Ibid., Sept. 18, 1899, May 19, 1902.
[47] Ibid., Oct. 4, 1896, Mar. 29, Dec. 13, 1897, Jan. 20, 1899.

Saving the Children:

The Women's Crusade Against Child Labor,
1902–1918

Judith N. McArthur*

THE INNOVATIONS OF THE PROGRESSIVE ERA in Texas have traditionally been described as male initiatives, agendas promoted by re-
form-minded governors and interest groups such as farmers, organized
labor, and prohibitionists. Except for a nod to the suffragists and an
occasional reference to the Woman's Christian Temperance Union, the
historical literature has failed to notice any female players in the
drama; the assumption has prevailed that because women did not hold
political office they did not take any meaningful part in politics.[1] Yet

* Judith N. McArthur received her Ph.D. from the University of Texas at Austin
and teaches American social history at the University of Houston-Victoria. She
coedited *Citizens at Last: The Woman Suffrage Movement in Texas* and is working on
a study of Texas women in the Progressive era.

[1] See James A. Tinsley, "The Progressive Movement in Texas" (Ph.D. diss.,
University of Wisconsin, 1953); Maurice Sochia, "The Progressive Movement in Texas,
1900–1914" (M.A. thesis, Southwest Texas State Teachers College, 1959); Lewis L.
Gould, *Progressives and Prohibitionists: Texas Democrats in the Wilson Era* (Austin:
University of Texas Press, 1973); Robert S. Maxwell, "Texas in the Progressive Era,
1900–1930," in *Texas: A Sesquicentennial Celebration,* ed. Donald W. Whisenhunt
(Austin: Eakin Press, 1984); Robert A. Calvert and Arnoldo De León, *The History of
Texas* (Arlington Heights, Ill.: Harlan Davidson, 1990), chap. 10, "Progressivism in
Texas"; and Larry D. Hill, "Texas Progressivism: A Search for Definition," in *Texas
Through Time: Evolving Interpretations,* eds. Walter L. Buenger and Robert A. Calvert
(College Station: Texas A&M University Press, 1991). Evan Anders, in a recent review
of the literature, has noted the need for research on women's role in politics and social
reform. See Anders, "Populism and Progressivism," in *A Guide to the History of Texas,*

despite the fact that women were excluded from voting booths and Democratic party councils during most of the Progressive Era, they were an integral part of the reform coalition, and their influence on public policy and legislation was substantial.[2] Denied a formal voice in the political process, women used their voluntary associations as the entree to politics that they lacked as individuals.[3]

Two such groups, the Texas Federation of Women's Clubs and the Texas Congress of Mothers (now the Texas Congress of Parent-Teacher Associations), played a significant but unacknowledged role in securing and enforcing child labor legislation in Texas.[4] Both were organi-

---

eds. Light Townsend Cummins and Alvin R. Bailey, Jr. (New York: Greenwood Press, 1988), 78.

[2] Historians of women, however, in still-unpublished work, have documented the extensive activity of women's associations during this period. See Megan Seaholm, "Earnest Women: The White Woman's Club Movement in Progressive Era Texas, 1880–1920" (Ph.D. diss., Rice University, 1988); Elizabeth Hayes Turner, "Women's Culture and Community: Religion and Reform in Galveston, 1880–1920" (Ph.D. diss., Rice University, 1990); Judith N. McArthur, "Motherhood and Reform in the New South: Texas Women's Political Culture in the Progressive Era" (Ph.D. diss., University of Texas at Austin, 1992); Elizabeth York Enstam, "They Called It 'Motherhood': Dallas Women and Politics, 1895–1920," paper presented at the Texas State Historical Association annual meeting, Mar. 3, 1989 (copy in author's possession). Jacquelyn McElhaney's work-in-progress on Isadore Callaway will profile an important Progressive journalist and clubwoman.

[3] See Paula Baker, "The Domestication of Politics: Women and American Political Society, 1780–1920," *American Historical Review*, LXXXIX (June, 1984), 620–647; Katherine Kish Sklar, "Hull House in the 1890s: A Community of Women Reformers," *Signs: A Journal of Women in Culture and Society*, X (Summer, 1985), 659–677; and Anne Firor Scott, *Natural Allies: Women's Associations in American History* (Urbana: University of Illinois Press, 1991), 141–174, for a discussion of how women used their own organizations as a base for political activism.

[4] Passing references to the presence of women's organizations in the Texas child labor reform campaign appear in Texas Bureau of Labor Statistics, *First Biennial Report, 1909–1910* (Austin, 1910), 8; Alexander J. McKelway, "Child Labor Campaign in the South," *Survey*, Oct. 21, 1911, p. 1025; and Clyde Norman, "Child Labor Legislation in Texas," unpublished ms., 1936, p. 5, Labor Movement in Texas Papers, 2E309 (Barker Texas History Center, University of Texas at Austin; hereafter cited as BTHC). Discussing child labor legislation in the South, Dewey W. Grantham in *Southern Progressivism: The Reconciliation of Progress and Tradition* (Knoxville: University of Tennessee Press, 1983), 178–199, notes, without elaboration, the presence of women in the reform coalitions in nearly every state. Hugh C. Bailey, *Liberalism in the New South: Southern Social Reformers and the Progressive Movement* (Coral Gables: University of Miami Press, 1969), 153–188, similarly notes women only in passing. By

zations of middle-class white women who justified their public activity by expanding "woman's sphere" to encompass all matters relating to child welfare.[5] Each organization had a standing committee that monitored legislative sessions and determined which measures the membership would advocate or oppose. Each also joined with various other single- and mixed-sex organizations to form coalitions that pressed for specific social welfare reforms: in the child labor struggle these were the Child Welfare Conference of Texas, the Texas Conference of Charities and Correction, and the Texas Child Labor Committee.

Nevertheless, the Federation of Women's Clubs and the Congress of Mothers were not a monolithic force; the image of united motherhood that they presented to the public concealed tensions and territorial rivalries.[6] The older and larger Federation of Women's Clubs, whose interests encompassed literature, fine arts, conservation, history and government, and education as well as child welfare, was already well established when the Congress of Mothers made its appearance. Organized nationally in 1897 and in Texas in 1909, the Congress drew its membership from Kindergarten associations, child study groups, and school mothers' clubs that had previously joined the Federation of Women's Clubs. Club leaders viewed it as an upstart organization encroaching on the TFWC's child welfare and school reform work. The two organizations competed for members and influence, maintaining separate agendas even though they shared the same goals.

---

contrast, Mary Martha Thomas in "The 'New Woman' in Alabama, 1890–1920," *Alabama Review*, XLIII (July, 1990), 163–180, shows for one state the detail that historians of women are bringing to light on the same subject.

[5] Both the Federation of Women's Clubs and the Congress of Mothers had parallel African American organizations, but no records of the Texas branches are known to exist. In practice, child labor legislation applied only to white children; black youngsters worked in agriculture and domestic service, which were not among the occupations covered by the law.

[6] Ella Caruthers Porter, founder of the Texas Congress of Mothers, characterized the relationship between the TFWC and the TCM as one of "friction and inharmony." See Ella C. Porter to Mrs. S. J. Wright, Nov. 22, 1909, Texas Federation of Women's Clubs Papers [uncatalogued] (Blagg-Huey Library, Texas Woman's University, Denton; hereafter cited as TWU); Porter to Anna Pennybacker, Mar. 28, 1912, box 2M14, Mrs. Percy V. Pennybacker Papers (BTHC). Many individual women were members of both organizations; the tension seems to have existed primarily at the office-holding level.

Working separately, they were responsible for the two most significant advances in the effort to restrict child labor in Texas: the child labor law of 1911 and the appointment of a woman as the state's first child welfare inspector in 1918.

Texas and the other southern states entered the twentieth century carrying the double burden of the highest child labor and illiteracy rates in the country. Twenty-five percent of southern cotton mill operatives were under fifteen, and the proportion of working children aged ten to fifteen was four times higher in the South than in the northern states in 1900.[7] Although Texas had only a handful of cotton mills at the turn of the century, the state labor press publicized the fact that boys and girls as young as eight worked twelve-hour days in the stifling heat and oppressive humidity necessary to keep thread from breaking in the spinning rooms.[8] Breathing air thick with cotton dust while they tended whirring machinery, child workers might make fifty cents a day, depending upon their speed and dexterity.[9] Young boys could also be found working in coal mines, quarries, and sawmills, where even grown men risked injury and sometimes death.

Texas was one of five southern states in which labor unions launched the first phase of child labor agitation; the resulting statutes, all passed by 1903, set a minimum age of twelve for work in factories and mills.[10] A child labor law was one of the first measures sought by the Texas State Federation of Labor's legislative committee, after it was created in 1902. It began planning immediately for the 1903 legislative session, securing endorsements from the Democratic party and the Texas Federation of Women's Clubs.[11]

The TFWC was then only five years old and just beginning to expand its interests beyond literature and the arts. At the national level, however, the General Federation of Women's Clubs had already

[7] Walter I. Trattner, *Crusade for the Children: A History of the National Child Labor Committee and Child Labor Reform in America* (Chicago: Quadrangle Books, 1970), 36–40.

[8] James Carrington Maroney, "Organized Labor in Texas, 1900–1929" (Ph.D. diss., University of Houston, 1975), 61.

[9] Dallas *Morning News*, Apr. 26, 1908.

[10] Grantham, *Southern Progressivism*, 181–187.

[11] Maroney, "Organized Labor in Texas," 61–63; Joint Labor Legislative Board of Texas, *Report of the Joint Labor Legislative Board, on all Matters Affecting the Interests of Labor that Were Considered by the Twenty-eighth Legislature* (San Antonio, [1903]), 3–4.

formed a Committee on Industrial Problems Affecting Women and Children with Florence Kelley, the former Illinois factory inspector who headed the National Consumers' League, as chair. Kelley mailed out a pamphlet of child labor facts, complete with bibliography and resource list, asking that each club in the General Federation investigate the extent of child labor regulation in its own state and devote at least one meeting to discussing industrial problems. At the General Federation's biennial convention in 1902, a circular tabulating child labor statutes in the states was distributed; each delegate could see how her state compared with the rest of the country. Jane Addams of Hull House spoke on the suffering behind the statistics and the moral and mental waste that child labor inflicted on the nation.[12]

With this inspiration, the TFWC took up child labor at its annual convention later that year. Isadore Callaway, who was also known to readers of the Dallas *Morning News* as the witty and satirical columnist "Pauline Periwinkle," read a paper denouncing the industrial exploitation of children. When President Anna Pennybacker, a former high school teacher and author of a popular school history of Texas, subsequently addressed the assembled women on the need for a state child labor bill, her speech "struck a new note of advance" for the state's clubwomen, the federation's historian wrote years later. The delegates passed a resolution "heartily" endorsing the demand for a law to prohibit the employment of children under twelve and "most earnestly" urging the state legislature to act in the upcoming session. The Joint Labor Legislative Board, organized at the beginning of 1903 by delegates from various city labor councils and one from the TSFL's legislative committee, did the actual lobbying work. The state's first child labor law passed in 1903. It established minimum ages of twelve to work in factories and mills and fifteen for employment in mines and quarries.[13]

---

[12] On women's clubs see Karen J. Blair, *The Clubwoman as Feminist: True Womanhood Redefined, 1868–1914* (New York: Holmes & Meier, 1980). Anne Firor Scott, "The New Woman in the New South," *South Atlantic Quarterly*, LXI (Autumn, 1962), 473–483, and *The Southern Lady: From Pedestal to Politics, 1830–1930* (Chicago: University of Chicago Press, 1970), 150–163, analyzes the club movement in the South. Seaholm, "Earnest Women," does the same for Texas. See Mary I. Wood, *The History of the General Federation of Women's Clubs* (New York: The Federation, 1912), 139, 145–148, on clubwomen and child labor.

[13] Stella L. Christian (ed.), *History of the Texas Federation of Women's Clubs*

Reformers soon realized that the 1903 act was only a paper statute, "shamefully violated in every particular," according to the state federation of labor.[14] The legislature did not create any enforcement machinery until 1909, when, under pressure from the Joint Labor Legislative Board, it finally authorized a Bureau of Labor Statistics consisting of a commissioner and one deputy. The inspector of mines almost immediately reported to the new labor bureau that underage boys were working in nearly all the state's coal mines. The commissioner of labor's first visits to factories and cotton mills in 1909 resulted in the removal of more than 100 children, and he reported that employers dismissed "considerable more" in voluntary cooperation.[15] It was evident to child welfare advocates that stronger enforcement and a more comprehensive law were necessary.

Late in 1910 a coalition of child labor reformers began forming in anticipation of the next legislative session in 1911. The state federation of labor had passed a resolution calling for a new child labor law earlier in the year; the Texas Congress of Mothers now issued the same demand at its October convention. The Texas Federation of Women's Clubs followed suit at its own convention a month later. Child labor would likewise be on the agenda of the organizing convention for a state conference of charities and correction scheduled for after Thanksgiving. The National Child Labor Committee had also anticipated forming a Texas committee, but decided against crowding another convention into the same month. Instead, the NCLC's southern field secretary, Alexander J. McKelway, made plans to attend the charities conference and meet afterward with individuals interested in forming a state child labor committee. All of these groups hoped that the 1911 legislature could be persuaded to pass a stronger child labor law. Since such legislation exempted agricultural work, they also sought compulsory education and free textbook statutes that would take tenant farmers' children out of the fields.[16]

(Houston: Dealey-Adey-Elgin, 1919), 88 (quotation); Minutes, Fifth Annual Meeting, Nov. 17, 1902, Texas Federation of Women's Clubs Papers (TWU). The text of the Texas law appears in *General Laws of Texas*, Twenty-eighth Leg., Reg. Sess. (1903), 40. Illiterate children were barred from employment until age fourteen.

[14] Texas Federation of Labor, *Proceedings of the Thirteenth Annual Convention* (Austin, 1910), 16.

[15] Texas Bureau of Labor Statistics, *First Biennial Report, 1909–1910*, 12–13.

[16] Texas Congress of Mothers, Minutes, Second Annual Meeting, Oct. 14, 1910,

The decision to join forces stemmed from a special conference called by the Congress of Mothers. On October 15, the day after closing their convention in Austin, the leaders of the Congress of Mothers convened the state's first child welfare conference. All organizations working for child welfare had previously been invited to send delegates, and representatives assembled from a dozen groups, including the Federation of Women's Clubs, the Woman's Christian Temperance Union, and the YWCA. With Mothers' Congress president Ella Caruthers Porter in the chair, the delegates concluded that their separate agencies could be more effective if they coordinated their efforts to educate public opinion and exert pressure on the legislature. To this end the University of Texas, represented by Dr. A. Caswell Ellis of the education and extension departments, was designated to issue a call for a planning conference in December.[17]

While the conference call was circulating, the Federation of Women's Clubs moved aggressively to identify itself with child labor reform. When the Texas Conference of Charities and Correction organized in Houston on November 28 and 29, it created a child labor committee consisting of three representatives from organized labor and three well-known clubwomen: Anna Pennybacker, Isadore Callaway, and Maggie Barry, a professor of literature at North Texas Female College. On November 29, the Texas Federation of Women's Clubs opened its own annual convention in San Antonio under the leadership of Mrs. S. J. Wright, who had declared her presidential term (1909-1911) the "administration of the child." After passing the resolution endorsing child labor legislation, the TFWC created a special ad hoc committee to pursue this goal in Austin.[18]

---

box 32A, Texas Congress of Parents and Teachers Headquarters, Austin; San Antonio *Express*, Dec. 2, 1910; Texas State Federation of Labor, *Proceedings of the Thirteenth Annual Convention*, 16–17; Francis H. McLean, "Passage to Texas," *Survey*, Nov. 19, 1910, p. 291; Francis H. McLean to C. E. Evans, Mar. 18, 1910, and Owen J. Lovejoy to "Dear Friend," Nov. 23, 1910, box 4J283, Conference for Education in Texas Papers (BTHC).

[17] "Conference for the Conservation of Child Life," *Texas Motherhood*, I (Nov., 1910), pp. 32–33; Dallas *Morning News*, Nov. 27, 1910. In calling a state conference on child welfare the Texas Congress of Mothers was following the earlier example of the national body, which had convened an International Congress on the Welfare of the Child in Washington, D.C., in 1908 in conjunction with the annual convention.

[18] Houston *Chronicle*, Nov. 28, 1910; Houston *Post*, Nov. 29, Nov. 30, 1910. The

When the fledgling child welfare conference assembled again for its planning conference during the Texas State Teachers' Association convention in Abilene on December 28, both club and mothers' congress women were elected to office. The organization formally adopted the name Child Welfare Conference of Texas and elected as president Adella Kelsey Turner, a past president of the Federation of Women's Clubs, whom governors Campbell and Colquitt had appointed to represent Texas at the National Child Labor Conference. A. Caswell Ellis was elected chair of the executive committee, whose female members were Nettie B. Ford of the Congress of Mothers and Mrs. Harris Masterson of the YWCA.[19]

The Child Welfare Conference agreed that the executive committee should survey the state's child welfare needs, choose one or more issues on which to focus, and coordinate the group's efforts. Preference would be given to those reforms with the greatest chance of passing in the upcoming legislative session. Each organization was to send its suggestions to the executive committee, which would meet in Austin in January. The Federation of Women's Clubs immediately pressed ahead to ensure that its proposed child labor restrictions would be on the CWC agenda. The day after the Child Welfare Conference adjourned, the Federation's special child labor committee met with the labor commissioner in Austin to decide how a bill should be drawn for the legislature. They agreed that the commissioner would draft it, asking for a minimum age of fifteen in factories and mills and provisions for improving safety and sanitation.[20]

The TFWC's ad hoc labor committee, accompanied by a member of its regular Legislative Outlook Committee whose husband had been chosen to introduce the bill in the senate, was present to make its case when the executive committee of the Child Welfare Conference met as planned in January to choose legislative goals. Not surprisingly, in

---

Texas Conference of Charities and Correction changed its name to the Texas Conference of Social Welfare in 1915. See Susie Kathleen Thompson, "The Texas Conference for Social Welfare" (M.A. thesis, University of Texas at Austin, 1939), for an overview of its work.

[19] Dallas *Morning News*, Dec. 30, 1910.

[20] Ibid., Dec. 29, Dec. 30, 1910, Jan. 16, 1911. For a biographical sketch of A. Caswell Ellis, see Austin *American*, Aug. 20, 1917; for Turner see *Texian Who's Who* (Dallas: The Texian Co., 1938).

view of the TFWC's fait accompli in securing a draft and a sponsor, the executive committee selected child labor legislation as one of its three goals; the others were school hygiene and sanitation and compulsory education.[21]

The clubwomen's child labor bill was the only one of the three measures supported by the Conference for Child Welfare that passed in the 1911 legislative session. The Texas Federation president, Mrs. S. J. Wright, announced the victory triumphantly in the press, thanking the legislators on behalf of the state's ten thousand clubwomen; she also expressed special thanks to the labor committeewomen, to Adella Turner and Caswell Ellis of the Child Welfare Conference, and to the retiring and incoming commissioners of labor.[22] Significantly, she did not mention the Congress of Mothers. Because the Federation of Women's Clubs had so clearly marked child labor legislation as its own, the Congress of Mothers had pursued different legislative priorities that emphasized its special work in the schools.[23] The Congress was responsible for suggesting the unsuccessful school sanitation proposals of which the TFWC, in turn, had taken no notice, although it too was strongly interested in school improvement. Despite the overlap in their child welfare goals, each group marked its own legislative territory and remained aloof from the other.

The child labor law of 1911 established a minimum age of fifteen to work in factories and mills, the highest such limit imposed by any southern state at that time, and a minimum age of seventeen for work in dangerous occupations such as mining and quarrying.[24] Nevertheless, it still failed to meet the standards of the National Child Labor Committee's Uniform Child Labor Law by not imposing an eight-hour maximum on hours of labor, not forbidding night work, and not requiring documentary proof of age. Parents who needed children's

---

[21] Dallas *Morning News*, Jan. 26, 1911.

[22] Ibid., Mar. 20, 1911.

[23] The Texas Congress of Mothers had suggested bills to require medical inspection of children in the public schools and to abolish the public drinking cup, both of which failed in the 1911 legislature. Ibid., Jan. 16, Feb. 6, 1911.

[24] National Child Labor Committee, *Proceedings of the Seventh Annual Conference* (New York, 1911), 141; *General Laws of Texas*, Thirty-second Leg., Reg. Sess. (1911), 75–76. The law also forbade anyone under fifteen to work "in any capacity in the manufacture of goods for immoral purposes, or where their health may be impaired or their morals debased."

earnings in order to make ends meet could subvert the law by swearing that underage sons and daughters were old enough to work. Middle-class clubwomen, who knew little of the hard realities of working-class life, believed that this happened infrequently; they were slow to grasp the concept of a family wage and prone to attribute child employment to the laziness or greed of working-class fathers.

Clubwomen continued to press for more stringent standards, more rigorous enforcement, and compulsory education, which re-formers of both sexes believed would be the most effective child labor law of all. The TFWC's Social Service Committee, chaired by Estelle B. Sharp, included child labor among its mandates. Summarizing the committee's work in 1914, she pointed out that Texas had still not enacted the Uniform Child Labor Law and was one of only six states, all in the South, still without a compulsory education statute.[25] In a long article published just before the opening of the Thirty-fourth Legislature in 1915 (which finally passed a compulsory education bill) Sharp reminded clubwomen that they were pledged "to remove the stain of child labor from the honor of Texas."[26]

Women's voluntary associations also pursued their child-saving work through the Texas Child Labor Committee, which emerged as a permanent organization out of the Conference for Child Welfare. Caswell Ellis and Adella Turner were again leaders; this time she served as secretary and he as chair. Nettie B. Ford and Mrs. Harris Masterson continued to represent the Congress of Mothers and the YWCA; WCTU president Nannie Webb Curtis represented temperance women.[27] In the fall of 1913 the Texas Child Labor Committee brought the National Committee's field investigator and photographer, Lewis Hine, to Texas for undercover work. His discovery that messenger boys as young as eleven and twelve regularly delivered telegrams and drug-store packages to the red light districts—and on their own learned to offer their services as guides to out-of-town businessmen—led the

[25] Estelle B. Sharp, Reports of the Social Service Committee, Texas Federation of Women's Clubs, 1912, 1914, box 2G186, Mrs. Walter B. Sharp Papers (BTHC).

[26] Houston *Post*, Jan. 17, 1915.

[27] Correspondence regarding the activities of the Texas Child Labor Committee can be found in the Alexander Caswell Ellis Papers, box 2P359 (BTHC). For the membership of the committee see Edward N. Clopper to A. Caswell Ellis, Jan. 22, 1917.

reformers to emphasize a cause and effect relationship between the street trades, moral corruption of youth, and juvenile delinquency.[28]

But the child labor coalition had no real legislative successes after 1911 beyond extending the fifteen- and seventeen-year age limits to some additional occupations, such as messenger services.[29] By then the lobby of businessmen and manufacturers who championed the New South Creed of industrial progress and swore that labor restrictions would drive them out of business was too strong to overcome.[30]

Faced with the state legislature's continuing intransigence, organized women lent support to the National Child Labor Committee's efforts to secure a federal child labor bill. Unlike some southern members of the NCLC, most notably Edgar Gardener Murphy, who resigned in protest, Texas women voiced no objection to federal legislation. Isadore Callaway promoted it in her "Pauline Periwinkle" column as a solution to the eternal objections that restricting child labor would subject Texas industries to unfair competition from those in neighboring states without such laws.[31]

Texas women repeatedly endorsed the legislation that would eventually pass Congress as the Keating-Owen Law forbidding interstate shipment of the products of child labor. The Dallas Council of Mothers, at the request of the National Congress of Mothers, asked every minister in the city to deliver a special sermon on January 23, 1915, as part of a nationwide effort to generate favorable public sentiment for

---

[28] See correspondence between Ellis and Hine, 1913; "Field Notes of Lewis V. Hine, Child Labor Conditions in Texas" (typescript); and [Lewis Hine,] "The Night Messenger Service of Texas and its Relation to the Red Light Districts" (typescript), Ellis Papers, box 2P359 (BTHC).

[29] Amendments in 1917 extended the age fifteen limit to workshops, theaters, and messenger services, and forbade the employment of anyone under seventeen in a brewery or a "disorderly house, bawdy house, or assignation house." Children between twelve and fifteen could be exempted in hardship cases decided by a county judge, but they were limited to a ten-hour day and a forty-eight-hour week. *General Laws of Texas*, Thirty-fifth Leg., Reg. Sess. (1917), 104–106.

[30] Tinsley, "Progressive Movement in Texas," 136. The Texas Commercial Secretaries Association represented businessmen and industrialists in the legislature, with the result that whenever restricted hours legislation did pass, it was always in considerably weakened form.

[31] Dallas *Morning News*, Jan. 24, 1916. I am indebted to Jackie McElhaney for sharing this citation from her files. See Bailey, *Liberalism in the New South*, 172–175, for Murphy's position.

the bill.[32] When the Keating-Owen bill was again before the House of Representatives the following year, "Pauline Periwinkle" urged all friends of children to send their congressmen an "avalanche" of letters and telegrams. If victory were to be won, she asserted, "organized womanhood must take to the field."[33]

The Keating-Owen Law, passed in 1916, was a short-lived success invalidated by the Supreme Court two years later. At the same time, however, the nation's participation in World War I opened an unexpected door for women. Enforcing the child labor law had always been a problem, but the need to boost industrial production during the war increased the demand for workers enormously. The state labor commissioner discovered during inspections that "the child labor law has almost been set aside in some places."[34] Investigators from the Bureau of Labor Statistics found that the violations invariably could have been avoided without causing production declines and "in many cases the cry of emergency was only a thinly veiled excuse for profiteering and exploitation."[35]

Organized women therefore seized the unique opportunity that arose when President Woodrow Wilson declared that beginning on April 6, 1918, the nation would observe "Children's Year," a campaign to cut infant mortality and establish "irreducible minimum standards for health, education, and work for the American child." Children's Year was the brainchild of Children's Bureau chief Julia Lathrop and the Woman's Committee of the Council of National Defense, which had invited her to serve as executive chair of its Department of Child Welfare.[36] One of Children's Year's published goals was "to maintain

[32] Dallas *Morning News*, Jan. 23, 1915. The measure was at that time called the Palmer-Owen bill.

[33] Ibid., Jan. 24, 1916.

[34] Austin *American*, July 24, 1918. Not the least of the problems in enforcing the labor law was the power of entrenched local interests. The labor department followed a policy of pressuring employers for voluntary compliance and seldom referred cases to the county attorneys for prosecution. As the reporter explained: "Mr. Jennings says it is a regrettable thing, but nevertheless true, that a conviction or lack of conviction in the different cases alluded to are [*sic*] controlled largely by local influence and officials."

[35] Texas Bureau of Labor Statistics, *Fifth Biennial Report, 1917–18* (Austin, 1918), 18.

[36] Jessica B. Peixotto, "The Children's Year and the Woman's Committee," *Annals of the American Academy of Political and Social Science*, LXXIX (Sept., 1918),

standards of child-labor and school-attendance laws under war-time pressure."[37] With the prestige of the federal government behind them, the Texas Congress of Mothers began almost immediately to press for the appointment of a special child welfare inspector in the Bureau of Labor Statistics, which in 1918 still had only four deputies to police the state's 245 counties.

Leadership was vested in the Congress of Mothers because its founder, Ella Porter, and president, Mrs. E. A. Watters, were appointed to direct Children's Year in Texas by the Woman's Committee of the Council of National Defense in Washington. The Federation of Women's Clubs participated through the Texas Division of the Woman's Committee of the CND, chaired by former TFWC president Dora Fleming. She and other prominent clubwomen, as well as the leaders of a number of other organizations, served on the state Children's Year Advisory Committee.[38] But the Texas Congress of Mothers led the campaign for a child welfare inspector just as the TFWC had monopolized the drive for the 1911 child labor law. As had been the case with the Child Welfare Conference, many organizations were committed in name, but only one was actively at work. On June 5, 1918, Watters wrote to Gov. William P. Hobby formally requesting him to create the child welfare inspector position.[39]

The women appealed directly to the governor because the regular biennial session of the legislature would not convene until 1919, but

257–258, 259 (quotation), 260–262. Children's Year was modeled on successful efforts of European governments, concerned about loss of life on the battlefields, to cut child mortality rates at home.

[37] U.S. Department of Labor, Children's Bureau, Children's Year Working Program, Children's Year Leaflet No. 3 (Washington, D.C.: U.S. Government Printing Office, 1918), 9.

[38] "Report of the Child Welfare Department, Woman's Committee of National Defense, State of Texas," box 2J364, Texas War Records (BTHC); Mrs. E. A. Watters and Mrs. Ella Caruthers Porter to Minnie Fisher Cunningham, May 9, 1918, Minnie Fisher Cunningham Papers, box 19, folder 282, Houston Metropolitan Research Center, Houston Public Library. The Dallas *Morning News*, June 1, 1918, lists the members of the Children's Year Advisory Committee, which included both women and men.

[39] Texas Congress of Mothers, Dallas Council of Mothers, to William P. Hobby, June 5, 1918, Lala Fay Watts Papers, in possession of Lillian Watts Green, New Braunfels, Texas. There is also a copy in the Governor William P. Hobby Papers (Archives Division, Texas State Library). See also Minutes, Tenth Annual Conference, November 6-8, 1918, box 32A, Texas Congress of Mothers Papers.

the timing of the request was important in another respect. Hobby had earlier called a special legislative session to deal with war-generated problems, and before adjourning in March the lawmakers had granted women the right to vote in primary elections. Women would cast their first ballots in the July Democratic primary, where Hobby was running hard against the impeached former governor, James Ferguson. Women's groups were solidly supporting Hobby, who under pressure from liberal Democrats had been gradually abandoning his conservative views and moving into the Progressive orbit. Since the newly enfranchised women were forming Women's Hobby Clubs all across the state, the Congress of Mothers expected a favorable hearing from the young governor whose campaign they were promoting. President Watters's letter was endorsed, probably with politics in mind, by Lala Fay Watts, who in addition to being president of the Dallas Council of Mothers and of the Texas Second District Congress of Mothers was chair of the Dallas Women's Hobby Club.[40]

Hobby, however, replied noncommittally and referred the request to Commissioner of Labor T. C. Jennings for an opinion on the "authority and necessity" of such a position. Jennings, who was a former chair of the Joint Labor Legislative Board and an ally of the women reformers, responded sympathetically to a subsequent telegram from Watts but was unable to offer any immediate assistance. He replied that the attorney general advised that a new position could only be created by the legislature, but promised to do everything in his power to promote it in the next regular legislative session in 1919 or in any special one that the governor might call before then.[41]

There is no further correspondence on the matter, but Hobby authorized the child welfare inspector position on September 15, despite the attorney general's adverse opinion, and appointed Watts herself to fill it.[42] The reason may well have been the new women

[40] For biographical information on Watts see *Texian Who's Who: A Biographical Dictionary of the State of Texas* (Dallas: Texian Co., 1937); Texas Federation of Women's Clubs, *Who's Who of the Womanhood of Texas*, I, 1923–1924 (Fort Worth: The Federation, 1924); and Mrs. Claude DeVan Watts, biographical file (BTHC). Information on the Woman's Hobby Committee is found in "Woman's Hobby Committee Will Instruct Voters," unidentified newspaper clipping, Watts Papers.

[41] William P. Hobby to Mrs. Claude DeVan Watts, June 7, 1918, Governor William P. Hobby Papers, series II, Letter Press Book, May 25–June 8, 1918, (Archives Division, Texas State Library); T. C. Jennings to Watts, June 19, 1918, Watts Papers.

[42] Jennings to Watts, Sept. 26, 1918, Watts Papers.

voters' high visibility in the July primary, which Hobby won by a landslide. In a handwritten notation later added at the bottom of the original letter of request, Watts wrote that Hobby had refused to consider it, and she had gone to Austin in September to talk to him personally. She may have reminded him that 386,000 women had registered to vote in the primary; that as head of the registration campaign in Dallas County she was personally responsible for nearly 17,000 of them; and that Ferguson himself, who had belatedly tried to court the female electorate, was admitting that the women had apparently voted ten to one for Hobby.[43] Women had demonstrated that they could be a power at the polls, and with passage of the federal full suffrage amendment conceded to be inevitable even by its opponents, Hobby might well have considered it expedient to conciliate this proven female constituency.

The campaign against child labor reveals that women were equal participants with men and catalysts in achieving important victories. Its broader significance, however, lay in its effect on the women themselves. In the process of lobbying to protect children, Texas women learned how to translate their domestic concerns into policy initiatives and rally public support. The new roles as experts on social problems and child welfare that women designed for themselves in the Progressive era brought them legislative successes and administrative authority. In 1903 organized labor led the battle for child labor and women followed; by 1911 women were in the front ranks, and by 1918 they had claimed the field for themselves.

[43] Dallas *Morning News,* July 5, 12, 1918; *Ferguson Forum* (Temple), Aug. 1, 1918.

The "Next 'Big Job'":

Women Prison Reformers in Texas, 1918–1930

PAUL M. LUCKO*

A FEW MONTHS after the Texas Legislature granted women the right to vote in the state's primary elections in 1918, Minnie Fisher Cunningham, who led the suffrage campaign, wrote a colleague that the "next 'big job' in Texas is prison reform." From the time women received franchise rights in Texas, they have played significant roles in prison reform movements. Especially during the decade that followed their suffrage victory, prohibition drive, and involvement in anti-vice crusades associated with Texas military camps in World War I, leaders of the women's movement embarked upon an endeavor intended to effect a fundamental alteration in the nature of the state's penal system.[1]

---

* Paul M. Lucko, a former research associate with the *Handbook of Texas* revision project, is a doctoral student in American history at the University of Texas at Austin. He is writing a history of the Texas prison system.

[1] Minnie Fisher Cunningham to Mrs. T. A. Coleman, Nov. 8, 1918, Minnie Fisher Cunningham Papers (Houston Metropolitan Archives, Houston Public Library). Gov. William P. Hobby signed the primary suffrage bill on March 26, 1918. For a discussion of the primary suffrage bill enacted by the Texas legislature in March 1918 and other aspects of the women's suffrage campaign in Texas see A. Elizabeth Taylor, *Citizens At Last: The Woman Suffrage Movement in Texas* (Austin: Ellen C. Temple, 1987), 13–48, 165; Lewis L. Gould, *Progressives and Prohibitionists: Texas Democrats in the Wilson Era* (Austin: University of Texas Press, 1973), 234–235; Emma Louise Moyer Jackson, "Petticoat Politics: Political Activism Among Texas Women in the 1920s" (Ph.D. diss., University of Texas at Austin, 1980), 1–16. For an indication of World War I anti-vice work see letter from Minnie Fisher Cunningham to Mrs. Percy V. Pennybacker, Aug. 31, 1917, in Mrs. Percy V. Pennybacker Papers (Eugene C. Barker Texas History Center, University of Texas at Austin; hereafter cited as BTHC). The letterhead of the preceding document lists a number of cooperating women's organi-

Historians Estelle Freedman and Nicole Hahn Rafter have recently written about the social feminist impulses which inspired women reformers to establish separate prisons for female criminals in the United States; these same impulses also motivated the leaders of Texas women's organizations to seek the rehabilitation of a far larger population of male felons. Though women received the assistance and encouragement of men, most of the goals and particularly the ideological underpinnings of the post-World War I movement resulted directly from the efforts of women activists. This paper concludes that reformers closely associated with the women's movement advanced a program that would have patterned Texas prisons after the most modern facilities in the United States long before a Federal judge ordered a drastic revision in the character of Texas penology.[2]

Historians have constructed the concept of social feminism as a means of explaining a certain genre of political activism that accompanied the women's suffrage movement in the United States. Convinced that women's separate sphere encompassed a morality superior to that of men, leaders within a national network of women's organizations advocated an extension of "female moral guardianship from the home to the society." Buttressed by "faith in the intrinsically moral, nurturing, and domestic nature of women," social feminists maintained that their efforts could correct critical social problems such as crime, child labor, poor working conditions, and alcohol abuse.[3]

Conscious of the devastation crime caused for "the families of those we convict," one Texas clubwoman discerned a "direct link"

---

zations such as the Woman's Christian Temperance Union, The King's Daughters, Texas Farm Women, and Texas Press Women.

[2] Estelle B. Freedman, *Their Sisters' Keepers: Women's Prison Reform in America, 1830–1930* (Ann Arbor: University of Michigan Press, 1981), 39, 45–47, 63; Nicole Hahn Rafter, *Partial Justice: Women in State Prisons, 1800–1935* (Boston: Northeastern University Press, 1985), 45–46. During the last quarter of the nineteenth century numerous American women participated in meetings of the National Prison Congress and National Conference on Charities and Correction. Before suffrage women served on boards of charities in at least half of the states and administered women's prisons.

[3] Freedman, *Their Sisters' Keepers*, 39; Rafter, *Partial Justice*, 46; William L. O'Neill, *Everyone Was Brave: A History of Feminism in America* (New York: Quadrangle Books, 1971), 51, 77, 83–84, 352–353. Freedman discusses social feminism and female networks in "Separatism as Strategy: Female Institution Building and American Feminism, 1870–1930," *Feminist Studies*, V (Fall, 1979), 512–529.

between the home environment and criminal behavior. "Society never allows . . . children to forget their heritage of crime and disgrace," she explained. Although humanitarian considerations exerted an important influence upon women prison reformers in Texas and the United States during the period of this study, the most ambitious reformers hoped to use prisons as mediums for the rehabilitation of convicted felons. Mindful of the tradition of failure and controversy that surrounded American prisons under male direction, a club leader from New York urged women to involve themselves in prison reform. "Men have certainly made a terrible mess of prison work," she told Texas reformer Elizabeth Ring in 1921. "It is time we women had more to say about such matters, for there is certainly more of women's emotions and heart needed in such work." "One thing is sure," she concluded, "we could not make a worse botch of the job than the men have done."[4]

Although the Texas Federation of Women's Clubs had adopted prison reform resolutions as early as 1910, the state's women did not begin an intensive campaign until 1918. By that time the Texas Prison System, administered by a three-man Board of Prison Commissioners, resembled that of most southern states. An enclosed penitentiary that housed about 400 prisoners and contained a few small shops and factories existed at Huntsville, but the vast majority of the state's 3,750 convicts lived and labored on fifteen farms owned or leased by the state in East Texas and on the Gulf Coast and the Red River. During much of the period of this study the number of white convicts slightly exceeded the number of African Americans; prisoners of Mexican descent constituted approximately 10 percent of the prison population. Excepting the Goree Farm for women and the Wynne Farm at Huntsville for physically disabled prisoners, state officials conducted the farms in a plantation fashion, utilizing gang labor to raise cotton, sugar cane, and other commercial crops in what was usually an unsuccessful attempt to make the prison system self-supporting.[5]

[4] Mrs. C. A. Atkins to Officers and Members of City Federation, July 1913, Elizabeth L. Ring Papers (BTHC); Mrs. R. C. Talbot Perkins to Elizabeth Ring, Mar. 8, 1921, ibid.

[5] Stella L. Christian (ed.), *The History of The Texas Federation of Women's Clubs* (Houston: Dealey-Adey-Elgin Co., 1919), 253. The state prison began in 1849 as a single penitentiary at Huntsville. From February 1867 to December 1912 the state

An investigating committee of the Thirty-fifth Legislature issued a massive report on the status of state departments and institutions in February 1918. A lengthy section concerning the prison system catalogued a multitude of serious problems such as the existence of crowded and dilapidated convict housing, filthy bedding often covered with vermin and insects, and shortages of food and clothing. Maintaining that "no particular effort was made toward reforming the prisoners," investigators found that state officials failed to separate young convicts from older convicts and neglected to operate schools as required by law. At the Imperial Farm in Sugarland, guards often hung prisoners from chains attached to their arms in a manner which swung them up with their toes barely touching the ground, often

---

contracted large numbers of prisoners to private employers, including railroads, mining companies, and plantations. The convict lease system returned profits to the state treasury, but continued controversies ultimately led to its abolition. The state hoped to profit from prison farms in place of the leases. For the early history of Texas state prisons see Donald R. Walker, *Penology for Profit: A History of the Texas Prison System, 1867–1912* (College Station: Texas A&M University Press, 1988), 13–21, 42–54, 145–151, 191–197; Herman Lee Crow, "A Political History of the Texas Prison System, 1829–1951" (Ph.D. diss., University of Texas, 1964), 23–48, 179–182, 299–301; *Report of the Committee of the Senate and the Central Executive Committee of the House of Representatives Composing A Legislative Committee to Investigate the Departments of the State Government and the State Institutions Under Simple Resolutions of the Thirty-fifth Legislature of the State of Texas* (n.p., 1918; cited hereafter as *A Legislative Committee to Investigate the Departments of the State Government*), 27–30, 241–242, 247–250, 257–258. Fifteen farms on 56,017 acres owned by the state and 34,191 acres leased by the state existed at the time of the 1917 investigation. By the end of 1930 the prison system consisted of 5,000 prisoners housed at the Huntsville Penitentiary and on eleven farms consisting of more than 73,000 acres of state-owned land. Anglo-Americans composed approximately 50 percent of the prisoners, African Americans comprised another 40 percent, and prisoners of Mexican ancestry made up the remaining 10 percent. Texas Prison Board, *Annual Report*, 1930: 6-D. Blake McKelvey describes southern prison systems in "A Half Century of Southern Penal Exploitation," *Social Forces*, V (Oct., 1934–May, 1935), 112–123, and in *American Prisons: A History of Good Intentions* (Montclair, N.J.: Patterson Smith, 1977), 215–216. The Texas system earned a profit during the World War I era of 1916–1918 when farm prices reached an exceptional level. See *A Legislative Committee to Investigate the Departments of the State Government*, 244–249; J. E. Pearce, "History of Efforts at Reorganizing and Relocating the Penitentiary System of Texas," unpublished manuscript in Prisons Vertical file and Scrapbook (BTHC). The prison also profited from farming operations in 1924 and 1927 but lost in other years during the period covered by this study. *Annual Report*, 1924: 9, 1927: 1, 1928: 2, 1929: 12-C, 1930: 2.

causing a loss of consciousness. Employees beat prisoners with wet ropes or pistols, kicked and spurred them, and permitted prison dogs to attack convicts; state law permitted officials to whip prisoners with a leather strap or "bat" two and one-half inches wide and twenty-four inches long, but some guards apparently used larger instruments and ignored regulations that required the presence of a physician at all beatings. Other evidence indicated that officials forced ill prisoners to work and allowed intoxicated guards to supervise convicts.[6]

The Texas Federation of Women's Clubs responded to the 1918 investigation by passing resolutions that demanded the humane treatment and rehabilitation of state convicts. Requesting that the governor place a woman on the Board of Prison Commissioners and that women retain exclusive control over female prisoners, the Federation also suggested that at least two women trained for social welfare work receive appointments at every prison farm in the system. The Texas League of Women Voters, the Texas Prison Association, and the Texas Prisoners Protective Association joined the Federation of Women's Clubs in prison reform. By 1922 the Joint Legislative Council, or "petticoat lobby," consisting of representatives from the women's clubs and League of Women Voters, as well as the Texas Congress of Mothers and Parent Teacher Association, the Woman's Christian Temperance Union, and the Federation of Business and Professional Women's Clubs, began a period of activism that included prison reform among its many legislative goals.[7]

Apart from ameliorating inhumane conditions in Texas prisons, women reformers desired to correct important social ills by rehabili-

---

[6] *A Legislative Committee to Investigate the Departments of the State Government*, 29–30, 259–260, 266–271, 276–282.

[7] *Texas Federation of Women's Clubs Annual-1919–1920*, 78–81; Ermina Thompson Folsom Papers (Archives Division, Texas State Library, Austin; hereafter cited as TSL); Jackson, "Petticoat Politics," 88–90, 98; Dallas *Morning News*, Apr. 28, Aug. 30, Sept. 6, 1921; Jessie Daniel Ames to Elizabeth Ring, Oct. 7, 1920, Ring Papers; Florence Floore to Ring, Jan. 28, 1921, ibid.; Elizabeth Speer to Ring, Sept. 5, 1921, ibid. For a list of member organizations within the Joint Legislative Council, see a professional card in McCallum Family Papers (Austin-Travis County Collection, Austin Public Library, Austin); Norman Brown, *Hood, Bonnet, and Little Brown Jug: Texas Politics, 1921–1928* (College Station: Texas A&M University Press, 1984), 8. Also see unpublished manuscript concerning the impact of woman suffrage in Jesse Daniel Ames Papers (TSL) for a discussion of various reform efforts by the Texas League of Women Voters.

tating criminals. Voicing impatience with legislative investigations that publicized atrocities and scandals without solving prison problems, they lobbied for an investigation or "scientific survey" by experts not associated with the Texas Legislature or the prison system. The quest for an outside study revealed the relationship between the reformers and the social justice progressive movement of the pre-World War I era that persisted among women political activists in southern states during the 1920s. In a series of articles for the Dallas *Morning News* in 1921, Caroline Palmer argued that "if we are wise . . . we will get investigators who will, instead of simply muckraking, study the system in every detail and make constructive and practical suggestions." Florence Floore, president of the Texas Federation of Women's Clubs, also expressed similar reservations about past investigations and reform attempts by stating: "It can be said that nobody but . . . experts know what is being done in other states. . . . We are anxious to avoid any more exposés or amateur surveys, attended possibly by indecent publicity."[8]

The women's suffrage campaign and the crusade during World War I to "make the world safe for democracy" had inspired political activism during and after the war. Noting the paradox between Ameri-

---

[8] Jessie Daniel Ames, Mrs. S. M. N. Marrs, and Florence Floore to My dear Fellow Citizen, undated manuscript, Starlin Marion Newberry Marrs Vertical file (BTHC); Floore to Elizabeth Ring, Feb. 11, 1921, Ring Papers; Carrie Weaver Smith to Floore, June 25, 1921, ibid., Elizabeth M. Speer to My dear Mr. —, Dec. 12, 1922, McCallum Papers; Elizabeth Ring to Julia Jaffray, June 19, 1920, Ring Papers. See Palmer's articles in Texas State Penitentiary Board Papers, 1921–1927, Texas Prison Exhibition Clippings, 1921–1927 (BTHC). Florence Floore indicated that Ring directly inspired the Palmer articles. Floore to Ring, Jan. 28, May 2, Aug. 5, 1921, Ring Papers; Floore to R. B. Creager, Dec. 8, 1922, ibid. Anne Firor Scott discusses the progressive movement by women's organizations in the Southern states during the 1920s in *The Southern Lady: From Pedestal to Politics, 1830–1930* (Chicago: University of Chicago Press, 1970), 178, 184–187, 191–199, 210. Also see Anne Firor Scott, "After Suffrage: Southern Women in the Twenties," *Journal of Southern History,* XXX (Aug., 1969), 298–318; Jackson, "Petticoat Politics," vi–vii, 96–101, 150, 598. See David J. Rothman, *Conscience and Convenience: The Asylum and Its Alternatives in Progressive America* (Boston: Little, Brown and Co., 1980), 50–60, and Samuel Walker, *Popular Justice: A History of American Criminal Justice* (New York: Oxford University Press, 1980), 127–129, 149–158, 169–173, for attitudes toward science, investigation, and treatment that characterized criminal justice reforms during the Progressive Era. Presidents of the three organizations to Sen. Guinn Williams, Jan. 24, 1923, Ring Papers.

can war goals and conditions in Texas prisons, a San Antonio clubwoman asked in despair: "Can we afford to send our best blood across the waters that Humanity may not die off the Earth? While we at home are tolerating such horrors?" Through a national network of women's clubs and suffrage groups, Texas leaders established contacts and alliances with female social justice advocates who desired a variety of reforms in such areas as child welfare, alcohol abuse, education, working conditions, and juvenile delinquency. Women in other states informed their Texas counterparts about prisons that attempted to prepare convicts for a return to civilian life instead of simply using them for the purpose of securing revenue for the state treasury.[9]

A national organization that included renowned penologists emerged as the most important prison reform group in the state. By 1920 Texas prison reformers led by Florence Floore, Jesse Daniel Ames, and Ina Caddell Marrs had become acquainted with Julia Jaffray of the National Committee on Prisons and Prison Labor (CPPL), based in New York City. Initially formed to prevent male convict labor competition against female garment workers, the CPPL included men and women dedicated to comprehensive prison reform throughout the United States. The CPPL provided consulting services by retaining social scientists to conduct surveys of state and federal prisons.[10]

[9] Mrs. T. A. Coleman to Minnie Fisher Cunningham, Sept. 21, 1918, Cunningham Papers. Texas women, for instance, frequently corresponded and met with Julia Jaffray of the General Federation of Women's Clubs and the National Committee on Prisons and Prison Labor. Julia Jaffray to Sarah King, Dec. 21, 1921; Jaffray to Elizabeth Ring, Jan. 5, 1922, Ring Papers; Julia Jaffray to Ring, Sept. 14, 1920, ibid.; Ring to Dear Club Women, Nov. 1, 1920, ibid.; Jaffray to Ring, Nov. 12, 1920, ibid.; Harriet N. Leary to Ring, Feb. 3, 1921, ibid.; Jaffray to Ring, Mar. 22, 1921, ibid.; Dr. Carrie Weaver Smith to Ring, Aug. 6, 1921, ibid.; *Texas Federation of Women's Clubs Annual-1919–1920*, 79–86; Jackson, "Petticoat Politics," 1–16; "Presidents of the Three Organizations" to Sen. Guinn Williams, Jan. 24, 1923, Ring Papers.

[10] Well-known penologists associated with the National Committee on Prisons and Prison Labor activists included E. Stagg Whitin, Adolph Lewisohn, Julia Jaffray, George Gordon Battle, Bernard H. Glueck, and Thomas Mott Osborne. Julia Jaffray, *The Prison and The Prisoner: A Symposium* (Boston: Little, Brown, and Co., 1917), title page; National Committee on Prisons and Prison Labor, "A Practical Prison System," pamphlet in McCallum Papers; Jessie Daniel Ames, Florence C. Floore, and Mrs. S. M. N. Marrs to My dear fellow citizen, undated, in S. M. N. Marrs Vertical file; Minnie Fisher Cunningham to National Committee on Prisons and Prison Labor, June 11, 1920, Ring Papers; Ring to Jaffray, June 19, 1920, ibid.; Jaffray to Ring, Sept. 12, 1920, ibid. The National CPPL opposed prison contract labor competition against

The penal philosophy embraced by the CPPL emphasized the burden that crime caused for the families of male offenders and sought to train convicts in vocational skills they could utilize after their release from prison. Because the CPPL also objected to convict competition against free workers, the organization proposed that prisoners only manufacture goods for consumption by governmental agencies. Opposed to the plantation style commercial prison farming that prevailed in most southern states, the CPPL recommended that prison agricultural operations produce only food crops and livestock for consumption by prisoners and others under the care of state institutions. This "state's use system" would possess the dual advantage of lowering incarceration costs while training prisoners for productive labor that should prevent them from committing new crimes.[11]

Texas prison reformers organized a state chapter of the CPPL at Austin in January 1923 with the assistance of Julia Jaffray. Leaders in the Texas CPPL included Elizabeth Speer as executive secretary, Elizabeth Ring as first vice-chairman, and Jessie Daniel Ames as recording secretary. Jane McCallum, chairman of the Joint Legislative Council,

---

free men and women workers. The CPPL began in 1909 after female garment workers asked the General Federation of Women's Clubs to help prevent competition from male prisoners employed in contract garment production. See National CPPL, "The New Experiments in Social Service Work at Sing Sing," *Prison Leaflets*, No. 50, ibid. Also see a 1918 transcript from "Trade Union Conference of The Woman in Industry Service of The United States Department of Labor," reprinted in Judith Sealander (ed.), *Records of The Women's Bureau of the Department of Labor, 1918–1965: Part 1* (Frederick, Md.: microfilm, University Publications of America, Inc., 1986), 96–107.

[11] For a description of the CPPL's penal philosophy see pamphlet by the National Committee on Prisons and Prison Labor, "How Human Waste is Being Saved," McCallum Papers; National Committee on Prisons and Prison Labor, *Report Presented to the Annual Meeting, April 14, 1930*, 14–16, Ring Papers; Texas Committee on Prisons and Prison Labor, *The Texas Prison Survey*, V (Aug., 1924), 14–15, 25–27, 71. Also see various clippings in the Texas Prison Exhibit; Elizabeth Speer, "What Does A Practical Prison System Call For?" unpublished manuscript in McCallum Papers. An unpublished memorandum by an unknown author not only reflected Texas reformers' disdain for past legislative investigations but also described the CPPL's purpose and goals. "In Re: A Survey of Prison Conditions in Texas," Ring Papers. Also see comments by a New York prison reformer whose goals paralleled those of Texas women. "Mrs. Charles H. North, Chairman, Committee on Institutional Relations, New York State Federation of Women's Clubs," unpublished manuscript, ibid. For a description of the state's use system see McKelvey, *American Prisons*, 122–124, 151, 227, 250–251, 292, 306.

and Minnie Fisher Cunningham participated on the CPPL's Executive Committee. The women reformers, who also recruited a number of prominent business and professional men to occupy visible positions in the CPPL, helped solicit financial contributions from prominent Texans that funded the CPPL's survey of the Texas Prison System during 1923 and 1924.[12]

The survey report suggested policies consistent with the National CPPL's goals and urged Texas to pay wages for prison labor, end corporal punishment, and separate prisoners according to age and rehabilitation potential. Calling for the dissolution of the Board of Prison Commissioners, the CPPL recommended that the state establish a gubernatorially-chosen board that would hire an expert manager to supervise the system. The report's most controversial proposal

---

[12] Julia Jaffray attended the organizational meeting and frequently advised Texas CPPL members. Jaffray to Ring, Sept. 4, Nov. 1, 1920, Mar. 22, 1921, Jan. 5, 1922, Mar. 16, 1923, Ring Papers; "Report of Organizational meeting of Texas Committee on Prisons and Prison Labor," unpublished manuscript, ibid.; Jaffray to Elizabeth Speer, Jan. 26, 1928, ibid.; Jaffray to Ring, Sept. 26, 1922, May 28, 1930, ibid. Jessie Daniel Ames, Ina Caddell Marrs, Elizabeth Speer, Mrs. Claude De Van Watts of the Woman's Christian Temperance Union, and Sarah King also attended the organizational meeting, as did such male reformers as law professor Charles Shirley Potts and journalist Tom Finty. Well-known male CPPL members included railroad promoter Robert Homes Baker, humanitarian Henry Cohen, and journalist George Waverly Briggs. Representatives from the Texas Congress of Mothers and Parent-Teacher Association, the Texas League of Women Voters, the Graduate Nurses Association of Texas, the Woman's Christian Temperance Union, the Texas Federation of Woman's Clubs, and the Texas Federation of Business and Professional Woman's Clubs, as well as other social welfare organizations, served on the CPPL's advisory committee. Financial donors included Ima Hogg, Tom Hogg, Morris Sheppard, Jesse Jones, H. J. Lutcher Stark, I. H. Kempner, George Sealy, and Ross Sterling. Dallas *Morning News*, Mar. 10, 1923; Elizabeth Speer to Committee member, Feb. 24, 1925, Henry Cohen Papers (BTHC); "Minutes of Meeting of Texas Committee on Prisons and Prison Labor," Sept. 12, 1927, unpublished manuscript in ibid.; Speer to Ima Hogg, June 8, 1924, ibid.; Speer to H. J. Lutcher Stark, Aug. 11, 1924, ibid.; "Minutes of Meeting of Executive Committee of the Texas Division of the National Committee on Prisons and Prison Labor, Fort Worth," June 14, 1923, unpublished manuscript, Ring Papers. Statewide donations, National CPPL assistance, and foundation grants funded the survey which the Texas legislature authorized but refused to finance. Texas Committee on Prison and Prison Labor, *Summary of the Texas Prison Survey*, V. 1, 1; Ring to my dear friend, June 25, 1923, ibid.; "Report of Institutional Relations For the Years 1920–1921," unpublished manuscript in ibid.; "Memorandum: In Re: A Survey of Prison Conditions in Texas," unpublished manuscript, ibid.

advocated the construction of a single penal colony near Austin and the sale of all existing prison properties. Emphasizing vocational training and manufacturing, the new prison facility would sharply reduce commercial prison farming. Relocation proponents also argued that an Austin site might permit greater access to medical and educational expertise and should enhance legislative oversight of penal operations. More than other aspects of the program, relocation assumed a symbolic importance for prison reformers. "The prison system of Texas needs a fresh start amidst newer and different surroundings," one woman observed.[13]

Robert Homes Baker, chairman of the Texas CPPL, praised Texas women's organizations for their protracted involvement in prison reform. "They have been willing to assume the program from year to year until they see its completion," Baker commented. During Gov. Pat Morris Neff's administration (1921–1925) women reformers helped avert a proposed contract between the prison system and a private manufacturer for the purchase of garments produced at the Huntsville Penitentiary; they also supported the prison commissioners' ban against the chaining of prisoners, although Neff vetoed a bill that would have prohibited whipping. Sen. Harry Hertzberg, a close ally of women reformers, successfully sponsored a bill that created a Penitentiary Advisory Board to inspect prison facilities and issue quarterly reports. Neff, however, largely subverted a provision designed to place a woman activist on the board when he chose Sarah King, who advocated humane treatment for prisoners but failed to endorse much of the CPPL's broader reform agenda. A Neff political supporter with no previous interest or training in penology, King disappointed more knowledgeable women reformers by recommending that prison officials continue to whip convicts. "I can see that there is nothing that will

---

[13] Texas CPPL, *The Texas Prison Survey*, V (Aug., 1924), 1, 8–13, 25–27, 71–74, 86–87; Pearce, "History of Efforts at Reorganizing and Relocating"; Texas CPPL, "Minutes of the Executive and Survey Committee Meeting," Nov. 13, 1924, McCallum Papers; Speer, "The Texas Penitentiary System and Taxation," unpublished manuscript, ibid.; Speer, "What Does A Practical Prison System Call For?" unpublished manuscript, ibid.; Texas Committee on Prisons and Prison Labor, "For Abolishing the Board of Prison Commissioners," pamphlet, ibid.; "The Prison Amendment," unpublished manuscript by unknown author, ibid.; Speer, "Release Sunday March 8, 1925," unpublished manuscript, Ring Papers.

take the place of the strap when you are dealing with the low grade of Mexican and negro prisoners," King once reported.[14]

Another legislative investigation in 1925 uncovered a number of scandals that involved financial wrongdoing, conflicts of interest,

[14] R. H. Baker to Mrs. W. H. Potter, President, Texas Federation of Women's Clubs, Nov. 22, 1928, Ring Papers. Neff entered office with a pledge to strictly enforce state criminal statutes. Although he advocated humane treatment for prisoners, he denounced "mush-headed, faint-hearted sentimentalists" and drastically curtailed the early release of felons from the prison system by abolishing the Board of Pardon Advisors. Pat Neff to Board of Prison Advisors, Jan. 22, 1921, Pat Morris Neff Papers (The Texas Collection, Baylor University, Waco); Neff to The Members of the Senate and House of Representatives, Feb. 1, Feb. 3, 1921, Governors' Papers: Pat Morris Neff, Letter Press Book (TSL); Neff to members of the Thirty-eighth Legislature, Jan. 13, Jan. 23, 1923, ibid.; Neff to The Members of The Senate and House of Representatives, Jan. 15, 1925, ibid.; Carrie Weaver Smith to Ring, June 25, Aug. 6, 1921, Ring Papers; Jaffray to Ring, Aug. 29, 1921, ibid. See a copy of the proposed contract with the Reliance Manufacturing Company of Chicago, dated April 1923, in the Texas Prison Exhibit; also see a copy of Senate Joint Resolution Number 2, introduced by Sen. Charles A. Murphy, in ibid. This resolution opposed the Reliance contract. See undated clipping from Dallas *Morning News*, in ibid.; Speer to Ring, May 11, 1923, Ring Papers; Speer to Ring, Apr. 21, 1923, ibid.; C. M. Caldwell to Ring, May 15, 1923, ibid.; "Minutes of Meeting of Executive Committee of the Texas Division of National Committee on Prisons and Prison Labor, Fort Worth," unpublished manuscript in Ring Papers, ibid.; Jackson, "Petticoat Politics," 110–127; Harry Hertzberg to Mrs. A. N. McCallum, Jan. 10, 1923, McCallum Papers; Dallas *Morning News*, Aug. 30, Sept. 6, 1921; Speer to Ring, Sept. 5, 1921, Ring Papers; Floore to Ring, Jan. 27, 1921, ibid. J. A. Herring, Chairman of the Board of Prison Commissioners, advised Neff to veto the bill that outlawed whipping but recommended that Neff sign the bill creating the advisory board. He suggested, however, that Neff appoint "friends to this position" who would not attempt to embarrass the Neff administration. Herring also advised Neff to sign a meaningless prison relocation bill that lacked legislative funding. Herring to Neff, Feb. 16, Aug. 2, 1921, Governors' Papers: Neff. Sarah King joined the Texas Committee on Prison and Prison Labor but often opposed its major goals and was never an important member in the organization. King disliked Hertzberg. See Mrs. J. E. King to Neff, Aug. 2, Aug. 9, Sept. 8, 1921, Governors' Papers: Neff; Neff to King, Dec. 10, 1921, ibid.; Kate Friend to Ring, Sept. 21, Sept. 22, 1921, Ring Papers. Leading women reformers hoped Neff would select the more experienced Elizabeth Ring for the woman's position on the board. Jessie Daniel Ames to Ring, Sept. 9, 1921, ibid.; Ames to Ring, undated, Ring papers; Sarah C. King to Ring, Dec. 20, 1921, ibid. Julia Jaffray of the National CPPL viewed King's selection as a disappointment. Jaffray to King, Dec. 21, 1921, ibid.; Jaffray to Ring, Jan. 5, 1922, ibid. King's reform recommendations stressed palliative measures designed to produce more humane prisoner treatment without altering the nature of a plantation penal system. King to Ring, Mar. 15, 1922, ibid.; Supervisory Board of the State Penitentiaries to Neff, Jan. 6, 1923, J. T. Herrington Papers (The Texas Collection, Baylor University); "Report of

widespread physical abuse of prisoners by state officials, and employee-operated whiskey stills at a time of national and state prohibition. The investigating committee issued a report that recommended
systemic changes similar to those suggested by the CPPL survey.
Although Gov. Miriam A. Ferguson vetoed a relocation bill in 1925,
the CPPL and various women's organizations enthusiastically participated in a November 1926 campaign for a state constitutional amendment authorizing the legislature to abolish the three-person Board of
Prison Commissioners and to create a new administrative system.[15]

Numerous women's organizations also backed Dan Moody's candidacy for governor during 1926 and campaigned vigorously for his
victory over Ferguson in the Democratic primary the same year.
Moody supported much of the CPPL program, including relocation
to Central Texas, and signed a 1927 bill through which the legislature
reorganized the prison system's management pursuant to the 1926
amendment. The new law permitted Moody to appoint a nine-person,
unsalaried Texas Prison Board which hired a manager for the system.
Initial appointees to the board included several male members of the
CPPL, with Robert Homes Baker as chairman; the board retained
Elizabeth Speer as its executive secretary.[16]

Organizational meeting of Texas CPPL," unpublished manuscript, Ring Papers; *General Laws of Texas, Thirty-seventh Legislature, 1921, First Called Session* (Austin: 1921),
228–229. The law established the advisory board for a six-year period; the legislature
did not renew the board after its expiration.

[15] Dallas *Morning News*, Feb. 26, 1925; *Ferguson Forum* (Temple), Jan. 29, Feb.
12, 19, 26, 1925. For details on the 1925 scandals see various clippings in the Texas Prison
Exhibit. Dallas *Morning News*, Jan. 15, Jan. 24, Jan. 27, Jan. 30, Jan. 31, Feb. 2, Feb.
3, Feb. 11, Feb. 20, Feb. 24, Feb. 25, Feb. 26, Feb. 27, Mar. 6, Mar. 18, 1925. Ferguson
argued that the $200,000 appropriated by the legislature was inadequate for relocation. Miriam Ferguson to Secretary of State, Apr. 2, 1925, McCallum Papers; Austin
American-Statesman, Apr. 2, 1925; Frank M. Stewart and Joseph L. Clark, *The Constitution and Government of Texas* (Dallas: D. C. Heath and Co., 1936), 85; Speer to
Members, Oct. 28, 1926, McCallum Papers; "Statement of Work done by the Texas
Committee on Prisons and Prison labor," unpublished manuscript, Ring Papers;
"Bulletin February 1926–" unpublished manuscript, ibid.; Dallas *Morning News*, Apr.
17, 1926; Galveston *Tribune*, May 3, 1926; Galveston *News*, May 3, 1926.

[16] Jane McCallum to Mrs. D. H. Doom, June 3, 1926, McCallum Papers;
"Executive Committee of Texas Women Citizens' Committee Dan Moody For Governor," unpublished manuscript, ibid.; Jackson, "Petticoat Politics," 318–347; *General
and Special Laws of the State of Texas Passed by the Fortieth Legislature at the Regular
Session*, 298–307; Charlotte A. Teagle, *History of Welfare Activities of the Texas Prison*

Speer's employment gave women reformers an influential voice in the prison system. Unlike Sarah King, Speer, who had participated in the women's suffrage and anti-vice campaigns during World War I, had an extensive background in prison reform. One of six women to serve on the Department of Delinquency for the General Federation of Women's Clubs, she had also acted as executive secretary of the Arkansas Commission on Charities and Correction. During her career Speer had visited prison units throughout the United States, headed the Texas League of Women Voter's Prison Reform Committee, attended the organizational meeting of the Texas CPPL, directed the CPPL's survey of the Texas Prison System in 1923, and led the ratification campaign for the 1926 constitutional amendment. Baker, chairman of the CPPL and the Texas Prison Board, praised Speer as "the only person in Texas that I know who has had a thorough training in criminology and penology," noting that her sound judgment and realistic perspective transcended "morbid sentiment."[17]

Baker readily deferred to her advice concerning prison matters, although Speer's critics, such as former Gov. James E. Ferguson, described her as "a female politician" who lacked "sense." From 1927 to 1929 the board attempted under Speer's leadership to implement facets of what historians have labeled "progressive penology." Working to limit corporal punishments, the board fired farm managers and guards who mistreated prisoners, encouraged recreational and educational pursuits, and permitted prisoners to establish a welfare league

---

Board, 1927–1940 (Austin: Texas Prison Board, 1940), 11–12. In addition to Baker other Texas CPPL members on the board included Rabbi Henry Cohen of Galveston, attorney Wilmot M. Odell of Fort Worth, and Dr. Arthur C. Scott of Temple.

[17] Minnie Fisher Cunningham to Mrs. Percy V. Pennybacker, Aug. 31, 1917, Mrs. Percy V. Pennybacker Papers (BTHC); Elizabeth Ring to Julia Jaffray, June 19, 1920, Ring Papers; *Report of The Charities and Correction Commission of Arkansas May 1, 1919 to December 31, 1920* (Prescott, Ark.: Picayune Point, 1921), 12; W. M. Odell to Walter C. Woodward and Edgar Witt, Feb. 12, 1929, *Senate Journal of the Forty-first Legislature of Texas Regular Session* (Austin: 1929), 728–744; "Notes on Executive Committee Meeting of Texas Committee on Prisons and Prison Labor in Dallas on February 7, 1923," unpublished manuscript, Ring Papers; "Report of State Chairman of Committee on Social and Industrial Conditions Texas Federation of Women's Clubs November 1922," unpublished manuscript, ibid. Julia Jaffray complimented Speer's "excellent work . . . in Arkansas, [as] nationally known." Robert Homes Baker credited Speer for passage of the 1926 amendment, praising her "splendid work." R. H. Baker to J. A. Phillips, July 21, 1927, ibid.; R. H. Baker to Lee Simmons, Nov. 28, 1927, McCallum Papers.

that promoted democracy and self-help policies similar to those in many northern states.[18]

Prison employees and members of the legislature, however, frequently voiced disapproval of Speer and other members of the progressive board. Sen. William Doddridge McFarlane contended that Speer had destroyed employee morale by denying farm managers "permission to whip the inmates for the worst forms of disorder." Farm manager B. B. Monzingo complained vociferously about Speer and Baker. Annoyed by "a bawling out" that he received for handcuffing "rank prisoners," Monzingo blasted reformers for expressing an excessive interest in "picture shows, ball games, radios, boxing gloves, and music," while neglecting prison farming. "I was afraid to work the convicts . . . for fear that I would get a bawling out, or fired, from Mrs. Speer or Mr. Baker," Monzingo told the legislature. Monzingo also charged that Speer and Baker wasted money by employing a dietitian and "a high priced canning lady to . . . superintend the canning of . . . vegetables." "We did not need a Dietician [sic] for we had a good many [sic] prisoners who were as good cooks [sic] as could be found anywhere," observed Monzingo.[19]

Before the end of 1930, the last full year of Dan Moody's administration, the prison reform effort characterized by Minnie Fisher Cunningham in 1918 as "the next 'big job'" effectively concluded. The

---

[18] R. H. Baker to Simmons, Nov. 28, 1927, McCallum Papers; *Ferguson Forum* (Temple), Mar. 14, 1929. See list of fired guards in Texas Penitentiary Collection, Oct. 28, Nov. 28, 1929 (TSL); Baker to B. B. Monzingo, Jan. 8, 1929, Cohen Papers. For a description of "progressive penology" see Rothman, *Conscience and Convenience,* 119–122; also see Thomas Mott Osborne, *Society and Prisons: Some Suggestions For A New Penology* (1918; reprint, Montclair, N.J.: Patterson Smith, 1975), vi–x, 152–184; John Stratford to Henry Cohen, Oct. 12, 1928, Cohen papers; Eugene V. Simons to Cohen, Mar. 1, 1929, ibid. Prisoners also inaugurated publication of a newspaper, *The Echo.* See *The Echo* (Huntsville), Nov., 1928; Teagle, *History of Welfare Activities,* 154–157.

[19] R. H. Baker to Simmons, Nov. 28, 1927, McCallum Papers. Although Lee Simmons of Sherman served on the new board, he and Judge A. H. Carrigan of Wichita Falls adopted a minority position in opposition to progressive penological policies. R. H. Baker to Dan Moody, Nov. 14, 1929, Governors' Papers: Daniel J. Moody (TSL); Baker to Simmons, ibid.; Simmons to W. H. Mead, May 23, 1929, Cohen Papers; A. H. Carrigan to Baker, Nov. 12, 1928, ibid.; *Ferguson Forum* (Temple), Apr. 11, 1929; *Texas Senate Journal, Forty-first Regular Legislature,* 589; Simmons to Baker, Nov. 19, 1929, Governors' Papers: Moody; A. H. Carrigan to Hon. R. S. Sterling, n. d., Governors' Papers: Ross S. Sterling (TSL); *Texas Senate Journal, Forty-first Regular Legislature,* 1929, 424–426.

legislature's failure to relocate the prison system, despite persistent urgings by Moody, women's groups, and other reformers, signified the demise of a lengthy campaign. A movement largely inaugurated by private citizens seeking to impose sweeping changes on the state's penal system had failed to achieve its broad goal of creating an industrial and educationally-oriented correctional apparatus. The Texas Prison System remained an austere Southern institution dependent upon plantation-style commercial farming and brutal disciplinary measures, probably because most state leaders, imbued with prevailing cultural attitudes, could not recognize the merits of a more advanced penology. Nonetheless, the reformers enjoyed modest successes, including the adoption of an administrative structure that remains largely intact to the present day. Moreover, the penological ideology derived from the female-influenced CPPL had formed the basis for the discussion of prison issues during much of the 1920s.[20]

Interest by Texas women in prison affairs, however, did not disappear after the failure of relocation in 1930. Florence Floore and Charlotte Teagle served on the Texas Prison Board during the 1930s, although they did not demand major operational changes. Future reform movements also featured prominent roles by Texas women. A 1947 campaign by the Texas State Council of Methodist Women promoted massive improvements in the system's physical facilities, though not an appreciable alteration in the character of Texas penology. Beginning in 1967 Francis T. Freeman Jalet, an attorney for the Federal Office of Economic Opportunity, rendered important legal

[20] The Forty-first Legislature appropriated $575,000 to revamp existing properties without relocating the system. Believing that the bill failed to correct "fundamental defects," Moody allowed the measure to become law without his signature. He failed to veto the bill because he recognized the necessity for alleviating immediate prisoner overcrowding. Moody called a record five special legislative sessions primarily to consider the relocation plan. *General and Special Laws of the State of Texas Passed by the Forty-first Legislature, Fourth and Fifth Called Session* (Austin: 1930), 215–219; "Statement from the Executive Office," Mar. 22, 1930, unpublished manuscript in Governors' Papers: Moody; "Statement from the Executive Office," Mar. 27, 1930, ibid.; Austin *American-Statesman*, Mar. 22, 1927; Houston *Post Dispatch*, Feb. 17, 1927; Houston *Press*, Mar. 13, 1930. See an editorial in the Houston *Post Dispatch*, Apr. 23, 1927, for a discussion of the prison relocation controversy. Also see various clippings in the Texas Prison Exhibit; *The Mirror* (Houston), Mar. 15, 1930, in Ring Papers; Houston *Post Dispatch*, Feb. 7, 1930; Ring to "Madam Chairman and Delegates to the State League of Women Voters," undated, in Ring Papers.

assistance to Texas inmates. Her activities led directly to the filing of a prisoners' lawsuit in 1972 which culminated in the *Ruiz v. Estelle* ruling of 1980. In that case, Federal Judge William Wayne Justice issued an order which required a transformation of the state's penal policies. More than fifty years earlier, however, women prison reformers in Texas had assiduously lobbied for an alternative penology that would have emulated the most modern correctional units in the United States without intervention by the federal government.[21]

[21] Teagle, *History of Welfare Activities,* 16–24; *Annual Report of the Texas Prison Board,* 1935: 3, 1941: 3 (Charlotte Teagle's name does not appear after the 1941 *Annual Report*); Mrs. C. T. Schaedel to Beauford H. Jester, Feb. 17, 1947, Governors' Papers: Beauford H. Jester (TSL); Texas State Council of Methodist Women to Dear Friend, Oct. 7, Oct. 11, 1947, ibid.; L. D. Ransom to Schaedel, Oct. 6, 1947, ibid.; Geraldyne Havard to Jester, Aug. 29, 1947, ibid. The Jester Records contain numerous letters and telegrams from Methodist women's organizations that advocated prison reform. For a discussion of reforms by Jester and prison system director Oscar Byron Ellis, see Ben Crouch and James W. Marquart, *An Appeal To Justice: Litigated Reform of Texas Prisons* (Austin: University of Texas Press, 1989), 30–38; Steve J. Martin and Sheldon Ekland-Olson, *Texas Prisons: The Walls Came Tumbling Down* (Austin: Texas Monthly Press, 1987), 18–19, 29–58. For interpretations of the *Ruiz* case see ibid., 235–247; Crouch and Marquart, *Appeal,* 221–238; *Ruiz v. Estelle,* 503 *Federal Supplement* 1265 (1980). Especially see pages 1385–1391 for federal Judge William Wayne Justice's analysis of pre-*Ruiz* penology in Texas.

Professional, Feminine, and Feminist:

Annie Webb Blanton and the Founding

of Delta Kappa Gamma

Debbie Mauldin Cottrell*

IN THE SECOND HALF OF THE NINETEENTH CENTURY, American women formed a coalition with the teaching profession that remains to this day. The broadening of educational opportunities in general, which created a greater need for teachers, coupled with the depletion of male educators during and after the Civil War opened the way for women to establish themselves as educators and subsequently dominate the profession. As the number of women teachers grew, teaching increasingly was viewed as an extension of traditional female roles; the profession became feminized, although, significantly, not necessarily glorified. In 1881 a guidebook for wage-earning women noted that teaching had become popular employment for educated females "principally because it is one of the few means of money-making in which a lady may openly engage without compromising her social standing." Another later observation on teaching as appropriate work for women noted that "it was genteel, paid reasonably well, and required little special skill or equipment." On a more positive note historian Anne Firor Scott has observed that in the South "every additional schoolroom created a new job for a woman, and by the turn of the century

* Debbie Cottrell is a doctoral candidate in American history at the University of Texas at Austin. This essay is part of her larger work entitled *Pioneer Woman Educator: The Progressive Spirit of Annie Webb Blanton,* which will be published by Texas A&M University Press in 1993.

women schoolteachers constituted a growing cadre of professional women."[1]

Scott's quotation somewhat oversimplifies the slow process by which women moved from finding social acceptance as educators to attaining true professional status within that arena. Lower salaries, limited opportunities for advancement, pressure to resign upon marriage—these and other problems plagued female educators well into the twentieth century, often relegating teaching to the status of semi-professional rather than professional work for women. Although several organizations for women teachers subsequently were created in an attempt to encourage professionalism and unity, in 1929 Texas educator Annie Webb Blanton determined that there remained a need for a carefully structured organization to address more directly the issue of professionalism for women teachers. Her subsequent creation, Delta Kappa Gamma, emphasized feminism, femininity, and meritocracy as a means of uniting selected teachers to raise professional standards for female educators.[2]

Delta Kappa Gamma must be seen as a direct result of the experiences of its founder. Blanton began her career as a rural teacher in La Grange in 1887. Never overly interested in marriage, she pursued a degree at the University of Texas while teaching in the Austin schools and later joined the first faculty of North Texas State Teachers College in Denton as an English instructor. In Denton Blanton blossomed

---

[1] Sarah Eisenstein, *Give Us Bread But Give Us Roses: Working Women's Consciousness in the United States, 1890 to the first World War* (London: Routledge and K. Paul, 1983), 77 (1st quotation, attributed in Eisenstein to Ella Rodman Church's 1882 book *Money-Making for Ladies*); Alice Kessler-Harris, *Out To Work: A History of Wage-Earning Women in the United States* (New York: Oxford University Press, 1982), 56, 68, 235; Leslie Woodcock Tentler, *Wage-Earning Women: Industrial Work and Family Life in the United States, 1900–1930* (New York: Oxford University Press, 1979), 1–2, 81–82; John Mack Faragher and Florence Howe (eds.), *Women and Higher Education in American History* (New York: W. W. Norton and Company, 1988), 60, 150; Nancy Hoffman, *Women's "True" Profession: Voices from the History of Teaching* (Old Westbury, N.Y.: The Feminist Press, 1981), xvii (2nd quotation); Anne Firor Scott, *The Southern Lady: From Pedestal to Politics, 1830–1930* (Chicago: University of Chicago Press, 1970), 110–111, 115 (3rd quotation).

[2] Faragher and Howe, *Women and Higher Education*, 60; Kessler-Harris, *Out To Work*, 56, 68, 235; Tentler, *Wage-Earning Women*, 1–2, 81–82; Eunah Temple Holden, *Our Heritage in the Delta Kappa Gamma Society* (2 vols.; Austin: n.p., 1960, 1976), I, 7.

into a seasoned educator and astute follower of Texas and teacher politics. She worked for women's rights, including suffrage; became a leader in the Texas State Teachers Association; and eventually became the first woman elected to statewide office in Texas, when she won her race for state superintendent of public instruction in 1918. Following this feat, she earned graduate degrees and spent the rest of her life teaching at the University of Texas. Hard work, persistence, and fortunate timing all contributed to Blanton's enormous professional success. Cognizant of her rather unique role in Texas education, and always interested in helping female colleagues, she realized that her experiences could be useful to other women. Uniting women in a professional society offered her a direct way to share her experiences and increase the potential of women to exert a positive influence on the teaching profession.[3]

Blanton's participation in women's clubs directly influenced her creation of Delta Kappa Gamma. Because such clubs often emphasized educational reform, Blanton found a natural interest in participating in them, often in leadership roles. Her friendship with state and national club leader Anna Pennybacker, as well as the interaction and support Blanton shared with Texas club women when she ran for office in 1918, indicate the consistent influence of women's clubs in her life. Two themes were clear in these organizations: a commitment to extend women's influence and a desire to improve society by utilizing women's superior abilities. These clubs offered a network for communicating about issues important to women, they emphasized organizational and leadership skills, and they were socially acceptable. When she founded Delta Kappa Gamma, Blanton was seeking similar broad results within a more specific framework.[4]

[3] Faragher and Howe, *Women and Higher Education,* 60. Background information on Blanton is from Debora Lynn Cottrell, "Annie Webb Blanton: Texas Educator and Feminist" (M.A. thesis, University of Texas at Austin, 1989).

[4] Megan Seaholm, "Earnest Women: The White Women's Club Movement in Progressive Era Texas, 1880–1920" (Ph.D. diss., Rice University, 1988), 1, 4, 11–12, 184, 215; Karen J. Blair, *The Clubwoman as Feminist: True Womanhood Redefined, 1868–1914* (New York: Holmes and Meier Publishers, 1980), 15, 57, 63, 93, 117–118; Anne Firor Scott, "The 'New Woman' in the New South," *The Southern Atlantic Quarterly,* LXI (Autumn, 1962), 473–483; Scott, *The Southern Lady,* 158, 208; Ruthe Winegarten, *Texas Women: A Pictorial History from Indians to Astronauts* (Austin: Eakin Press, 1986), 66, 100; Judie Walton Gammage, "Quest for Equality: An Historical Overview of Women's Rights Activism in Texas, 1890–1975" (Ph.D. diss., University of North Texas, 1982),

Blanton's ideas for her new organization gradually took shape throughout the 1920s. Teaching at the University of Texas, she quietly formulated plans to pursue a very straightforward goal: she wanted to remove barriers that limited the professional opportunities for women educators. From her Denton days, when her lifestyle had encompassed close professional and personal interaction with competent female colleagues, Blanton found the company of such women enjoyable and stimulating, and from it she recognized that women educators with similar interests and capabilities constituted a potentially powerful group if they could be organized in a united fashion. This idea, along with the success she saw various women's clubs attain, seemed to Blanton to belie suggestions that women were not capable of working together well. After Delta Kappa Gamma was founded, Blanton recalled that while she served as state superintendent a man told her that women's inability to stand together was hurting the teaching profession and the quality of education in Texas. This encounter reinforced her initial thoughts about the need for a group such as Delta Kappa Gamma.[5] She traced the progression of her ideas for organizing the group this way:

> I saw that women in their progress towards equality with men, educationally and politically, had won each step in advancement by the demands of groups of intrepid women who did stand together. I thought that if we are to learn leadership, it must be chiefly in women's organizations. finally

14, 18–19; Annie Webb Blanton to Anna Pennybacker, Sept. 15, Oct. 26, 1917, Mrs. Percy V. Pennybacker Papers (Eugene C. Barker Texas History Center, University of Texas, Austin; cited hereafter as BTHC); Blanton to Pennybacker, June 27, 1918, ibid.; Teacher's Report, 1927–1928, University of Texas President's Office Records (BTHC); Mrs. Lee Joseph to William Seneca Sutton, June 23, 1923, William Seneca Sutton Papers (ibid.)

[5] Ann Fears Crawford and Crystal Sasse Ragsdale, *Women in Texas: Their Lives, Their Experience, Their Accomplishments* (Burnet, Tex.: Eakin Press, 1982), 196; Theresa Fechek to Debbie Cottrell, Nov. 11, 1986, interview; *The Delta Kappa Gamma Bulletin,* X (June, 1944), 25; Clara Parker, *Annie Webb Blanton, Founder . . . the Delta Kappa Gamma Society* (Austin: Delta Kappa Gamma Society, 1949), 31; Holden, *Our Heritage,* I, 8, 19; Margaret McDermott and James Kilgore to Debbie Cottrell, Sept. 9, 1988, interview; "Annie Webb Blanton Memorial Resolution," Annie Webb Blanton folder, Clippings file: Biographical (BTHC).

I evolved the idea that we might accomplish more through a special organization working together for what women teachers especially need. This, I thought, should be composed of experienced teachers, more or less permanently in the profession. It seemed to me that such an organization would be more likely to succeed, if the ties binding its members together were rather close, and thus evolved the idea of a professional fraternity for women teachers.[6]

Blanton determined that her plans could only be successful if she sought members who were committed to teaching as a profession and who were willing to expend the necessary time and energy. A sense of feminist meritocracy, then, informed her organizational ambitions. She also believed that by including in the new group representatives from all levels of the teaching profession, she would be better able to foster a sense of mutual understanding and appreciation among women teachers. From her earliest dreams about the society, Blanton envisioned a distinctive group of female educators whose joint efforts would result in both increased opportunities and long overdue recognition for women teachers, who since the turn of the century had comprised the majority of the teaching profession. Blanton had a general sense of wanting to help all women educators, but her plans more specifically addressed aiding those who were outstanding yet were being limited by gender discrimination. A key to understanding Delta Kappa Gamma and her involvement in it is to recognize that Blanton was much less interested in women who planned to teach only briefly, women who were not willing to work hard, or women who were not of her own class and race.[7]

Before seeking potential members for the new organization, Blanton carefully thought through some other specific purposes she wished to

6 *The Delta Kappa Gamma Bulletin*, X (June, 1944), 25.
7 Parker, *Annie Webb Blanton, Founder*, 33–34; *Pioneer Women Teachers of Texas* (Austin: Delta Kappa Gamma Society, Alpha State Organization, n.d.), 6; Holden, *Our Heritage*, I, 7–8; Margaret Berry to Debbie Cottrell, Apr. 1, 1989, interview; *The Delta Kappa Gamma Bulletin*, XLIII (Fall, 1976), passim; Mary Beth Rogers, *Texas Women, A Celebration of History* (2nd ed.; Austin: Texas Foundation for Women's Resources, 1986), 63; various Blanton correspondence, Delta Kappa Gamma Alpha State Organization Records, The Woman's Collection (Texas Woman's University, Denton; cited hereafter as TWU).

pursue. She was especially concerned with improving academic opportunities for women and thus wanted the society to maintain a scholarship fund for members to continue their education. She also believed that the development of a professional spirit should be an outgrowth of the group and thus chose to emphasis experience over scholarship as a membership criterion.[8]

These desires and dreams that were solidifying in Blanton's mind in the late 1920s continued to reinforce three basic beliefs which she had long held: that merit, not gender, should determine leadership roles in education; that cooperative efforts could be very positive; and that the potential of feminine leadership was unlimited. References to feminism were more implicit than direct in Blanton's plan for Delta Kappa Gamma, but it is clear that the group's purpose was not only to improve opportunities for professional women educators through gender unity but also to attempt to end the male-dominated hierarchy in public schools. Blanton's proposal encompassed her belief that women could emphasize their femininity (i.e., their differences from men) without accepting professional inequality or lesser career aspirations. This approach of seeking equal opportunities for women within a context of traditional femininity was consistent throughout Blanton's life and defined her feminist spirit.

Blanton's first direct step towards founding Delta Kappa Gamma was to approach potential members whose professional careers and attitudes she found appropriate. She wanted a small group, carefully chosen, to join her as founders and then help her organize and enlarge the membership. She sent fourteen women educators whom she knew professionally a letter outlining her plans. Even though all of the women she wrote lived in Texas, Blanton foresaw the organization extending nationwide and presented her plans in this vein. Eleven women accepted Blanton's proposal and assisted her in preparing the group's constitution. Although it was difficult for these founders, and later any member, to consistently match Blanton's commitment to Delta Kappa Gamma, the original members who joined her in 1929 played the significant role of confirming her ideas and energizing her dreams. As she said,

---

[8] *The Delta Kaopa Gamma Bulletin*, XXXVII (Fall, 1970), passim; XLIII (Fall, 1976), passim; University of Texas Memorabilia file (BTHC); Crawford and Ragsdale, *Women in Texas*, 197–198; Holden, *Our Heritage*, II, 162.

There were none among the Founders who ridiculed my notion that we were about to begin a great organization for women teachers. Their faith strengthened my own courage and determination.[9]

Among her University of Texas colleagues who became founders were Anna Hiss, director of physical training for women; Helen Koch, psychology instructor; Ruby Terrill, dean of women and associate professor of classical languages; and Cora Martin, elementary education faculty member. These university women were joined by secondary history instructors (and sisters) Ray and Sue King of Fort Worth and math teacher Lalla M. Odom of Austin. Elementary educators who accepted Blanton's invitation were Mamie Bastian, a principal in Houston; Ruby Cole, a San Antonio principal; Mabel Grizzard, a rural supervisor and teacher in Waxahachie; and Lela Lee Williams, an administrator in Dallas elementary schools. Blanton used the contacts she had made during her career as a Texas educator to insure that her co-founders represented a variety of educational positions and geographical regions within the state, and also were women she knew personally and judged to possess the character she was seeking for her new society.[10]

On Saturday, May 11, 1929, the new group met in the drawing room of the Faculty Women's Club in Austin, where Blanton initiated the selected women into Delta Kappa Gamma. The group elected Blanton as its first president, finalized the constitution, and organized committees to begin the work of incorporation and expansion.[11]

[9] *The Delta Kappa Gamma Bulletin,* X (June, 1944), 25.

[10] Holden, *Our Heritage,* I, 8, II, 19; Anna Hiss Gymnasium, University of Texas, Austin, August, 1989, site visit; Program for the Delta Kappa Gamma Society International Alpha State, Texas, Fifty-Ninth Annual Convention, June 16–18, 1988, San Antonio, 4 (copy in possession of author); *Our Golden Anniversary, Delta Kappa Gamma, 1929–1979* (copy of publication at Delta Kappa Gamma headquarters, Austin); Ruby Terrill Lomax and Cora Merriman Martin folders, Clippings file: Biographical (BTHC); Margaret C. Berry, *The University of Texas: A Pictorial Account of Its First Century* (Austin: University of Texas Press, 1980), 163, 184; Texas State Teachers Association to Debbie Cottrell, Apr. 26, 1989 (original in possession of author); Better Schools Campaign Materials, Frederick Eby Papers (Texas Collection, Baylor University, Waco).

[11] *The Delta Kappa Gamma Bulletin,* V (June, 1939), 5; X (June, 1944), 25. The group's name was initially Kappa Gamma Delta, but when it was discovered that a

Although the organization considered itself national, the twelve members determined at that point to limit their membership to Texas for several years before attempting broader growth. As president from 1929 to 1933, Blanton's duties included leading the organizing of new chapters, an effort she relished. In a later recollection she put this work into context:

> [We] were strongly of the opinion that an organized body of women teachers selected from among the best in the profession united by bonds of friendship and by the force of common purposes—for the betterment of women teachers and the improvement of the schools generally—would have an opportunity for rendering real service to education.[12]

To begin to accomplish the expansion goals, select teachers from across the state were notified of Delta Kappa Gamma's founding, then Blanton sent letters explaining the group's aims in August 1929 to those who had expressed an interest in the new organization. The correspondence noted that the new society was to consist of women who had proven their success as teachers, shown leadership in professional organizations, and exhibited an unselfish professional spirit. To keep the society honorary, a maximum of one-tenth of the total number of teachers in any school system or higher education facility would be admitted. Blanton signed these letters as "Dalton Katherine Graham," a pseudonym with the same initials as Delta Kappa Gamma and one she thought would keep male educators from learning of and criticizing her plans. This secrecy indicates that she expected male criticism, but no evidence remains as to the specific individuals she perceived to be potentially troublesome.[13] In fact, the University of

---

national aeronautical fraternity already existed with that name, Blanton's group became Delta Kappa Gamma. (See Holden, *Our Heritage,* I, 7, II, 19.)

[12] *The Delta Kappa Gamma Bulletin,* III (Nov., 1936), 50.

[13] Holden, *Our Heritage,* II, 138–139, 162; *The Delta Kappa Gamma Bulletin,* II (June, 1936), 7; III (Nov., 1936), 50. *The Delta Kappa Gamma Bulletin,* XLIII (Fall, 1976), passim, notes that Blanton and the eleven co-founders risked job security because male educators frowned on the group's founding. It is difficult to assess what the other co-founders faced in terms of criticism, but the written documentation in the organization's history offers no specific evidence of serious employment threats to them or Blanton.

Texas's support of Delta Kappa Gamma was clear, as evidenced by a later letter from Dean B. F. Pittenger of the school of education to university President Homer P. Rainey, written in response to Blanton's request for a rather long absence from teaching to organize chapters in the Northwest. Pittenger wrote:

> I am suggesting its approval for two reasons: first, I believe that the development of this organization which now enlists several thousand of the leading women educators in almost every state; and which was originated and promoted by Professor Blanton personally, is a real contribution to American education. Secondly, I feel that Miss Blanton's long and effective service to the state of Texas warrants this consideration.[14]

By 1933 Blanton's efforts at expansion had resulted in forty-seven chapters in Texas, Alabama, Oklahoma, and Missouri, with a total membership of 1,500. State conventions were annual events and continued growth seemed assured. Blanton noted that some men believed the organization existed to fight them and that many women not asked to join resented Delta Kappa Gamma, but "we all learned to laugh at checks and criticisms, and go calmly ahead." By this time Blanton knew that Delta Kappa Gamma would fulfill her dreams and that the risks of failure had been successfully minimized. She believed that the success stemmed from her own contacts, hard work, and attention to detail— her letters of instruction to new chapters often ran to twenty-five pages in longhand—as well as the continued recruitment of the right kind of members, often with the advice of local male school superintendents and university officials. The success of these first few years motivated her to aim for even more growth in the future.[15]

In 1933 Blanton decided that her term as president would end. This change did not reflect any decrease in her commitment to Delta

[14] B. F. Pittenger to Homer P. Rainey, Apr. 10, 1940, University of Texas President's Office Records (BTHC).

[15] Holden, *Our Heritage*, II, 19–20, 39, 139; *The Delta Kappa Gamma Bulletin*, II (June, 1936), 7; X (June, 1944), 26 (quotation). By utilizing school superintendents and university officials around the country, Blanton indicated her willingness to take the advice of males in identifying potential members, although final acceptance always came from Delta Kappa Gamma members.

Kappa Gamma, but rather indicated her desire to have a non-Texan become president to aid in expansion efforts and to allow herself to take on new duties for the growing group. From 1933 to 1945 Blanton's control of the organization remained intact: she served as executive secretary and thus kept the group's headquarters in her home; she was editor of the organization's *Bulletin;* and she was directly involved in the selection of state and national officers.[16]

The level of emotional and physical involvement that Blanton contributed to Delta Kappa Gamma in these years was intense, but she did obtain desired results. She inaugurated the group's scholarship fund, created an annual achievement award, and projected the group's expansion into foreign countries. Membership included the most prominent female educators, including those who served as state superintendents across the country and numerous women who were leaders in the National Education Association. Blanton continued to travel and organize new chapters, and at her death Delta Kappa Gamma existed in all forty-eight states and Washington, D.C., with a total membership of almost 23,000; thirty-five states were organized by Blanton alone. She also saw the group continue its efforts for teachers' retirement funds and salary equity for women teachers. Delta Kappa Gamma was not solely responsible for the eventual success of these efforts, but it was an important contributor. Blanton's commitment to Delta Kappa Gamma was recognized by members, as they endowed a scholarship in her name; gave her the society's first national achievement award; presented her with monetary gifts, in appreciation of her personal time and financial sacrifice to the group, and a scrapbook of letters and other memorabilia; and purchased a car to assist her in her organizational travels.[17]

---

[16] *The Delta Kappa Gamma Bulletin,* X (June, 1944), 26, 29; XV (Summer, 1949), 22; Phyllis Ellis to Debbie Cottrell, July 14, 1988, interview; Jeanette Hastedt Flachmeier, *Pioneer Austin Notables* (2 vols.; Austin: privately published, 1975, 1980), II, 14; *Daily Texan* (Austin), Oct. 3, 1945; Holden, *Our Heritage,* I, 20, II, 140; *Our Golden Anniversary;* Minutes, Delta Kappa Gamma Alpha State Organization Records, The Woman's Collection (TWU); University of Texas President's file for Annie Webb Blanton (Office of the Executive Vice President and Provost, University of Texas, Austin; cited hereafter as OEVP); Birdella Ross to Debbie Cottrell, Aug. 11, 1988 (original in possession of author).

[17] *The Delta Kappa Gamma Bulletin,* III (June, 1937), 12; VI (Nov., 1939), 7; VII (Jan., 1941), 21; XLIII (Fall, 1976), 3; University of Texas Memorabilia file (BTHC); Crawford and Ragsdale, *Women in Texas,* 197–198; Mabelle and Stuart Purcell et al.,

In addition to providing Blanton with an opportunity to use her leadership skills and to pursue her goals for women teachers, as well as giving her a sense of personal and professional reward for her efforts, Delta Kappa Gamma also became a significant outlet for Blanton to express feminine and maternal traits within the realm of professionalism. Although Blanton never minimized her own femininity around her male colleagues, she always had been more comfortable and more inclined to express all sides of her personality in the company of women. Thus, within Delta Kappa Gamma, it was natural for her, as its leader, to show a wide gamut of emotions and preferences, including many not directly expressed in her classroom or other career endeavors. She emphasized to the group the significance of wearing its jewelry and of dressing properly at all times, and to honor pioneer women educators she began a collection of dolls dressed in period costumes, which she displayed at each annual convention. As editor of *The Bulletin,* she included articles on the value of literature, music, and social activities for members and also ran baby pictures of the original founders.[18] Blanton's writings in *The Bulletin* frequently referred to her maternal connection to the group and indicated the range of roles inherent in parental relationships. She scolded members for submitting information incorrectly to *The Bulletin* and fussed when they were irresponsible about their membership duties.[19] Conversely, she could take the role of proud and boastful parent, referring to new chapters as young offspring in need of care, and calling herself and enjoying being called Delta Kappa Gamma's "mother."[20] In 1939 she wrote, "A mother who has several children who express their affection and appreciate her past

This Is Texas (Austin: privately published, 1977), 37–44; University of Texas President's file for Annie Webb Blanton (OEVP); Teacher's Report 1936–1937, University of Texas President's Office Records (BTHC); Holden, *Our Heritage,* I, 20–21, II, 20; *Pioneer Women Teachers of Texas,* 6; Minutes, Delta Kappa Gamma Alpha State Organization Records, The Woman's Collection (TWU); Ellis to Cottrell, July 14, 1988, interview.

[18] Holden, *Our Heritage,* I, 22, II, 39–41; *The Delta Kappa Gamma Bulletin,* I (Mar., 1935), 17; I (May, 1935), 6; II (June, 1936), 46; V (Jan., 1939), 6; VI (Nov., 1939), 11; VII (Nov., 1940), 16; VII (June, 1941), 8–10; *Our Golden Anniversary;* Ellis to Cottrell, July 14, 1988, interview; Blanton to Fannie Lu Yeager, Feb. 22, 1934, Delta Kappa Gamma Alpha State Organization Records, The Woman's Collection (TWU).

[19] *The Delta Kappa Gamma Bulletin,* I (Mar., 1935), 17; I (May, 1935), 6; Blanton to Yeager, Feb. 22, 1934, Delta Kappa Gamma Alpha State Organization Records, The Woman's Collection (TWU).

[20] *The Delta Kappa Gamma Bulletin,* III (June, 1937), 13, 48; V (June, 1939), 6.

efforts is fortunate; but what of the mother who has 10,000 'children,' who delight to do her honor!"[21] And five years later, shortly before her death, she observed, "Like all doting mothers, I have often looked upon you, as too wonderful to be true."[22] She also could reflect and encourage members and pride them (and herself) on their accomplishments, as she did in a 1939 editorial in *The Bulletin:*

> Delta Kappa Gamma must have filled a felt need or it could not have grown so rapidly. And its prestige must be established in each new state, by the character of our members, by the purposes for which we exist, by the worthwhile activities in which we engage, by the beauty of the fellowship which animates our personal relationships.[23]

This aspect of Blanton's interaction with Delta Kappa Gamma suggests that in many ways the society became her extended family. Her closest friends were members, and her social activities were almost all related to Delta Kappa Gamma. It was not that the organization replaced any other part of her life; after Delta Kappa Gamma had been founded she actively maintained her teaching duties, her scholarly endeavors, her interest in rural education, her familial responsibilities, and her memberships in other organizations. Rather, it was that the society filled a need in a part of her life that was not quite complete. It provided a widening enhancement of friendships with professional women that long had been important to her, it created opportunities for family-like relationships, and it gave her a sense that her efforts and ideas might continue after her death. The membership of Delta Kappa Gamma took Blanton's dominance in stride, dwelling on her positive contributions and usually understanding when she encouraged them to do better. When the first volume of the organization's official history appeared in 1960, grateful appreciation to Blanton was evident, and this explanation of her approach to the group was included:

> If at times she was possessive, it was normal for her to be protective of her progeny; if positive in her opinions, it was

---

[21] Ibid., VI (Nov., 1939), 7.
[22] Ibid., X (June, 1944), 4.
[23] Ibid., V (June, 1939), 6.

because her experiences had been so broad; if exacting, it was because she expected above average response from the upper ten percent of the profession; if ambitious, it was because of her great hopes for the usefulness of The Delta Kappa Gamma Society.[24]

The toll of years of activity and intense commitment to numerous causes, but especially to Delta Kappa Gamma, gradually began to slow Blanton in the 1940s. In 1941 she determined that after four more years she would no longer serve as executive secretary of the organization. By declaring in advance her intention to decrease her organizational duties, Blanton allowed time for the society to plan for future leadership. This planning, as well as the structure of national officers already in place, allowed for an easy transition period upon Blanton's death at age seventy-five in 1945.[25]

At her death, the accomplishments of Delta Kappa Gamma were clear. A strong committee system kept the organization involved in issues pertaining to equal opportunity and increased visibility for women teachers, as well as major education issues. Annual conventions provided opportunities to meet colleagues from around the country and to hear such prominent speakers as Mary Ritter Beard and Judge Sarah T. Hughes. A secure state and national scholarship program was in place to aid members in pursuing graduate work.[26]

Within all of this activity was a sense of the importance of femininity and social propriety of members. Feminism was an inherent contributor to Blanton's creation of Delta Kappa Gamma, but it was carried out in the group in a non-doctrinaire manner, providing a common ground for leading women educators and allowing them,

[24] Holden, *Our Heritage,* I, 21. See also *The Delta Kappa Gamma Bulletin,* VIII (Nov., 1941), 12, for acknowledgement of Blanton as the stabilizing force of the organization.

[25] Holden, *Our Heritage,* I, 21, II, 6, 20, 140; Minutes, Annual Conventions, Delta Kappa Gamma Alpha State Organization Records, The Woman's Collection (TWU); Eugenia Hill Ramsey to Debbie Cottrell, Oct. 23, 1988, interview; *The Delta Kappa Gamma Bulletin,* X (June, 1944), 4.

[26] "Annie Webb Blanton Memorial," Booklet, Dallas Independent School District, 21–73 (in possession of author); Minutes, Annual Conventions, Delta Kappa Gamma Alpha State Organization Records, The Woman's Collection (TWU); *The Delta Kappa Gamma Bulletin,* IV (June, 1938), 30; V (June, 1939), 5–6; VI (Mar., 1940), 12; VI (June, 1940), 17–19; XLIII (Fall, 1976), passim.

as it had Blanton, to pursue professional femininity without fear or embarrassment. Similar to the women's clubs which its founder knew so well, the organization focused on reform (in the professional sense), encouraged self-improvement, maintained a certain eliteness, and never deviated from the mainstream of American educational concerns.

Upon her death, *The Delta Kappa Gamma Bulletin* noted that the organization was Blanton's greatest and most compelling interest, as well as the realization of her greatest dream.[27] Perhaps as meaningful for Blanton as seeing her dream fulfilled was knowing that the organization she looked upon as a dear child would continue after her death and that the reforms she had worked for her in her lifetime as an educator would continue to be addressed. Despite the domination of her strong personality in Delta Kappa Gamma for sixteen years and despite the certainty and force with which she made decisions in the organization, the group managed to extend beyond her personality and move forward in the years after her death. The 1950s brought a move to new headquarters in Austin. The organization later ended its racially segregated policies, and by the late 1980s had more than 160,000 members in the United States and twelve other countries. International and state scholarships, an educational foundation, and annual awards provide continued monetary support to women teachers today.[28] In sum, the ideas of professionalism encouraged by its founder have been continuously addressed.

Delta Kappa Gamma succeeded not only because Blanton used her energy and influence to nurture it, but because she recognized the need for emphasizing women's role as professional educators. Astutely utilizing the themes of feminism and femininity within the organization, Blanton created a long-lasting society with unique historical significance. She built on women's traditionally accepted role in the classroom to move women educators several steps closer to professionalism.

---

[27] *The Delta Kappa Gamma Bulletin,* XII (Nov., 1945), 31.

[28] *Daily Texan* (Austin), Jan. 9, 1955; Fechek to Cottrell, Jan. 31, 1987, interview; Walter Prescott Webb, H. Bailey Carroll, and Eldon Stephen Branda (eds.), *The Handbook of Texas* (3 vols.; Austin: Texas State Historical Association, 1952, 1976), III, 237; San Antonio *Light,* June 18, 1988. Numerous annual Delta Kappa Gamma scholarships of $2,500 are listed in Gail Ann Schlachter, *Directory of Financial Aids for Women, 1987–88* (Redwood City, Cal.: Reference Service Press, 1987), 395.

Bonnet in the Ring:

Minnie Fisher Cunningham's Campaign for Governor of Texas in 1944

PATRICIA ELLEN CUNNINGHAM*

WHEN MINNIE FISHER CUNNINGHAM ran for governor of Texas in 1944, the United States was in the final year of World War II and President Franklin D. Roosevelt was running for an unprecedented and highly controversial fourth term of office. Texas was virtually a one-party state, but there was great discord between the liberal and conservative factions of the Democratic Party. The state's political climate was extremely reactionary, resulting in "harsh antilabor laws, the suppression of academic freedom, a segregationist philosophy, elections marred by demagoguery and corruption, the devolution of the daily press, and a state government that offered its citizens, especially the minorities, very few services."[1]

Texas politics were controlled by corporate interests, particularly oil. The conservative Democrats thought that New Dealers were "too intimate with the labor movement and had saddled the country with too many wartime restrictions and high-handed bureaus."[2] The incumbent governor, Coke R. Stevenson, was a conservative Democrat.

* Patricia Ellen (Trish) Cunningham received her B.A. in aesthetic studies from the University of California at Santa Cruz in 1976 and her M.A. in journalism from the University of Texas at Austin in 1985. Her master's thesis was about Minnie Fisher Cunningham's race for governor in 1944. "Minnie Fish" was Trish Cunningham's great-great-aunt.

[1] George Norris Green, *The Establishment in Texas Politics: The Primitive Years, 1938–1957* (Norman: University of Oklahoma Press, 1979), xi.

[2] Ibid., 46.

He had previously served as lieutenant governor and was appointed governor in 1941 when his predecessor, "Pappy" O'Daniel, became a U.S. senator in a special election. Whereas "O'Daniel had kept the state in an uproar . . . [Stevenson] was quiet and inoffensive . . . [and] seldom became excited or ruffled. . . . His popularity grew as the people saw [him in] contrast to O'Daniel. . . ."[3]

Stevenson "was personable in many ways, but he . . . [had] a mean steely eye."[4] His looks and demeanor prompted journalists to call him "Calculatin' Coke."[5] It was said that Stevenson could "keep quiet longer and use fewer words in breaking his silence than anyone else who has loomed large in Southern politics."[6] The governor himself said that

> when he was a boy . . . in the rough hill country of southwestern Texas he noticed that even crafty coyotes . . . got into trouble by yapping. So he usually [kept] his lips tightly clamped on the stem of his pipe. Disdainful of political platforms, . . . he . . . made only two definite campaign promises in thirty years of political life. . . .[7]

Stevenson was a staunch proponent of states' rights. He blasted the bureaucracy of federal government but made no personal attacks on the popular president. Stevenson enjoyed a lucrative income from oil leases and was especially critical of the federal administration's wartime policy on oil rationing. He believed that Texas alone could produce plenty of oil, not only for the war but for domestic consumption as well.[8]

[3] Seth Shepard McKay, *Texas Politics, 1904–1944: With Special Reference to the German Counties* (Lubbock: Texas Tech Press, 1952), 392.
[4] Walter Hall to David McComb, June 30, 1969, Oral History Collection, LBJ Library (cited in Green, *The Establishment in Texas Politics,* 82).
[5] Green, *The Establishment in Texas Politics,* 77.
[6] Edmunds Travis, "Coke Stevenson, Rancher Governor," *Southwest Review,* XXX (Autumn, 1944), 25.
[7] Lewis Nordyke, "Calculatin' Coke," *Saturday Evening Post,* CCXVII (Oct. 28, 1944), 14.
[8] Coke R. Stevenson to Tommy Dean Ball, July 11, 1962, interview, cited in Tommy Dean Ball, "The Life of Coke R. Stevenson, Governor of Texas" (M.A. thesis, Sul Ross State College, 1963).

The exigencies of World War II were a bane to Stevenson, but for women it was a time of opportunity and action. The shortage of manpower on the home front created an enormous demand for women to fill crucial roles in the public sphere.[9] With so many men so far from home, the liberal Democrats were having a difficult time finding a good candidate to oppose Stevenson. They tried to coax J. Frank Dobie into running, but he was teaching in England and had no intention of returning to Texas for a quixotic campaign.[10] Dobie's protege and friend, John Henry Faulk, said,

> When . . . nobody . . . would run except a bunch of unknown weirdos, [Minnie Fisher Cunningham] said, "Well, I've decided to do it myself." It was a hopeless thing—she knew that. But she said someone had to . . . voice . . . opposition to Coke Stevenson.[11]

Faulk said that "Minnie Fish," as she was known to her friends,[12] was

> a very un-ostentatious person. . . . She was interested in issues and principles, not . . . fame or acclaim. . . . She was a solid, right, earthy, good, incorruptible, enlightened person. She . . . believed in a set of principles and would do anything to see them excel.[13]

Minnie Fish was no novice in politics, either. Her father, Horatio White Fisher, served two terms in the Texas legislature before she was born. As a child in the late nineteenth century, she accompanied him to political meetings in Huntsville, eight miles from their home, and enjoyed talking politics on the long ride home through the piney

[9] William H. Chafe, *The American Woman: Her Changing Social, Economic, and Political Roles, 1920–1970* (New York: Oxford University Press, 1972), 137–138.

[10] John Henry Faulk to Patricia Ellen Cunningham, 1983, interview.

[11] Ibid.

[12] Her maiden name was Fisher, which she said her mother told her never to drop from her name. Family history recorded by Rosamond Fisher Stewart, Conroe, Texas. She signed nearly all of her correspondence "Minnie Fisher Cunningham." According to those who knew her, she also liked the nickname "Minnie Fish" very much.

[13] Faulk to Cunningham.

woods.[14] Later, as a young wife in 1904, she helped carry the vote for her husband, B. J. (Bill) Cunningham, in his successful bid for election as Walker County attorney.[15] But she came into her own politically during the fight for woman suffrage.

In 1915, Minnie Fisher Cunningham was elected president of the Texas Woman Suffrage Association,[16] having previously led the suffrage movement in Galveston. She quadrupled the number of local associations across Texas and organized the state by senatorial district, striving to get motivated chairmen to carry every district, precinct, and block.[17] Under her leadership, Texas women won the right to vote in primary elections in 1918, two years before women were enfranchised nationwide by the Nineteenth Amendment to the Constitution of the United States. Being able to vote in the primaries was a real coup for Texas women because Texas was virtually a one-party state.[18]

In 1919 and 1920, Minnie Fisher Cunningham served on the staff of the National American Woman Suffrage Association in Washington, D.C., lobbying for the federal amendment. In 1920, she helped transform the national organization into the League of Women Voters, and in 1924, she chaired its national campaign to urge women to vote. Also in the 1920s, she served on the Democratic National Committee, substituting for vice chairman Emily Newell Blair, and was executive secretary of the Woman's National Democratic Club.[19] In 1928, she came home to Texas to run for the United States Senate. She was the first Texas woman to vie for that office.

Minnie Fish was a staunch New Dealer, and she returned to Washington from 1939 to 1943 to work as a public information specialist for the U.S. Department of Agriculture. She had been acquainted with the Roosevelts since 1922, when Eleanor Roosevelt was so moved by Cunningham's speech at the second annual convention of the

[14] Milwaukee *Journal,* Feb. 19, 1938, cited in Glenn K. Polan, "Minnie Fisher Cunningham" (M.A. thesis, Sam Houston State College, 1968), 12.

[15] Austin *American,* May 24, 1946.

[16] The organization was renamed the Texas Equal Suffrage Association the following year.

[17] They were mostly chairwomen, of course, but in the vernacular of the time, they were called "chairmen."

[18] Jane Y. McCallum, "Texas," in *The History of Woman Suffrage,* Vol. VI, *1900–1920,* ed. Ida Husted Harper (New York: J. J. Little and Ives, 1922), 630–643.

[19] Polan, "Minnie Fisher Cunningham," 55–59.

League of Women Voters that she wrote home to tell Franklin about it.[20] Minnie Fish's decision to run for governor was motivated largely by her outrage over a plot to defeat Roosevelt by unethical means and Stevenson's apparent connections with that conspiracy.

As election year 1944 began to take shape, the Texas "good ol' boys" had to face the unlikelihood of unseating Roosevelt by popular vote. They knew, however, that the citizens would not be casting their votes directly for the president, but for a slate of electors who were honor-bound but not legally obligated to reflect the will of the voters.[21] So the "good ol' boys" colluded with their cronies in South Carolina and devised a scheme to "steal" some votes in the electoral college. The presidential contest would then be thrown into the House of Representatives, where each state would have one vote, and the South would be disproportionately strong.[22] The scheme was to inundate the precinct, district, and state conventions with anti-Roosevelt forces who would pack the national convention and electoral college with "uninstructed" delegates and electors.

The anti-Roosevelt coup was "well financed and carefully planned in advance."[23] About a week before the precinct conventions, the chairman of the State Democratic Executive Committee sent a letter to precinct chairmen outlining the plan. As a result, delegations to the state Democratic convention were dominated by attorneys for oil and gas companies.

Soon after the delegates convened in the Senate chamber of the Capitol, Alvin Wirtz, who had previously served in Roosevelt's administration as undersecretary of the interior, moved that no person be made an elector unless he agreed to vote for the party nominee. His motion nearly created a riot,[24] and the convention chairman ruled it out of order. Then real pandemonium broke out, as Mrs. Alfred Taylor

---

[20] Eleanor Roosevelt, speech at the League of Women Voters Biennial Convention, May 1, 1940, cited in Joseph P. Lash, *Eleanor and Franklin: The Story of Their Relationship Based on Eleanor Roosevelt's Private Papers* (New York: W. W. Norton and Co., 1971), 262.

[21] Max Lerner, "Opinion: The Great Electoral College Conspiracy," *PM* (June 1, 1944), 2.

[22] Green, *The Establishment in Texas Politics,* 45–46.

[23] Nathan Robertson, "How Big Business Plotted Texas Anti-Roosevelt Revolt: GOP Worked with O'Daniel to Pack Democratic Convention," *PM,* June 1, 1944, 3.

[24] McKay, *Texas Politics, 1904–1944,* 434.

of Austin made her way to the rostrum and called on "every true Democrat" to follow her across the Capitol to the House of Representatives. The New Dealers surged out of the Senate chamber, waving a large picture of Roosevelt high overhead and singing "The Eyes of Texas."[25] The anti-Roosevelt delegates waved their handkerchiefs and made way for them to leave[26] as the organist played "God Be With You Till We Meet Again."[27]

Then the regular convention "went ahead, undisturbed, with the business of naming Governor Coke Stevenson to lead an uninstructed delegation" to the national Democratic convention in Chicago.[28] They also told their twenty-three electors not to cast their votes for the party nominee unless the national convention met three stringent demands. first, they wanted restoration of the so-called "two-thirds rule," which until 1936 gave Southern Democrats virtual veto power over the party's presidential nominee. Second, they wanted a plank in the national Democratic platform denouncing a recent Supreme Court decision that allowed blacks to participate in the Texas Democratic primary. And third, they wanted a guarantee that no one who bolted the regular convention would be seated as a delegate at the national convention. Since it was highly unlikely that the national convention would adopt these three measures, Texas citizens who voted for Roosevelt would be "completely disfranchised in the general election."[29]

The group that bolted did not organize a separate convention until they sent an envoy back to the regular convention to ask them once again to bind their delegates to support the party nominee. When the so-called "regulars" refused again, the "loyalists" announced that the will of the voters "should not be thwarted by a convention of republicans masquerading as democrats,"[30] and declared themselves a full-fledged convention, with Minnie Fisher Cunningham serving as parliamentarian.[31] The rump convention elected its own slate of delegates and electors, which gave Texas two rival delegations heading for the national convention.

[25] New York *Times,* May 24, 1944.
[26] Austin *American,* May 24, 1944.
[27] Green, *The Establishment in Texas Politics,* 47.
[28] "Texans Plot Third Party Against FDR," *PM,* May 25, 1944, 4.
[29] Green, *The Establishment in Texas Politics,* 47.
[30] "Pro-Roosevelt and Antis in Full Cleavage," Austin *American,* May 24, 1944.
[31] Ibid.

Meanwhile Stevenson, the state's highest-ranking elected official, never made an appearance at either convention. A reporter for the *Saturday Evening Post* observed that the governor had "a rare faculty for being away from the wrong place at the right time."[32] Nevertheless, the Texas "regulars" elected Stevenson to lead their uninstructed delegation to Chicago. When a newspaper editor in Amarillo asked his Austin correspondent what was going on down at the Capitol, he got "this terse reply: 'Coke in office. Smoking pipe. No comment.'"[33]

Minnie Fish was "boiling mad" that Stevenson refused to comment on matters of state.[34] "People in Texas don't like for their governor to hide in his office while the state Democratic convention is going on," she said.[35] She called Stevenson "an unseen force" behind the regular convention and said he was sympathetic to the resolutions adopted there.[36]

Minnie Fish probably saw the proverbial writing on the wall even before the convention took place. As chairman of the Walker County delegation, she may have been privy to the letter calling for the precinct and county conventions to send uninstructed delegates to the state convention. At any rate, she held a press conference to announce her candidacy on May 22, 1944, the day before the party split. She probably realized that with meager funds and a late start in the race, she had very little chance of winning. But she was savvy to the power of the press, and having previously run for U.S. Senate, she knew the power inherent in candidacy itself. She used her campaign to gain access to the media and proceeded to make Coke Stevenson as uncomfortable as possible with straddling fences.

As she told Carrie Chapman Catt, her mentor and friend since the fight for woman suffrage,[37]

[32] Nordyke, "Calculatin' Coke," 15.

[33] Ibid.

[34] Unidentified clipping, n.d. (ca. 1948) (Austin *American-Statesman* Library).

[35] Marshall *News Messenger,* June 11, 1944, reprinted in Corpus Christi *Caller Times,* n.d. (in Minnie Fisher Cunningham Papers, Houston Metropolitan Research Center, Houston Public Library, cited hereafter as HMRC).

[36] June 15, 1944. Variations of this story ran in several newspapers. Cunningham Papers (HMRC).

[37] Catt was formerly president of the National American Women Suffrage Association.

a small group of us said that after all we were only responsible to God for what we did ourselves and not for what other people did or did not do. So I announced as a candidate . . . and we made our campaign a straight, hot attack on the governor and his anti-war activities. . . .[38]

Her campaign had only one plank. "In seeking the governor's office," she said, "I have but one purpose, and that is to mobilize the strength and resources of the great state of Texas behind the men and women who are doing the fighting in this war."[39]

Nine candidates entered the race before the filing deadline. A headline in the Texarkana *News* said that the "Talents of Gov. Coke Stevenson's Opponents . . . Range From Ventriloquism to Seed Breeding."[40] The seven other opponents were Gene Porter, a Waco merchant; W. J. Minton, a newspaper editor in Sherman; "Doc" Carey, a Houston real estate agent and accomplished ventriloquist; Alex M. Ferguson, a seed breeder in Howe whose younger brother James and sister-in-law Miriam had previously served as governors of Texas; Martin Jones, a farmer in Nacogdoches; Herbert Mills, a Dickinson dentist; and William Grimes, a Houston attorney and ship fitter. Minnie Fisher Cunningham kicked off her campaign in Austin on Flag Day, June 14, 1944. At noon, she was the honored guest at a candidates' forum sponsored by the League of Women Voters of Texas. At eight o'clock that evening, at the Driskill Hotel, she delivered her keynote address

to an audience predominantly composed of women, who applauded so frequently she begged them to stop. There was frequent laughter as, step by step, she connected a tour Gov. Stevenson made in April and May with the votes of county delegations at the state democratic convention. . . .[41]

---

[38] Minnie Fisher Cunningham to Carrie Chapman Catt, Aug. 24, 1944, cited in Polan, "Minnie Fisher Cunningham," 83.

[39] Benavides *Facts,* June 2, 1944, in Cunningham Papers (HMRC).

[40] Texarkana *News,* July 13, 1944, in ibid.

[41] Austin *American,* June 15, 1944 (microfilm, Eugene C. Barker Texas History Center, University of Texas at Austin).

She called the electoral vote conspiracy "the most revolutionary movement that has appeared in my lifetime," and charged Stevenson with conspiring "to destroy the two-party system on which our government seems to rest."[42] She said,

> It may sound incredible to assert that Governor Stevenson has not kept faith with the people, but I am telling you he has not dealt with them with clarity and has not taken the leadership.
>
> By innuendo, implication, and insinuation, he has impeded the war effort and undermined morale.[43]

Minnie Fish's principal bases of support were women, soldiers, pensioners, and organized labor. Soldiers were dissatisfied with Stevenson because he wouldn't call a special session of the legislature to pass a law that would let them vote even if they hadn't paid their poll taxes while stationed overseas. Pensioners were unhappy with Stevenson because he cut their $30 monthly pensions by 10 percent as a means of reducing the state's deficit. Minnie Fish said it would be more fair if Stevenson favored a 10 percent income tax "on everyone, not just the most poverty stricken group in the state."[44] Her campaign had active labor support from the Congress of Industrial Organizations (CIO) political action committee, as well as the American Federation of Labor (AFL), the railroad brotherhood, the Texas Farmers Union, and the liberal wing of the Texas Farm Bureau.[45] But women were her most visible constituency. United Press correspondents said that hers was "largely a woman's campaign,"[46] with prominent women on the headquarters staff and women listed as the only contributors in her first campaign expense report. Most of her appearances throughout the state were sponsored by women's groups, such as the Texas League of Women Voters, the Corpus Christi Business and Professional Women, the Austin League of Women Voters, and the Tarrant County Women's Good Government League.

[42] Ibid.
[43] Houston *Chronicle,* June 15, 1944, in Cunningham Papers (HMRC).
[44] Taft *Tribune,* June 15, 1944, and Ralls *Banner,* June 16, 1944, in ibid.
[45] Gardner Jackson, "'Minnie Fish' Perils Connally Machine," *PM,* May 23, 1944.
[46] Unidentified clipping, July 7, 1944, in Cunningham Papers (HMRC).

The Texas press seemed more preoccupied with the novelty of a woman running for governor than with what she had to say. One reporter cleverly observed that a woman had "tossed her bonnet into the political ring."[47] The University of Texas Students Clipping Bureau compiled newspaper accounts of the race from dailies and weeklies all over the state; a study of those clippings forty years later revealed that 65 percent of the headlines alluded to gender.[48]

Minnie Fisher Cunningham was not the first woman to run for governor of Texas, nor was she the last. On January 15, 1991, just three months after this paper was presented at the Women and Texas History Conference, its author was among the 20,000 Texans who surged up Congress Avenue to the Capitol in Austin to witness the inauguration of Ann Willis Richards as the forty-fifth governor of Texas. As Richards took the oath of office, she became the first woman elected governor of the state since 1935, and the first Texas woman elected governor in her own right.

Minnie Fisher Cunningham was one of four women whose bids for the governorship blazed the trail for Richards. Edith Therrel Wilmans ran in the Democratic primaries of 1926 and 1928, finishing fifth of six candidates and last of four, respectively.[49] Miriam A. Ferguson ran in 1924, 1926, 1930, and 1932, and was elected on her first and last attempts. Frances Tarlton (Sissy) Farenthold made it into the runoff in 1972, and ran again in 1974.

Wilmans, who in 1914 helped organize the Dallas Equal Suffrage Association and in 1918 was licensed to practice law, became the first woman elected to the Texas legislature in 1922. She was also the first woman to preside as speaker of the House, and in 1924 Gov. Pat Neff appointed her as a special judge of the Texas Supreme Court.[50]

Farenthold, who was the only woman to serve in the Texas House from 1969 to 1973, led a group of reform legislators called the "Dirty

---

[47] *State Observer,* June 12, 1944, in ibid.

[48] Patricia Ellen Cunningham, "Too Gallant a Walk: Minnie Fisher Cunningham and Her Race for Governor of Texas in 1944" (M.A. thesis, University of Texas at Austin, 1985).

[49] Mike Kingston (ed.), *1990–91 Texas Almanac* (Dallas: Dallas Morning News, 1989), 361.

[50] Sarah Weddington, Jane Hickie, and Deanna Fitzgerald, *Texas Women in Politics,* eds. Elizabeth W. Ferea and Marilyn P. Duncan (Austin: Foundation for Women's Resources, 1977), 6–7.

Thirty" in opposition to the speaker of the House, who was implicated in the illegal manipulation of stock transactions.[51] In the 1972 Democratic gubernatorial primary, she finished second among seven candidates with 28 percent of the vote, but lost to Dolph Briscoe in the runoff. Briscoe defeated her again in 1974.[52]

Unlike the others in this coterie, Miriam A. Ferguson was never a great proponent of women's rights. When questioned about woman suffrage in 1916, while her husband James E. (Jim) Ferguson was governor, Miriam replied, "Personally, I prefer that men shall attend to all public matters."[53]

"Ma" Ferguson, as she was dubbed by the press, was the first woman actually elected governor of Texas, but she "was governor in name only."[54] She ran because her husband had been impeached in 1917 and was forever barred from holding office. Jim did most of the talking in his wife's campaigns, assuring the crowds that by electing her, they would get two governors for the price of one. Once she was elected, he set up an office next to hers. Although Miriam did overrule her husband occasionally and matured politically during her tenure in office, Jim was nevertheless "the real power. He attended the meetings of state boards, agencies, and commissions with or without her, received political callers, and 'advised.'"[55]

Jane Y. McCallum, who in 1917 had called Gov. Jim Ferguson "the implacable foe of woman suffrage and of every great moral issue for which women stood,"[56] had no kinder words for his wife. A newspaper clipping among her papers, probably written by McCallum herself, said that "Ma" was "called the first woman Governor of Texas," but was, in fact, "the first proxy Governor of the State, and, it is to be hoped, the last."[57]

[51] Ruthe Winegarten, *Texas Women: A Pictorial History From Indians to Astronauts* (Austin: Eakin Press, 1986), 139.

[52] Kingston (ed.), *Texas Almanac*, 363.

[53] Norman D. Brown, *Hood, Bonnet, and Little Brown Jug: Texas Politics, 1921–1928* (College Station: Texas A&M University Press, 1984), 219.

[54] Ibid., 269.

[55] Ibid.

[56] McCallum, "Texas," in *The History of Woman Suffrage*, Vol. VI, *1900–1920*, 634.

[57] Unidentified clipping, Jane Y. McCallum Papers, Austin History Center, Austin Public Library. It was probably written by McCallum and published in the Austin *American* during "Ma" Ferguson's first term as governor of Texas.

Minnie Fisher Cunningham was nobody's proxy. Like Wilmans before her and Farenthold and Richards later, she was running in her own right.

In 1944, the editor of the *State Observer* said that Minnie Fish's candidacy offered Texas women an opportunity "to prove or disprove their fitness to engage in political activities," but that he would understand if men didn't take her campaign seriously. "The disposition of the male of the human species to view any serious efforts of women lightly, is 'age old,' if not . . . inherent," he said in an editorial. With that disclaimer, he placed the burden of electing her squarely on women's backs—as if they could do it alone. He said her candidacy was

a direct and definite challenge to Texas women to "prove their metal" [*sic*] . . . . If the women of Texas . . . have the vision to apprehend this opportunity to elect one of their sex, who has the experience and ability to fill the Governor's chair with distinction and honor, opportunity is knocking at their door. . . .

Will the women of Texas grasp this opportunity and "Rise to the occasion?" Time alone will tell.[58]

Three and a half weeks later, the same editor wrote, "The whole result hinges on the efforts put forth by the women. . . ."[59]

The editor of the Arlington *Citizen* took a different view. After conducting an informal survey of voters across the state, he concluded that women would not vote as a bloc for Minnie Fisher Cunningham. He wrote: "Many women voters said that they believed it would be good for Texas to have a woman governor and would vote for one, but a MAJORITY of those interviewed stated most positively that the governor's job is 'no job for a woman', and that they would not vote for one under any circumstances. . . ."[60]

Although the editor personally felt that a woman governor would be "a wholesome change" for Texas, he urged his readers not to vote for her. He wrote, "the friends of Coke Stevenson are turning heaven

58 *State Observer*, June 19, 1944, in Cunningham Papers (HMRC).
59 Ibid., July 13, 1944, in ibid.
60 Arlington *Citizen*, July 15, 1944, in ibid.

and earth to get the opposition vote to line up behind the woman candidate, because [they] KNOW THAT A WOMAN CAN'T DEFEAT HIM in the run-off. . . ."[61]

Eighteen days before the primary, Minnie Fish took to the stump. "We hadn't intended to campaign," she said, "but we got a good number of requests. . . ."[62] Her friend Margaret Reading bought the gas, and they drove about 1,700 miles, stopping in seven cities and towns. It was said that as she campaigned, "she looked like a wren but behaved like an eagle."[63]

Their first stop was a Fourth of July celebration in her hometown of New Waverly. The population was about 400, but a crowd of 2,500 turned out for the event.[64] She devoted two days each to Houston, Dallas, Austin, and Corpus Christi, and made shorter stops in Fort Worth, Beaumont, and Coleman.

The evening of July 17, 1944, found her giving her third speech of the day at a political rally in Fort Worth. As she spoke, two rival delegations from Texas were traveling north on the same train to Chicago. The next morning, Minnie Fisher Cunningham told a Dallas reporter that the anti-Roosevelt delegation had proceeded to the national Democratic convention *without* Coke Stevenson. With that, she said her campaign had "accomplished its primary goal."[65]

At the national convention, the credentials committee recommended that both Texas delegations be seated, and that each delegate have half a vote. The Texas "regulars" tried to get sole representation, but were voted down by "an overwhelming chorus of 'noes.'" When the convention called for Texas's vote, the "loyalists" declared twenty-four for Roosevelt, and the uninstructed delegates split their votes, twelve for Roosevelt and twelve for Sen. Harry Byrd of Virginia.[66]

Back in Dallas, Minnie Fish made three fifteen-minute speeches by radio to women, soldiers, and all Texas voters, which were broadcast by stations in Dallas, Fort Worth, Houston, and San Antonio.[67]

[61] Ibid.

[62] Ronnie Dugger, "Spanning the Old to the New South: Minnie Fisher and Her Heroine Mother," *Texas Observer* (Nov. 21, 1958), 2.

[63] Liz Carpenter to Patricia Ellen Cunningham, Nov. 5, 1983, interview; Liz Carpenter quoted in Austin *American-Statesman,* Oct. 7, 1990.

[64] Huntsville *Item,* July 7, 1944, in Cunningham Papers (HMRC).

[65] Dallas *Morning News,* July 19, 1944, in ibid.

[66] McKay, *Texas Politics, 1906–1944,* 444–445.

[67] Austin *American,* July 19, 1944, in Cunningham Papers (HMRC).

She delivered her last radio address from Houston on July 21, and then went home to New Waverly to vote.

Despite her efforts to the contrary, the 1944 Democratic primary was, according to two United Press reporters, "Texas' quietest state political campaign in many years."[68] The Dallas *Times Herald* agreed that the race offered "little visible evidence that it was going on."[69] And a columnist for the McGregor *Mirror,* who was wringing sweat from his sleeves as he wrote, said, "Texas politics will never get hotter than this week's weather, even if Mrs. Minnie Fisher Cunningham should start a prairie fire of women voters in the modern trend of sexual equality."[70]

As the election returns rolled in, Stevenson "sailed through to an easy victory" with 85 percent of the vote.[71] He went on to another landslide victory over the Republican candidate in November.

Minnie Fisher Cunningham received 48,039 votes, less than 6 percent of the total votes cast in the primary. Nevertheless, the only woman among nine candidates placed second in the race, and no other candidate received half as many votes as she.

By her own measure, she had accomplished her goal. Four days before the primary, she told a reporter, "I just had to run. Otherwise [Stevenson] was going to take over the Texas delegation to Chicago. Well, we scared him out of going to Chicago. That means my campaign's a success." Anything else, she said, was "strictly plus."[72]

---

[68] N.p., July 7, 1944, in ibid.
[69] Dallas *Times Herald,* June 17, 1944, in ibid.
[70] McGregor *Mirror,* June 23, 1944, in ibid.
[71] Temple *Telegram,* July 23, 1944, in ibid.
[72] Dallas *News,* July 19, 1944, in ibid.

Domesticity and the Texas Oil Fields:

Dimensions of Women's Experience, 1920–1950

DIANA DAVIDS OLIEN*

HUNDREDS OF THOUSANDS of men, women, and children have lived and worked in the Texas oil fields since 1900, but oil field life is one of the least studied aspects of the evolution of modern Texas. When the history of petroleum development in Texas has been studied, moreover, it has usually been presented in the context of men's lives and work, a context in which women take minor and stereotypical roles. Carl Coke Rister's *Oil! Titan of the Southwest* is a good example of the male-oriented approach. When Rister mentioned women, he cast them either as upholders of civilization in the form of Sunday schools and civic groups or, as he put it, "working women" (prostitutes): they were either men's redeemers or ruination, with little intermediate ground admitted.[1] For the most part, women were simply given no part of oil field history.

In reality, oil field life encompassed women's experience, and large numbers of women lived in the Texas oil fields, taking neither stereotypical role of civilizer or soiled dove. Instead, they most often pursued

---

* Diana Davids Olien received a B.A. degree from Swarthmore College and M.A., M.Phil., and Ph.D. degrees from Yale University. She teaches women's history at the University of Texas-Permian Basin. She is the author of *Morpeth: A Victorian Public Career* and, with Roger M. Olien, a number of books on the petroleum industry, the most recent of which is *Easy Money: Oil Promoters and Investors in the Jazz Age.*

[1] Carl Coke Rister, *Oil! Titan of the Southwest* (Norman: University of Oklahoma Press, 1949), 155, 120, 167, 247.

the highly traditional goal of domesticity, a pursuit which, as Barbara Welter pointed out some years ago, was part of the nineteenth-century definition of women's proper social role.[2] They were, in short, keepers of homes. In the early twentieth-century oil field environment, however, the keeper of a home faced unusual obstacles, for the home often had neither a conventional physical structure nor a fixed location over time. For that reason, considering women's experience in the Texas oil fields with respect to domesticity raises two questions:

1) How did women realize the conventional American ideal of domesticity in the often unconventional living conditions of the oil fields; and

2) More speculatively, did the terms of that realization strengthen the traditional perspective of women's social roles as primarily domestic?

To begin, it is necessary to make a few observations about oil field life in Texas and the Southwest during the first half of this century. The period marked the opening up of the region's petroleum production and its eventual preeminence in national production of oil and gas. The pace of exploration was hectic and the number of discoveries throughout the region staggering.[3] As field after field opened up, a large mobile population followed activity from place to place. Its economic survival required mobility. Particularly in the decades before petroleum engineering permitted careful production management, in most fields exploration and production rapidly peaked and fell off; when action began to wind down, workers either had to look for jobs in new fields or follow their employers to them. Occasionally a field like East Texas would be so large and prolific that workers would not have to move with work for a number of years, but employment lasting little more than a year or only a matter of months was more usual. Thus, over a half century, hundreds of thousands of Texans, men, women, and children, would be part of an ongoing migration.[4]

---

[2] Barbara Welter, *Dimity Convictions: The American Woman in the Nineteenth Century* (Athens, Oh.: Ohio University Press, 1976), 31–34.

[3] For the sheer volume of Texas discoveries before the late 1930s see C. A. Warner, *Texas Oil and Gas Since 1543* (Houston: Gulf Publishing Co., 1939), 115–131.

[4] On oil field work and mobility, see Roger M. Olien and Diana Davids Olien, *Oil Booms: Social Change in Five Texas Towns* (Lincoln, Neb.: University of Nebraska Press, 1982), 21–39.

Oil field work was male work, and its culture, derived from rural life, emphasized "macho," emphatically male-oriented behavior. A worker was likely to win acceptance from his peers if he was physically strong, athletic, oblivious to danger or discomfort, hard-drinking, and periodically rowdy.[5] With its emphasis on male-oriented values, it is not surprising that oil field work reflected traditional patterns of gender discrimination in hiring. In the workplace, men commonly worked in small crews to do such labor as rig-building, roustabout work, or drilling; indeed, two-man crews usually served wells drilled with cable tools. In such small groups, the worker's ability to fit in, to conform to the group, was important, and here gender ruled out women's participation.[6] Many of the skills in oil field work were either learned on the job or carried over from male workplaces in a rural agricultural setting, both arenas to which women had little access. Much oil field work was heavy, dirty labor done out-of-doors in all weather; this too may have discouraged women from looking for oil field jobs.

But that did not mean women were unable to find employment when there was oil development. Many women found jobs indirectly created by oil, working as restaurant or boarding house owners, waitresses, nurses, teachers, laundresses, telephone operators, sales help, and office personnel. Some women found less respectable employment as bunco artists, fortune tellers, taxi dancers, and prostitutes. Like male workers, these female workers, too, moved with oil activity, and usually they had little choice. If they were married to oil field workers, their incomes were almost always supplementary, smaller than those of their husbands. That meant family economics would lead them to give up their work if their husbands found employment elsewhere.[7] Most women in the mobile population, however, did not

---

[5] On the "macho" character of oil field culture, see Roger M. Olien and Diana Davids Olien, *Life in the Oil Fields* (Austin: Texas Monthly Press, 1986), 8–9, 181–185.

[6] V. L. Cox to Roger M. Olien, Apr. 25, 1980, interview; Clarence Dunaway to Roger M. Olien, Apr. 30, 1980, interview; Don Dittman to Roger M. Olien, Apr. 6, 1979, interview ; W. H. "Steamboat" Fulton to Roger M. Olien, Oct. 27, 1979, interview; Mr. and Mrs. Joe Koesel to Diana Davids Olien, Mar. 27, 1982, interview; Hood May to Roger M. Olien and J. Conrad Dunagan, Apr. 19, 1978, interview; Clell Reed to Roger M. Olien, Apr. 6, 1984, interview.

[7] On women's employment in the oil field environment see Olien and Olien, *Oil Booms*, 87–93.

work outside the home. Their primary role was domestic, to create and maintain a home. This was the logical complement to the male's activity in the oil field; in macho culture, men were providers, economic supporters of homes women kept. For that matter, if men were hard-drinking and rowdy, women were to be orderly upholders of civilization, the obverse of the male role. In a sense, the pronounced and traditional understanding of the male roles in oil field culture demanded an equally traditional definition of female roles.

In the best of circumstances, creating a home under conditions of high mobility is challenging; when finding shelter to use as a home is difficult, the task is much harder. By geological happenstance, most oil discoveries took place in rural areas, locations often remote from population centers; in the Southwest, Oklahoma City was one of the few exceptions to this rule. Oil fields, moreover, often opened up in places where commuting from existing towns to work was out of the question. In the 1920s, for example, oil was discovered in the sand dunes of Crane and Winkler counties and in barren reaches of Pecos County, remote West Texas locations where there were no hard-surfaced roads. Near Burkburnett and in the East Texas oil field, rain and heavy oil field traffic turned dirt farm roads into virtually impassable mud sloughs.[8] Because of the rural location of much oil development and the lack of good roads, most field workers had to live at or within a short distance of their work site. When work at one site finished, it was time to move to the next, usually just as remote from town living.

Even when it was possible to live in a small town like McCamey, Desdemona, or White Oak and reach work, no small settlement was equal to the demand for shelter generated by an oil boom. (For that matter, larger towns usually were not equal to that demand.) Following an oil discovery, all lodgings in nearby towns would be snapped up. Male workers, traveling alone, were reduced to sleeping in cars; under trees; in barns, garages, cot or flop houses, barber chairs, hotel lobbies, and hallways; and on or under pool tables. But such makeshift arrangements could not suit married couples and families. For them,

[8] Mody C. Boatright and William A. Owens, *Tales from the Derrick Floor: A People's History of the Oil Industry* (Garden City, N.Y.: Doubleday, 1970), 78, 105; James A. Clark and Michel T. Halbouty, *The Last Boom* (New York: Random House, 1972), 126–127.

one- or two-room shacks, shotgun, or boxcar houses were often the only shelter available—when landlords did not balk at renting to couples with children. Sometimes families could not find even these substandard accommodations.[9]

Before the advent of the house trailer in the late 1930s, the common lack of family housing often brought mobile workers to improvise their own shelters from cheap lumber, crates and boxes, and flattened metal cans. One worker more creative than most housed his family in a structure made of flattened metal oil barrels.[10] But the most common expedient was the boarded tent. On reaching their work site, workers built eight- by twelve-foot plywood platforms, boxed them in with four-foot walls, and topped the walls with screened tent roofs. The tents gave temporary oil field settlements the familiar name "ragtowns"; when they existed on company-owned sites, collections of boarded tents and shacks were dubbed "poor boy camps."[11] No wonder mobile workers found even the small house trailers of the 1930s and 1940s a great improvement; the trailer court could seem like remarkable luxury compared to ragtown or poor boy camp!

Such were the shelters in which many oil field women were expected to practice conventional American domesticity, the surroundings they had to turn into comfortable homes. What was remarkable in the common experience of oil field women was their continual striving to minimize the unconventional nature of their domestic environments. Rather than act like campers and scale down domestic chores to adjust their lives to rugged living conditions, they were likelier to treat their tent or shack homes with the kind of care women's magazines recommended to suburban housewives in bungalows.

For example, though some families lived with no more than they could pack into two footlockers, many put conventional furnishings in their shacks or tents. Mrs. R. V. Melton, living in a twenty- by twenty-

---

[9]   Olien and Olien, *Oil Booms*, 43–47.

[10]   Mr. and Mrs. James Williams to S. D. Myres, Sept. 15, 1971, interview, Abell-Hanger Collection, Permian Basin Petroleum Museum, Library, and Hall of Fame, Midland, Texas (cited hereafter as AHC: PBPM).

[11]   C. P. Bowie, "Oil Camp Sanitation," Bureau of Mines Technical Paper 261 (Washington, D.C.: Government Printing Office, 1921), 6; Olien and Olien, *Life in the Oil Fields*, 87–107.

four-foot army surplus tent in Crane during the late 1920s, remembered that her household furnishings included "a two-burner oil stove, and we had two beds and a baby bed, a Victrola, a sewing machine, a dresser, a table, and chairs."[12] Mrs. R. V. Wilson, living in the same Crane ragtown in a fourteen- by twenty-foot shack, had a double bed, a trundle bed, two rocking chairs, and a convertible sofabed, or "sanitary couch"; the latter was kept in a lean-to tent attached to the shack for guests' lodging. She was proudest, however, of her kitchen and dining furnishings: "I had all my cooking equipment, and I brought it with me from Levelland to Crane. I had pretty nice chairs, and I had a fairly nice little dining table and chairs. And I had the prize: a Hoosier cabinet that was the nicest kitchen cabinet out there. In fact, it had a flour bin in it, and a sugar bin built in. . . ."[13]

From the 1920s onward, tent and shack dwellers had household appliances, albeit they tended to be small ones. Phonographs and radios were ordinary accessories where residents had electricity; 1920s tent dwellers without it had wind-up Victrolas.[14] Many ragtown housewives cooked on gas, rather than kerosene, stoves; there was never any lack of surplus gas in producing oil fields, but sometimes crude oil got into the gas lines, leaving stoves a daunting mess.[15] Tent and shack dwellers were likelier to have piped-in gas than modern plumbing. Running water was an amenity ragtown residents commonly did without, especially in arid West Texas, where drinkable water could be harder to find than oil. A McCamey tent dweller of the late 1920s, Bessie Leonard, recalled: "We had to buy water for everything. We'd pay one dollar a barrel for it. You took your bath in it, but you didn't throw it out. You kept it for your clothes, 'cause your clothes was full of sand. . . . Water was very precious."[16]

Using conventional household furnishings in a ragtown environment often meant making adaptations. Many tent dwellers used ordinary bedsteads and farmhouse tables, but they had to place the furniture

---

[12] Mr. and Mrs. R. V. Melton to S. D. Myres, June 10, 1970, interview (AHC:PBPM).

[13] Mr. and Mrs. R. V. Wilson to S. D. Myres, June 16, 1970, interview (AHC: PBPM).

[14] Mrs. Fred Keene to Diana Davids Olien, Mar. 21, 1978, interview.

[15] Mrs. Ruth Godwin to Roger M. Olien, Mar. 16, 1978, interview.

[16] Mrs. Fred Leonard to Diana Davids Olien, May 19, 1978, interview.

legs in cans of kerosene so that ants and other insects could not crawl up them. Tent housewives set tables conventionally, but because of insects and windborne grit, families sometimes ate meals under sheets draped over their heads and the table; as Bessie Leonard remembered, "We had many, many meals with our heads under a sheet."[17] Prized household items brought to the oil fields could be pressed to unusual uses; thus the children in a Wink tent household kept goldfish in their mother's cut-glass punchbowl. Some furnishings simply did not adapt readily to ragtown living. One shack homemaker had her carpets blow up and wrap themselves around her legs in a windstorm; another recalled how the wind blew up the linoleum on her shack's floor, making it necessary "to mash it down step by step." She added, "Oh, nobody knows what people went through and lived with at that time."[18]

But what people "lived with," in fact, was not what one would predict mobile people in primitive living quarters would have. Hoosier cabinets, dining tables, phonographs, sewing machines, gas ranges, carpets, and punch bowls were part of the department store or mail-order catalogue's allure to American consumers, the accessories of middle-class American domesticity. Oil field workers, often relatively well-paid compared to other blue-collar workers, could afford them and bought them. They did not forego the trappings of conventional domesticity because their living quarters were often totally unsuited to such furnishings: instead, one might say oil field housewives used them, in effect, to impose domesticity upon unsuitable surroundings. Confronted with a novel living environment, they responded with an aggressive reaffirmation of the conventional and traditional, however ill-adapted to existing conditions.

If women did not give up domestic accessories, neither did they abandon conventional and traditional housekeeping standards because they were living in tents or shacks. Yet the challenge the environment posed to conventional tidiness was formidable. Sticky crude oil and mud smirched clothing and dirtied floors. In arid West Texas, windborne sand could not be kept from tents and shacks, so women

[17] Ibid.
[18] Mrs. Clell Reed to Diana Davids Olien, Apr. 6, 1984, interview (quotation); Godwin to Roger M. Olien; Dr. Homer Johnson to Diana Davids Olien, Jan. 30, 1978, interview.

swept it up by the bucketsful; as one tent housewife said, "Every time it'd sand, I'd think, 'Well, I have to clean it up.' I couldn't stand it, you know."[19] Ragtown housewives made up beds with sheets, though by morning they could see body outlines in sand on the bed linen.[20] At holiday time, women attempted special meals despite their surroundings. Thus, Mrs. R. V. Melton mentioned, "On several occasions on this little two-burner oil stove, I prepared chicken, dressing, and all the trimmings, and we had a good feast with company in." Another West Texan, however, remembered the molded gelatin salad she made one Thanksgiving day; by the time she unmolded it and got it to the table, it was permeated with sand.[21]

In short, rather than modify routines away from conventional standards in response to their unusual conditions, these women, like many others, strove all the harder to attain them. Such behavior had a past parallel; as scholars like Sandra Myres and Joanna Stratton have found, pioneer women on the Western frontier tried to beautify cabins and sod houses and struggled valiantly at housekeeping.[22] But oil field women were more frequently mobile than their pioneer sisters and more influenced by the values of an increasingly consumer-oriented society. What they had and what they tried to do seems even more incongruous against their surroundings than the homemaking efforts of pioneer women. Their refusal to compromise on conventional domestic values and aspirations was striking indeed, an adamant adherence to traditional role.

There was one type of oil field living, however, that offered a middle-class alternative to the rigorous domesticity of ragtown. Troubled by high labor turnover rates in the 1920s, major oil company managers came to see comfortable, conventional housing as a perquisite that could keep valued employees with the company. As one executive put it, "When you hire a man, you [also] hire his wife."[23] Managers

[19] Keene to Diana Davids Olien.

[20] Ibid.; Reed to Diana Davids Olien.

[21] Melton to Myres (quotation); Dr. Merle Montgomery to Diana Davids Olien, Feb. 4, 1978, interview.

[22] Sandra L. Myres, *Westering Women and the Frontier Experience, 1800–1915* (Albuquerque, N.M.: University of New Mexico Press, 1982), 145–146; Joanna L. Stratton, *Pioneer Women: Voices from the Kansas Frontier* (New York: Simon and Schuster, 1981), 48, 52, 55–56.

[23] Quoted by Albert Raymond Parker, "Life and Labor in the Mid-Continent

realized that wives' discontent with substandard living conditions could push employees to look for other sorts of work. Their answer, the company camp, in effect attempted to transplant conventional suburban living to the oil field.

By contrast to makeshift ragtown arrangements, camp housing ordinarily consisted of tidy rows of sturdily-built modern bungalows with four or five rooms and screened-in porches. Houses had electricity, gas, company-purified water, and modern plumbing; they were often surrounded by mowed lawns and clipped hedges. When houses needed fresh paint, company crews did the painting, inside and out—in company-approved colors: in many camps that meant any color as long as it was white! In the 1950s Shell Oil supplied houses in its Denver City camp with window shades, carpets, light bulbs, bathroom tissue, and floor wax for wood floors. Camp housing limited expression of individual taste; painted walls could not be papered, and polished wood floors could not be covered with linoleum. No alterations could be made without company permission. Similar restrictions related to family pets; some camps permitted them, others did not.[24] These were trade-offs most camp dwellers accepted happily, familiar as they were with the alternatives.

In the company camp women could enjoy all the trappings of suburban domesticity except for the suburbs. They could have a home full of modern furniture and appliances. While children played on camp playgrounds, they could socialize in sewing circles, bridge clubs, and coffee klatches. They celebrated milestones in their lives with camp birthday parties and baby showers. There were company softball games, dances, parties, and picnics; most companies staged barbecues on July 4 and Labor Day. And when the company transferred their husbands, wives moved to another, similar company camp.[25]

Oil Fields, 1859–1945" (Ph.D. diss., University of Oklahoma, 1951), 167; see also F. B. Taylor, "Management Problems of Company Camps," *Petroleum Engineer* (Oct., 1935), 94–95.

[24] Koesel to Diana Davids Olien; Mr. and Mrs. C. E. "Steve" Cullum to Roger M. Olien, Aug. 12, 1980, interview; Mrs. G. C. McAuley to Diana Davids Olien, Mar. 24, 1984, interview; Mrs. Julius Zellmer to Diana Davids Olien, Sept. 9, 1983, interview. On life in Shell Oil company camps, see Lois A. Collins, "The Significance of Oil Company Camps in the Development of the Permian Basin," *Permian Historical Annual,* XXVIII (Dec., 1988), 85–104.

[25] Collins, "Significance of Oil Company Camps," 88, 95, 99, 103; Cullum to

Obviously company camp life was restrictive and demanded conformity. It also left little room for family privacy. As one former Humble camp resident recalled, "You must realize that you weren't that far away from your neighbor, and your neighbor was maybe your boss, his wife. Everything you did was being observed."[26] Such neighborly scrutiny in effect policed conformity to conventional behavior. Another Humble camp resident remembered: "You made faster, closer friends [in camp]. They were also nosy. They were also gossipy. And they never minded to look you straight in the eye and say, 'How much did you pay for that?' 'Are you pregnant?' 'Where were you last night?'" The compensation for such intrusion was the neighborly network of camp life; as this interviewee put it, "You never lacked for help."[27]

Camp dwellers not only knew one another's private lives, but they were well aware of each other's income brackets. Indeed, houses in many camps were arranged according to employee status in the company. The biggest and best houses were in the camp's front row, and in them lived top supervisory personnel. Moving back, house size and employee rank diminished, and the back row belonged to very junior professionals and gang pushers.[28] Thus a wife in a company camp lived with a constant visible reminder of her husband's company status, the sole determinant of her own social position in the camp community. No effort of her own could alter that position. Still, having any house in a company camp set one apart from those who did not qualify for company housing. Company camp housing meant both the attainment of economic aspiration and visible status. It was something to be envied, worked for, and longed for as an alternative to ragtown, for both women and men alike.

The company camp thus offered oil field women a self-contained, traditionally structured world, an oasis of middle-class living in the rough-and-tumble of oil field life. But the company camp in turn demanded that women restrict their lives to the traditional domestic role. A wife's presence in camp was not at her initiative, and she would

Roger M. Olien; Zellmer to Diana Davids Olien; Mr. and Mrs. E. W. Purdy to Diana Davids Olien, Apr. 10, 1984, interview.

26 Zellmer to Diana Davids Olien.
27 Purdy to Diana Davids Olien.
28 Zellmer to Diana Davids Olien.

never be called upon to help her husband do his work. Her husband alone was the provider, the achiever, the guarantor of family economic and social advancement. Her husband's upward mobility in the company hierarchy was likely to require geographical mobility; that, taken with the structure of camp life, offered no encouragement for a wife's independent career or economic initiative. Sheltered and domestic, her role was limited to being the complement of her successful husband-provider. And living that role was identified with realizing family economic aspiration.

Having looked at the ways in which women in the oil fields tried to realize the goal of conventional American domesticity in often highly unconventional surroundings, we may now come to grips with the second question we posed. With respect to domesticity, with respect to complementary roles for women-homemakers and men-providers, the industrial experience of the oil fields in Texas, and, for that matter, throughout the Southwest, worked to strengthen traditional values and reinforce old ideas of gender roles. The incongruities of ragtown domesticity, with its modern consumer accessories gracing tents and shacks, shows the direction of economic aspiration for women and men alike. In that context, the insular domesticity of company camps stood for the achievement of aspiration. In both environments, acceptance of traditional roles was the rule, and both taken together enhanced the value of female domesticity, in effect by identifying its acceptance with family economic advancement. Oil field living conditions, for the most part apparently incompatible with conventional domesticity, ended in enhancing its appeal and its strength.

By the end of the 1950s, ragtowns were part of the past, and company camps were being phased out. With the extension of well-paved roads to most Texas oil fields, both came to lack the reason for their existence. Those who once endured ragtowns could enjoy the relative comfort of modern mobile homes; those who once lived in camps now lived in towns. But when we remember how many thousands of persons lived in ragtowns and company camps now long gone, the importance of the widespread reinforcement those environments gave a traditional value and traditional gender roles begins to emerge. Indeed, from women's past in the Texas oil fields we can perhaps come to understand part of the strongly conservative tone of much in Anglo Texas culture today.

To Wed and to Teach:

The Myth of the Single Teacher

SYLVIA HUNT*

LEGENDS AND MYTHS about Texas and Texans abound; and with the current interest in women's history, Texas women have been animated in this genre.[1] In one popular history, the author states that

> Texas women were activists. They ran ranches, branded cattle, lobbied the halls of the Texas Legislature with the most hardened "good ole boys," wrote books, invented products, made big money, negotiated treaties, led strikes, ran hospitals, preached the gospel, got elected to public office and built major institutions. . . . Some Texas women were even quite outrageous. Many were outlaws in spirit, if not always in fact.

* Sylvia Oates Hunt teaches in the History Department of Eastern Michigan University in Ypsilanti, Michigan. She moved to Michigan with her husband in 1990 after a long association with East Texas Baptist University in Marshall, Texas. She completed her Ph.D. at the University of Texas at Arlington in 1992. Her research interests include the history of women teachers.

She would like to thank Kathleen Underwood and Henry Hood for their comments and critiques during the writing of this paper.

[1] The study of women's history is even newer in Texas than it is on the regional and national scene, possibly because Texas has not been included in studies either of the South or of the West even though it belongs in both. Ann Patton Malone has written a bibliographic essay, "Women in Texas History," in *A Guide to the History of Texas* (New York: Greenwood Press, 1988), eds. Light Townsend Cummins and Alvin R. Bailey, Jr. Not mentioned in that essay are two dissertations: Judie Walton Gammage, "Quest for Equality: An Historical Overview of Women's Rights Activism in Texas, 1890–1975" (Ph.D. diss., North Texas State University , 1982), and Megan Seaholm, "Earnest Women: The White Woman's Club Movement in Progressive Era Texas, 1880–1920" (Ph.D. diss., Rice University, 1988).

. . . Other Texas women expanded the range of allowable experiences for women by proving their extraordinary capabilities.[2]

Interestingly enough, a teacher's name can be attached to every category that is listed here, and more categories can be added: they were judges and superintendents of schools. From Lizzie Johnson Williams, who owned her own ranch, had her own brand, had her husband sign prenuptial agreements, and taught school from 1865 until 1880, when she found it more profitable to spend her time managing her investments; to Myra Belle Shirley, who taught school near Dallas in 1863, became the famous outlaw Belle Starr, and was gunned down in 1889, colorful women teachers fit these images. Although their life stories seem larger than life, they were real and far from legend or myth, and they made a difference in Texas history.

In searching for information about Texas teachers I found personal history documents for about 250 teachers who taught for some length of time from the mid-nineteenth century through the Depression, and some form of writing, either reminiscence, memoir, poem, or book, for about 100 of these women. The weaknesses of this sample are that it is small and it has been determined by availability of sources. The strength of the sample is that it allows the women's voices to come through. Most of the women in the sample were white, middle-class women, although a few were either Hispanic or black. Since the number of minorities included is so small, I have not attempted to generalize about their experiences.

Since historians generally have interpreted nineteenth-century women's history through the tenets of domesticity and/or separate spheres, the questions that have informed this study are 1) did Texas teachers uphold, exemplify, or believe in domesticity? and 2) was separate spheres a reality for them?[3] Answering these questions about

---

[2] Francis Edward Abernethy (ed.), *Legendary Ladies of Texas* (Dallas: E-Heart Press, 1981), 4.

[3] Among those addressing the historiography of women teachers and problems in establishing a theoretical base for this history are Courtney Vaughn-Roberson, "Historical Perspectives for the Study of Women Teachers," *Vitae Scholasticae*, II (Spring, 1983), 183–201, and Sally Schwager, "Educating Women in America," *Signs: Journal of Women in Culture and Society*, XII, No. 2 (1987), 333–372.

Texas women teachers has involved testing each personal history document and each woman's life history against the following commonly accepted tenets of domesticity: women were not individuals, but were part of a unit that was not complete without a husband on whom they were economically dependent; women were not to be heard in the political process except through private influence on their husbands; and, finally, the heightened dependence upon men which domesticity required made women more subordinate in a society in which independence was highly valued, making equality between men and women impossible.[4]

The difference in the findings of this study involves the position that domesticity is a rhetorical device, an artificial construct used by historians to analyze women's history. If it is valid, it should be substantiated in the rhetoric of those who were experiencing it. If it is not, then Linda Kerber's call for a paradigm change, at least in the realm of women teachers, is warranted.[5]

Adding the perspectives and the personal histories of women teachers, as several noted historians have done, shows that teaching not only gave women a livelihood at intellectually stimulating work, but that for these women domesticity, as defined above, was not a reality.[6] Indeed, Texas educators were acting, thinking, and talking as

[4] Barbara Leslie Epstein, *The Politics of Domesticity: Women, Evangelism, and Temperance in Nineteenth-Century America* (Middletown, Conn.: Wesleyan University Press, 1981), 2. For other references to domesticity see Nancy F. Cott, *The Bonds of Womanhood: "Woman's Sphere" in New England, 1780–1835* (New Haven: Yale University Press, 1977) and *The Grounding of Modern Feminism* (New Haven: Yale University Press, 1987); John Mack Faragher, *Women and Men on the Overland Trail* (New Haven: Yale University Press, 1979); Nancy Hoffman, *Woman's "True" Profession: Voices from the History of Teaching* (New York: McGraw Hill, 1981); and Shiela Rothman, *Woman's Proper Place: A History of Changing Ideals and Practices, 1870 to the Present* (New York: Basic Books, 1978).

[5] Linda K. Kerber, "Separate Spheres, Female Worlds, Woman's Place: The Rhetoric of Women's History," *Journal of American History,* LXXV (June, 1988), 9–39.

[6] Courtney Vaughn-Roberson argues that women teachers did operate under the philosophy of domesticity in her articles "Having a Purpose in Life: Western Women Teachers in the 20th Century," *Great Plains Quarterly,* V (Spring, 1985), 107–124, and "Sometimes Independent But Never Equal—Women Teachers, 1900–1950: The Oklahoma Example," *Pacific Historical Review* (Feb., 1985), 39–58. Among those who interpret the personal history documents of teachers as emphasizing their independence and the ability to earn a paycheck are Hoffman, *Woman's "True" Profession;* Polly Welts Kaufman, "A Wider Field of Usefulness: Pioneer Women Teachers in the

individuals rather than as part of husband/wife units; were participating in politics in overt ways; were economically independent, some both before and after marriage; and were working toward equality for women in society and the work force.

This essay centers on one of the more intriguing characteristics that has emerged through this research: the number of women who taught while they were married. Not only does this practice violate the general conception of women prior to World War II, but it also violates one of the most commonly agreed upon tenets of domesticity: the place of a married woman was at home.[7] Women were supposed to choose between a career and marriage.

For the inclusive years of my study, I found a total of forty-nine women who taught for some portion of the years they were married. The purpose of looking at married women is the same as for the larger study. I wanted to know what teaching meant to them, and I also wanted to find out if they were aware of any other constraints of domesticity, since at least these forty-nine were not hampered from combining a career and family. Although large numbers of single women were teachers, the lives and careers of these married women dispels the myth that until recently only single women were allowed to teach.

Between 1850 and 1890, Texas women shared the problems and turbulence of an unsettled country. Texas was rural and did not enjoy a uniform public school system. These characteristics are all evidenced in the writings of the married women teachers of my sample. In order

---

West, 1848–1854," *Journal of the West*, XXI (Apr., 1982), 16–25, and *Women Teachers on the Frontier* (New Haven: Yale University Press, 1984); Kathleen Underwood, "The Pace of Her Own Life: Teacher Training and the Life Course of Western Women," *Pacific Historical Review* (Fall, 1986), 513–530; and Geraldine J. Clifford, "History as Experience: The Uses of Personal-History Documents in the History of Education," *History of Education*, VII, No. 3 (1978), 183–196.

[7] Eli Ginzberg and Alice M. Yohalem, *Educated American Women: Self-Portraits* (New York: Columbia University Press, 1966), 3. Contrary to data presented here, these authors conclude that before the turn of the century alternative patterns of life were determined to a great extent by a more or less rigid environment. A woman who had completed higher education could generally pursue a career only at the cost of foregoing marriage and a family. If she married she had to withdraw from work and devote her abilities and energies to raising her children and participating in voluntary activities.

to teach, many of these women talked about taking county exams to obtain certificates and several noted that summer normals were available for the same purpose. Before 1890, these women needed to augment the incomes of their husbands during hard times, and they found that teaching was an interesting and rewarding way to do it. Cecilia Townsend's memoirs relate her feelings about her family's financial straits, about teaching in a school, and about what her capabilities meant to her. She noted that she began playing piano concerts in Austin after the Civil War in order to gain a following of private students:

> Feeling at first that we were entirely without means or income I began to think of making use of my musical talent to gain some money to live on. . . . I was induced to teach at a school during one session—It was held at the First Baptist church on the hill opposite the governors [*sic*] mansion— and I toiled there faithfully from morning until night, for many months.[8]

When she found out that her talent would bring her money, it was an even greater satisfaction to her and she had a great number of students. Townsend was lucky because her mother lived with her family and attended to all the home affairs, giving her the chance to devote all her time to music. After prosperity returned in 1870, she continued to teach in her home as she "had no other duties or cares to occupy my time." In 1871 her son was born and she did not mention teaching again. Although her memoirs do not evidence any concern with equality for women, Townsend was unselfconsciously broadening women's opportunities by being a married woman with a career. She matter-of-factly used her talents to gain an income when her husband's resources were insufficient, and her self-esteem and confidence grew in the process. She then chose to continue her career even after it was no longer economically necessary for the support of her family because it was intellectually stimulating. One could even speculate that it gave her the security of knowing that she could support herself if the need arose.

[8] Cecilia Townsend memoirs (Texas Collection, Baylor University, Waco).

Like women everywhere, several of these Texas educators started their teaching experiences with private schools in their homes, which can be construed as substantiating separate spheres. Most, however, expanded the home school into a more public setting outside their homes. At least three women from this sample gained statewide recognition for their excellent schools, and Willie Andrews was invited by a group of Austin citizens who donated a school site to move her school there. Her Austin Home Institute operated from 1888 until 1895 in affiliation with the University of Texas.[9]

Several women not only ran their own schools, they were the major means of support for the family. Rebecca Stuart Red provides an example of one such woman. Her memoirs tell how she protected her husband's ego in the process of running her school, and how she felt about teaching.

Red was the principal of Live Oak Female Seminary for over twenty years, beginning in the early 1850s. She married in 1854 and had a child in 1855, another in 1857, a third in 1859, and twins in 1861. In 1876 she and her husband opened Stuart Female Seminary in Austin. He was a doctor and taught science at the school, probably because his income as a doctor was insufficient. A letter that Red wrote in 1854 indicated that she did not plan to teach forever and described what teaching meant to her, as well as what it was like to teach while married:

> My time is pretty fully occupied now, have twenty seven scholars more than half of which write compositions. I rise at daylight and do not retire until ten. . . . A married woman must spend some time in talking to her husband and attending to his little wants. Mine is so modest that he will not ask me to do anything for him, if he sees me engaged in any way, and consequently I have to seem at leisure when in reality I have plenty to do. . . . I do not know when I will quit teaching, for above all other employments I like it best. I expect to teach the balance of this year and next year. By that time I suppose Dr. R. will have our house builded and will

---

[9] Willie Andrews Pioneer School Records (Eugene C. Barker Texas History Center, University of Texas, Austin).

want to go to housekeeping and of course I will not object. I think I will like housekeeping very much but I know I cannot be a good one and teach too, and ambition would prompt me to try to be such.[10]

Regardless of whether she built the house, she continued to teach and run the school, even after her husband's death, until her own death at the age of sixty. Her words here relate her enjoyment of teaching, but also indicate the inherent problem of being a working mother and wife: how to manage a household and career at the same time.

The overall picture of the married women teachers in my sample before 1890 indicates that teaching gave many of them a goodly portion, if not all, of their livelihoods for a large measure of their married lives. Some traveled on behalf of the schools they owned. They were interested in providing a quality education and their efforts in that direction were rewarded with successful and prominent schools. Many taught while having and rearing children. Several note the long hours and hard work involved, but also their enjoyment of teaching. These women were not economically dependent on their husbands; at most husband and wife were dependent on each other, and in some cases the husband may have been economically dependent on the wife. The relationships of which these women spoke were ones of mutual respect, love, and concern between husband and wife, not ones of subordination of wife to husband.

These women do not indicate that they were working to gain equality or broaden a circumscribed sphere. They do not indicate that their teaching while married and having a family violated any convention or caused any stir. They all seem to go about the business at hand with a most unselfconscious attitude.

After 1890, both Texas and the women in my sample underwent some changes. Although Texas was still very rural compared to many other states, this date marked the beginning of a transition from a rural to an urban Texas. The rudiments of a public school system can be

---

[10] Mabelle Umland Purcell, *Two Texas Female Seminaries* (Wichita Falls: Midwestern University Press, 1952), 258; Lel Purcell Hawkins, "A Texas Pioneer Teacher," unpublished manuscript in possession of the author.

found, and the establishment of state normal schools encouraged higher education for teachers. Several women from my sample taught in these normal schools and colleges, some were found in public school administration, and a few moved from teaching careers into politics. Three women earned doctoral degrees while they were married. Even some new patterns in marriage occurred, with several women living apart from their husbands in order to complete teaching assignments, continue educations, or engage in politics. And several noted that their salaries were used to hire household help. Again, these women wrote about how much money they made and changing jobs for higher pay. Several noted some forms of discrimination against women in the workplace. The recurrent characteristic of these women was the tremendous energy they displayed in accomplishing careers combined with being wives and mothers, and adding to all of this the time for church work, club work, and writing books. Once again none of them found these combinations out of the ordinary or in violation of acceptable norms. Some, however, began to talk about and work for equality for women.

Sue Huffman Warren Brady, for example, was named superintendent of a system with sixteen teachers in Fort Worth in 1880 and was credited with organizing and grading the public schools in that city and in Decatur. After her marriage, Sue Huffman Warren worked as a school principal. In 1883, she founded and carried on the Warren Female Institute until 1890, while serving as principal of four summer normals in the Dallas vicinity from 1883 to 1886. Her first husband died in 1889, and she remarried in 1892. In that same year, she was on the program of the National Education Association conference in Atlanta, Georgia. At the Woman's Congress of the 1893 Columbian Exposition, she presented a paper entitled "The Changing Ideals in Southern Womanhood." Her own words in this paper give proof of her belief in the intelligence and independence of women, to which her life history bears testimony:

The last thirty years have been one continuous school of toil, economy and sacrifice, but it has sent out graduates who eat the white bread of independence, and who carry in their hands the lantern of hard-earned experience, lighting the way to higher, truer, broader views of life. The sorrows of the woman of this period and their magical uprising have left their indelible impress upon the brow of the nineteenth century. The prodigious mental and moral force and the executive ability generated by this curriculum of hardship and responsibility, illumine and strengthen the character of the wide-awake womanhood of today.[11]

Brady related that she was overjoyed when women were admitted to the first normal schools in the South, and she affirmed education as a way of breaking down the barriers barring women from useful occupations. She observed in the women of her day a new attitude of mentoring, a new freedom to "roam at will the pleasant fields of all forms of activity," and a new release from "matrimony as the only condition to save her from a life of dependence."[12] Brady's changing ideals emphasize individuality and independence.

Jettie Felps's memoirs present a very different view of the teaching profession.[13] In 1907 she began teaching and was principal "of a school in a tough little town where my first love lived."[14] She married when she was twenty-four years old, and her husband began teaching with her. They attended the University of Texas in the summers and took their first degrees together. Felps continued her education by earning a master's degree from the University of Texas, and had a son at the age of thirty-six. She stated her opinion of woman's place candidly: "Surely anyone can see that women can be useful, not parasites, as so many are. . . . For my part, I believe that women should have a career the same as men."[15] She did not hold most teachers, herself excepted, in high regard:

I soon passed the county examination and began teaching, which I have later decided is nothing more than a trade

[11] Sue Huffman Brady, "Changing Ideals in Southern Womanhood," in *The Congress of Women*, ed. Mary Eagle (1894; reprint, n.p.: Ayer Co., 1974), 308.

[12] Brady, "Changing Ideals," 310.

[13] Besides her memoirs, Felps also published *Woman's Place and Influence* (Burnet, Tex.: n.p., 1955) and *Sidelights on Education* (Dallas: Story Book Press, 1949), among other books.

[14] Jettie Felps, *My Hectic Trek* (Boston: Forum Publishing Co., 1962), 43.

[15] Ibid., 50–51.

because of its inefficiency. How some of the would-be teachers cheated! Still some failed, though they had been teaching for years through "pull.". . . Some instructors might accomplish more in life by hoeing cotton instead of trying to teach.[16]

And her disdain for men, which soon after marriage extended to her "first love," is clearly indicated in the following passage: "A woman of sense walks among men, laughing up her sleeve at their didoes, uncontaminated by their thoughts of her, good or bad, but still loving them and wishing them well, with all of their faults and idiosyncrasies, though she wants none of them for husband."[17] Outright resentment characterized Felps's comments on equality in the workplace:

At first we (husband and self) taught separate small schools; but, as we continued to teach, we taught in larger and larger schools until Ernest was superintendent, making about twice my salary. I resented this, for I know that men in the teaching profession always drew better salaries, irrespective of what they did, or how well they taught. Any woman who has taught under her husband as superintendent, knows what a job she has! No doubt most husbands are alike in that they don't realize, maybe don't care, how much they heap upon their wives. Mine seem [sic] to think any work or subjects that none of the other teachers could handle I, of course, could. If a volley ball coach was needed, I was asked to take the work; if no one could teach Spanish, I would have to manage that some way. And ever since old Adam laid all the blame on Eve when things went wrong, I got the blame, especially on "blue Mondays" and other "blue days."[18]

Felps's most important goal was her education and her dream was to write, "because the written word lives on after the writer is dead."[19] She chose teaching because "Teaching and hoeing cotton were woman's

16 Ibid., 42, 77.
17 Ibid., 44.
18 Ibid., 83.
19 Ibid., 51.

occupations then, and I did not mean to make a field hand forever, though I prefer country life."[20] She lived apart from her husband in order to continue her education, and it is in this situation that Felps evidenced something of a guilty conscience, although she quickly absolved herself of responsibility: "When I think how lonely Ernest must have been living in the teacherage all alone, I wonder if I was not selfish in going to college; but both of us decided that the environment would be better for our son at Kingsville."[21]

In spite of her vitriolic personality, Felps accomplished a lot. She managed to earn three degrees and publish three books while teaching and rearing a son. Her views about life and women's place differ from many of those in print during her lifetime. Certainly equality for women in the teaching field was a concern to her and she was outspoken about it.

Unlike the Felpses, Edie Gist Williams Addison and her husband managed a relationship of love and respect while teaching together and sharing the responsibilities of rearing their two small children. In her memoirs Williams painted a vivid picture of the first time she voted and the way she and her husband handled voting against each other. She also commented on the issues of suffrage and prohibition:

> About this time two matters of importance were worrying the nation—and women in particular: woman suffrage and liquor.
>
> For as long as I could remember women had been struggling for the right to vote on issues that would affect their homes, their lives, and the future of their children.
>
> Women had been speaking and demonstrating since 1848. Susan Anthony, Lucy Stone, Carrie Nation—they'd fought so hard.
>
> Some men argued that women were so wrapped up in their homes that they didn't know what was going on outside of them. Others argued that if women were given the right to vote they would neglect their children, husbands, and homes.
>
> I was raising my children to be good citizens and loyal

---

[20] Ibid., 42.
[21] Ibid., 91.

Americans, so I certainly didn't consider myself too dumb to vote.

I don't think anything ever gave me a bigger thrill than the presentation and passing of the eighteenth amendment. Now I had a voice in the government of our great nation.

The issue of prohibition came up. Bert and I didn't discuss it—or rather, we didn't argue about it.

To me there was more involved than just open saloons. Women's rights were definitely being infringed on. A lady could not go into a saloon and drink a glass of wine. A woman was not even allowed to go in and drag her drunk husband out and take him home and put him to bed.

So whether a woman drank or didn't drink, she was generally against saloons.

When the day came to go to the polls and vote on the nineteenth amendment, I couldn't find anyone to stay with the children.

I carried Arthur in my arms and led Thelma by the hand and rode a street car to the polls.

A tremendous thrill swelled my heart—not just because I was voting for the first time, sharing in the making of the laws.

"How did you vote, Mrs. Williams?" Mrs. Wade asked.

"I voted for prohibition," I said proudly.

"And Bert voted against?" she said in amazement.

I nodded.

She shook her head. "Don't you know you just canceled Bert's vote? If I did that to Mr. Wade, he'd kill me!"

I just smiled. "Bert knows I have a mind. He expects me to use it."[22]

Williams expected to be treated with equality within her marriage, as well as within the political process in this country. She had the audacity to state her expectations openly because she was contributing financially to the support of her family. Her confidence in her intellect

---

[22] Edie Gist Williams Addison, *Pine Cones and Cactus* (San Angelo, Tex.: Anchor Publishing, 1980), 54.

and her ability to assert herself are characteristics that she more than likely obtained through her teaching. She also expressed great joy in being able to participate in the political process through voting and through the influence she had on her children.

In an oral interview some years ago, Cornelia Marschall Smith provided some insight into her situation as a married woman seeking the doctoral degree. Her life is indicative of the pattern for many women academics, who began teaching in the public schools and moved on into higher education as they were able. Smith, like many other women in this period, completed high school, obtained a state teacher's certificate, and taught in a private one-teacher school for one year. She entered Baylor University in 1915 and earned a bachelors degree in biology in 1918. That same year, she began teaching biology at Waco High School, where she remained until 1925, working at the same time on a masters degree in botany at the University of Chicago. She attended classes for two summers and one long term, and completed the degree in 1923. After she married in 1926, she and her husband entered Johns Hopkins University, where she earned the Ph.D. in 1928, and he completed his a little later. Smith then accepted a job at Baylor as assistant professor of botany, but she was only allowed to teach until 1930, when the Board of Trustees established a policy that prohibited husband and wife from teaching in the same institution. So from 1930 to 1935, she studied in the English department and continued researching and publishing articles. In 1935, Cornelia and her husband moved to John B. Stetson University, where she served as chairman of the biology department and her husband as dean. They returned to Baylor in the fall of 1940 and she served as chairman of the biology department, director of graduate studies in biology, director of the Strecker Museum, and taught a full schedule of biology courses for the next twenty-three years. Smith continued her research and publishing and found time to join civic and professional organizations. She was awarded many honors, including being named the Piper Professor of 1966, and she has been included in many biographical dictionaries, including *American Men of Science*.

Although she does not discuss what teaching meant to her, Smith does comment on "open marriages," by which she does not mean an open marriage in the current usage of the term: "And Mr. Smith in this process (Ph.D. degree) showing, I think, a thing that is frequently discussed at the present time is open-and-closed marriages. And I would say this [our relationship] is an exhibition, or shows that he believed in an 'open marriage.' In other words, he gave me an opportunity to go forward with my education. And he stepped aside and taught in Goucher College so that the money was available for me to continue with my degree. And also, he made it possible for me to receive my degree prior to his. And yet, the whole purpose in our being at Johns Hopkins was for him to get his Ph.D."[23]

Smith came from a modest background, and teaching provided her a living and enough money to get one graduate degree before she married. Her many honors and her involvement in student life indicate that she was a good and well-respected teacher. After marriage, her husband worked while she finished her Ph.D. and then she worked while he finished his, probably an uncommon practice in the 1920s. Then they both pursued careers in education while maintaining a life together. She certainly experienced discrimination during the five-year period in which Baylor would not allow both of them to teach; it is possible, however, that they decided mutually that he would be the one to teach because his salary was higher than hers.

Several women teachers commented specifically about the effects of teaching on families as well as the effects of families on teaching. Rowena Warfield taught for forty-four years in the Waco public schools. After many years of teaching, she married and had a family. When she was asked what effect her job had on her family she replied succinctly, "I couldn't see that it hurt them." She managed to keep good help; she had a cook, and later her sister came to live with them and took over the household duties.[24]

Marguerite Cooper was quite open in her reminiscences about teaching while she was pregnant. She commented that she married relatively late, at the age of thirty-four, and that she taught until shortly before the birth of each of her two children. I "just took a leave of absence, they didn't mind. I knew when to quit. And it was all the better for teaching. And then—then I went back," she stated matter-of-factly. When asked if she had always wanted to be a teacher, she replied, "Yes, yes. And I would do the same thing again. I think it's one

[23] Cornelia Smith, interview (Texas Collection at Baylor University; hereafter cited as TC).

[24] Rowena B. Warfield, interview (TC).

of the finest vocations that anybody could have, to teach somebody to better themselves."[25]

As with the women who taught before 1890, many teachers recorded that they taught because they could support themselves at something they enjoyed. They provided evidence of their professionalism by continuing their educations (some earned masters and doctoral degrees), belonging to professional organizations, and writing books and articles for scholarly journals. Long careers, some spanning thirty or forty years, were also typical of these married women teachers. Money was an important reason for their presence in the workplace.

Several women documented their awareness and experiences of the infringement of women's rights. Although the majority of them had daily routines that involved maintaining careers and families, the records show that several experienced discrimination in the workplace.

The most significant findings from this study are 1) the overriding reason that these women taught was to earn a salary, and 2) there were at least some women teachers in Texas who did combine a career and family. These findings lay to rest the myths that all women were economically dependent on men and that only single women taught school.

Clearly, if there had been no compensation for teaching, these women would have been doing something else. Especially in the early years of this study, the income meant the ability to buy the necessities of life. A little later, more women used their salaries to continue their educations; and later still, some women used the money to have household help and to travel for pleasure. Teaching meant that married women could contribute significantly to the family income, and in some cases be the family's sole support.

In combining a career and marriage, these women prove that not all teachers in Texas were unwed sixteen-year-olds with less than a high school education. Although many of them began teaching in just that way in order to support themselves before marriage, they either continued to teach after marriage or returned to teaching because their families needed the money or because that money opened new opportunities for them. The qualifying factor that emerged from this study

---

[25] Webb Cooper, interview (TC).

is that twelve of the forty-nine women taught as part of a husband/ wife team for at least a portion of their careers. Of these twelve, several married male colleagues, and these couples continued their careers together; others married men who wanted to engage in other endeavors but had to teach for a while because of a scarcity of jobs in their fields. Of the couples who continued teaching careers together in the public schools, the usual pattern after 1900 was that he was the superintendent and she was the principal/teacher, or he was the principal and she was the teacher. It is here that the influence of domesticity is felt most strongly. Women did not share equally in the opportunity to ascend the career ladder of the teaching field.

Throughout this study, the majority of women evidenced no awareness of the constraints of domesticity or of separate spheres. There is no evidence that the majority of them were engaged in an overt effort to gain equal rights for women. They were busy with the everyday routines of managing a job and a family. The large majority of these women were broadening women's sphere of operations in an unselfconscious way. They engaged in whatever interesting and challenging work they could find in order to maintain themselves and their families, and in the process several of them achieved leadership roles in education.

Teaching provided women with more than just economic independence. It gave them confidence in their own intelligence and capabilities. It gave them power over their own lives, as well as the lives of others. It provided them with a public existence at a time when few other women were allowed that experience. Finally, it gave them opportunities to excel and become leaders in their fields of endeavor. All of these things hardly add up to a picture of a retiring and subordinate woman.

Sepia Record as a Forum for Negotiating Women's Roles

SHERILYN BRANDENSTEIN*

ABOUT FIVE YEARS AGO I was conducting research on R. C. Hickman, a Dallas photographer, when I came upon a magazine for African Americans published in Texas in the 1950s. Early issues carried the title *Negro Achievements,* then the name changed to *Sepia Record* late in 1953. I was struck by the number of prominent articles on women, especially career women, in a magazine not intended specifically for women.

Around this time, I had a growing interest in the images in print media and how magazine graphics serve as arenas for negotiating ideas. One of the most significant of these negotiations in our century has had to do with gender roles.

I learned that several scholars already had analyzed the leading national magazines to find out how women were portrayed, i.e., how the Victorian ideals of white, middle-class womanhood were either endorsed or challenged. They had addressed how general-circulation magazines had portrayed women according to age and marital status. Only a few investigated whether and how black women were presented in mainstream magazines.

As I read this literature on gendered portrayals, I found little evidence of research on gender as portrayed in major African American periodicals. While a minority of white Americans reads such publications, blacks, especially urban blacks, are the targeted audience for these periodicals and have easy access to them. I assumed that if African Americans have had role expectations for women different

* Sherilyn Brandenstein, a former journalist, has an M.A. in American civilization from the University of Texas at Austin. She works in volunteer management and conducts independent scholarly research in Austin.

from the white, middle-class standard, a black magazine would be a good medium to examine for challenges and negotiations about women's proper place.

This article summarizes key conclusions from my investigation of *Sepia Record* (and *Negro Achievements*, its predecessor), developed more fully in my thesis, "Prominent Roles of Black Womanhood in *Sepia Record*, 1952–1954." First, the article discusses existing research on general-circulation magazine coverage of women and whether it matched the actual roles North American women were taking on in the decade after World War II. Then it describes *Sepia Record*, a Texas-based magazine for blacks, and provides highlights of its presentation of black women in the early 1950s.[1]

A review of the scholarship on portrayals of women in the major general-circulation magazines in the 1950s suggests that the dominant post-war concept of women's lives involved several mutually exclusive scenarios: 1) devoted wife-and-mother, whose unpaid work centered on home life and/or community service; or 2) the single woman or childless married woman employed in entertainment or in "female" service jobs. Typically, such jobs were conducive to finding a husband or fulfilling women's presumed needs to nurture. Women choosing professional, technical or business careers after male veterans had returned from World War II tended to be presented as exceptional. Some magazines went so far as to imply that they were frustrated or incompetent in jobs "better suited" to men.[2]

Betty Friedan, in her 1963 book *The Feminine Mystique*, accused the major U.S. magazines of using a pejorative tone in their coverage of women who sought or held jobs traditionally considered male. She also criticized the advertising industry for consistently promoting a housewife identity for female consumers in American magazines. Friedan identified the key role which industry assigned to women as homemakers to intensify consumerism after the war.[3]

---

[1] I have labelled periodicals directed toward a predominantly African American readership as either "black" or "African American," regardless of who published or edited them. I assume that a publication's identity is primarily determined by its target audience. Notwithstanding letters to the editors from white readers, *Sepia Record*'s primary audience comprised black adults.

[2] Betty Friedan, *The Feminine Mystique*, 20th Anniversary Edition (New York: W. W. Norton, 1983), 34–36, 42–44, 52–54, 67.

[3] Ibid., 58–59, 206.

Presumably, editorial content more accurately reflects women's status than advertising content. However, Matthews reportedly studied a sampling of *Time* and *Newsweek* issues from 1940, 1960 and 1980 and found that "women were infrequently pictured . . . in all roles except those of 'artist/entertainer' and 'spouse,'" typically in the "Entertainment" or "People" section. This pattern hardly changed across four decades.[4]

Belkaoui and Belkaoui gathered a sampling of general-circulation magazine advertisements from 1958 and the 1970s to learn how women were portrayed across fourteen years. In the 1958 group, they encountered familiar post-war stereotypes: 1) "Most women were shown in nonworking roles, often in the home;" 2) nearly all women portrayed in employed situations were presented as clerical, secretarial or blue-collar workers, i.e. low-income wage-earners; and 3) in leisure-time situations, female models, unlike their male counterparts, were shown as "decorative features" or "wrappings" for products.[5]

Analyzing female imagery in popular culture, Weibel traced the origins of portraying (white) American women as "housewifely, passive, wholesome and pretty" to nineteenth-century North American practices. She also stated that a sexy image of women in magazine content became increasingly prevalent after World War II, complicating traditional female ideals of "wholesomeness." Married or single, women shown as erotic icons were at peak child-bearing age, Weibel noted.[6]

Banta's study of "the American girl" in popular culture concluded that "Sexuality was clearly a marketable product by the 1890s, both as an item for direct sale and as a come-on for readers of the tabloid press." She labelled a new turn-of-the-century ideal of young womanhood "provocative winsomeness," a more subdued version of female sensuality than prevailed after 1945.[7]

By mid-century, the sexual persona was well-entrenched in magazine representations of American women. Hartmann has noted the

[4] Frances Goins Wilhoit (ed.), *Journalism Abstracts*, XX (1982), 86.

[5] Ahmed Belkaoui and Janice M. Belkaoui, "A Comparative Analysis of the Roles Portrayed by Women in Print Advertisements: 1958, 1970, 1972," *Journal of Marketing Research*, XIII (May, 1976), 170.

[6] Kathryn Weibel, *Mirror Mirror: Images of Women Reflected in Popular Culture* (Garden City, N.Y.: Anchor Books, 1977), 166, 168–169.

[7] Martha Banta, *Imaging American Women: Idea and Ideals in Cultural History* (New York: Columbia University Press, 1987), 620–622.

increased emphasis on female (hetero)sexual appeal during World War II in periodicals targeted specifically to men or to women. A study cited by Butler and Paisley found that more than 30 percent of the cigarette, beverage, automobile and airline advertisements drawn from a two-decade sampling of general magazines (1950–1971) presented women as physically alluring.[8]

This practice was so pervasive in the urban publishing industry that it cut across racial categories of marketing and magazine editing.[9] The findings of Jones and of Joseph and Lewis indicate that black women frequently have been portrayed as erotic icons in post-war African American magazines, aligning these periodicals with a dominant ideology promoting women's sexual role.[10]

For example, the obviously greater proportion of female popular entertainers than other employed women highlighted in Johnson Publications' *Ebony* magazine articles fit into the twentieth-century North American pattern of eroticized female imagery. Featuring African American celebrities already familiar to most readers—singers, dancers, and actresses who appeared in television and film—contributed to *Ebony*'s formula for maintaining steady sales nationwide through most of the post-World War II era. By the early 1960s, it had become the highest-circulation secular magazine among African Americans. Yet African American magazines' portrayals of women in the 1950s cannot be characterized as unidimensionally erotic.[11]

[8] Susan M. Hartmann, *The Home Front and Beyond: American Women in the 1940s* (Boston: Twayne Publishers, 1982), 198; Matilda Butler and William Paisley, *Women and the Mass Media: Sourcebook for Research and Action* (New York: Human Sciences Press, 1980), 99–101.

[9] Joseph and Lewis, as well as Carby, have noted that mainstream press portrayals of black women as explicitly sexual were hardly a new phenomenon. In fact, white writers historically have stereotyped people of color as sexually provocative, especially relative to whites. The change brought on by wartime conditions and by the mass media was to eroticize *white* middle-class women. The point is that this new mass-media trend influenced nearly all commercial magazines. See Hazel Carby, *Reconstructing Womanhood: The Emergence of the Afro-American Woman Novelist* (New York; Oxford University Press, 1987), 37, 39; and Gloria I. Joseph and Jill Lewis, *Common Differences: Conflicts in Black and White Feminist Perspectives* (New York: Anchor Press/Doubleday, 1981), 163.

[10] Jacqueline Jones, *Labor of Love, Labor of Sorrow: Black Women, Work, and the Family from Slavery to the Present* (New York: Basic Books, 1985), 270; Joseph and Lewis, *Common Differences*, 157, 159.

[11] Jones, *Labor of Love*, 270–272; Roland Edgar Wolseley, *The Black Press, U.S.A.* (Ames: Iowa State University Press, 1971), 63–64, 118.

Analyzing African American women's roles and activities in the first decade after World War II, Jones examined coverage of black women in Johnson Publications' *Ebony Magazine,* which became the best-selling magazine written for African Americans.[12] She stated that *Ebony* generally combined messages about various roles for women. Most issues carried imagery of bathing beauties and glamorous female celebrities, but also paid tribute to women achievers in the professions, skilled trades, business, and arts. Those who became the first or only black women in the U.S. to obtain prestigious positions received coverage, as did celebrities who spoke out advocating civil rights for members of their race.[13]

Jones admitted that, while *Ebony* did not accurately reflect the reality most black working women experienced, it did promote examples of "superwoman"—well-paid and competent working wife and mother—two decades before the white press did so. She notes the political signicance of a magazine in the 1950s conveying the ideas that "civil rights and good jobs went together, and that black women were equally entitled to both."[14]

In contrast to the dominant white-owned magazines, *Ebony* sometimes presented women in activist roles. Female celebrities and "famous wives" were credited for their opinions or actions on public issues as well as their ideas about fashions or homemaking. White Americans, especially women, typically focused on the private, domestic sphere, rather than public affairs just after World War II. Meanwhile, *Ebony's* featured subjects who had campaigned for racial integration and equal rights received respectful coverage. By showing African American women's participation, the magazine promoted both ideologies of gender equality and racial equality. Overall, its portrayals of female leaders probably put *Ebony* ahead of its time compared with most white-oriented general-circulation magazines.[15]

Still, as Goodman has noted, Johnson Publications' business strategy from 1945 to 1965 encouraged an editorial policy of minimizing overt social criticism. Indeed, in matters of gender, the magazine's

[12] Jones's observations are qualitative, as she drew on only a few issues from an entire decade to survey.

[13] Jones, *Labor of Love,* 270–274.

[14] Ibid., 269, 272–274.

[15] Ibid., 272–274.

disproportionate emphasis on entertainers and wives of famous men in the coverage of women complicated its role as a trailblazer.[16]

Moving beyond magazines' characterizations of women's lives in the 1950s, what do demographers say *real* American women were doing then? It's worth backing up a bit to assess the impact of World War II on American women's roles.

The biggest changes for women during World War II involved new waves of married and older women entering non-farm employment. Only about one-fifth of American wives were in the paid labor force by 1944, but they made up 75 percent of the female new-hires. For the first time in U.S. history, the number of married women exceeded the number of single women in the total female workforce.[17]

Another change was the substantial addition of older women to the ranks of the employed. Noting their long-term influence, Campbell has written:

> By 1945, half of all women workers were over thirty-five; slightly more than one in four was forty-five or older. The typical female worker had changed, from one who was younger and single to one who was older and married. This new pattern maintained itself through the post-war period.[18]

As I mentioned earlier, the overall percentage of African American women in the workforce had not changed that drastically during the war. The nature of the work shifted for some, but not most. The war years brought a drop in the number of black women in agriculture (down from 16 percent to 8 percent) and in domestic service, decreasing from three-fifths to roughly half of all black women employed. Meanwhile the percentage who were machine operatives climbed to 16 percent. Even more took jobs in commercial service.[19]

---

[16] Walter Goodman, "*Ebony:* Biggest Negro Magazine," *Dissent,* XV (1968), 404; Jones, *Labor of Love,* 272.

[17] D'Ann Campbell, *Women at War with America: Private Lives in a Patriotic Era* (Cambridge: Harvard University Press, 1984), 180–182; Hartmann, *The Home Front and Beyond,* 92–93; Ruth Milkman, *Gender at Work: The Dynamics of Job Segregation by Sex during World War II* (Urbana: University of Illinois Press, 1987), 63.

[18] Alice Kessler-Harris, *Out to Work: A History of Wage-Earning Women in the United States* (New York: Oxford University Press, 1982), 278; Campbell, *Women at War with America,* 78.

[19] Campbell, *Women at War with America,* 174; Hartmann, *The Home Front and Beyond,* 86; Jones, *Labor of Love,* 234.

When the United States converted to peacetime production, men took priority in the higher-paying industrial and business jobs. Many wives and mothers who had been new-hires returned to homemaking full-time. The consensus among North Americans during the postwar decade was that any woman who became a wife and mother already had a valid full-time career.[20]

Despite a dip in women's workforce participation in the first year after World War II, women soon returned to work by the thousands, but usually as part-timers. By the time the Korean War erupted in June, 1950, spot labor shortages had developed in secretarial, nursing, teaching, and social work positions. Of course, these vocations, typically filled by women, white *and* black, tended to provide lower wages than traditionally male positions. Yet a growing minority of families had to have the wife and mother working to be able to meet family expenses. In 1950, nearly one-third of all adult women worked for wages and roughly half of them were married.[21]

Proportionately more black women than white had wage-earning jobs. Furthermore, black working women were concentrated in domestic and institutional service positions.[22] By contrast, the profile of white American womanhood that emerges from the early 1950s is one of lives typically centered on home life, especially among married and older women. Even when women participated in school, church, and community affairs as volunteers, they generally performed extensions of the same functions women generally had at home.[23] Meanwhile, an increasing female minority within all races worked for wages away from home. For most of them, womanhood involved negotiations over competing family and employment roles.[24]

[20] Campbell, *Women at War*, 232; Douglas T. Miller and Marion Novak, *The Fifties: The Way We Really Were* (Garden City, N.Y.: Doubleday, 1977), 155; Norman L. Rosenberg, Emily S. Rosenberg, and James R. Moore, *In Our Times: America Since Word War II* (Englewood Cliffs, N.J.: Prentice-Hall, 1976), 64.

[21] Hartmann, *The Home Front and Beyond*, 93–94; Susan Estabrook Kennedy, *If All We Did Was to Weep at Home: A History of White Working-Class Women in America* (Bloomington: Indiana University Press, 1979), 204; Kessler-Harris, *Out to Work*, 303.

[22] Jones, *Labor of Love*, 234–235, 269.

[23] William Henry Chafe, *The American Woman: Her Changing Social, Economic and Political Roles, 1920–1970* (New York: Oxford University Press, 1972), 217–218; Eugenia Kaledin, *Mothers and More: American Women in the 1950s* (Boston: Twayne, 1984), 32–33.

[24] Kennedy, *If All We Did Was to Weep at Home*, 183–219; Ruthe Winegarten

Comparing the images of American women in the leading adult magazines of the 1950s with the actual roles women had, then, some but not all of the portrayals correlated. Showing women predominantly as wives and mothers in print seems to have reflected the majority of North American women's lives. Subscription magazines, as links between major advertisers and consumers, emphasized women's roles as purchasers of home furnishings, food, and fashions. Despite the steady rise in female employment, women were portrayed far less often than men as employed or in community leadership roles, except in such black magazines as *Ebony*.

General-circulation magazines promoted the ideology of young women, especially attractive single women, as erotic icons. Consequently, young female entertainers and models were presented in magazines in much greater proportion than their actual numbers in the population. It is worth noting that white-oriented American magazines began running profiles on selected African American performers, including women, during the 1940s and 1950s.[25]

By the time the major national magazines started featuring African American celebrities, most of these individuals already had received national publicity in national black magazines, periodicals about which many white Americans had only a vague awareness. *Ebony*, a large-format pictorial, and *Jet*, a pocket-size news digest also from Johnson Publications, were the most familiar examples of the national African American magazines to emerge after World War II. The field also included pictorials such as *Color* and *Our World*.

A publisher based in Fort Worth developed two regional African-American magazines, *The World's Messenger* and *Negro Achievements*, in the mid-1940s. By the 1970s, his successor had spun off four more magazines, all distributed nationally. These included a teen magazine, confessions and crime magazines, and a periodical about black entertainers, as well as *Sepia*, a monthly pictorial. *Sepia's* editors strove to make this magazine similar to *Ebony*, but it never had as many

---

(ed.), *I Am Annie Mae: An Extraordinary Women in Her Own Words* (Austin: Rosegarden Press, 1983), 67–70.

[25] On Dorothy Dandridge, see "Shy No More," *Life*, XXXI (Nov. 5, 1951), 65–70. *Look* ran "Portrait of an Actress," an Eartha Kitt profile, in vol. XVII (Oct. 6, 1953), pp. 72–73. For *Newsweek* stories on Marian Anderson and Harry Belafonte, see vols. XXXIII (Apr. 25, 1949), pp. 84–86, and XLIII (March 29, 1954), pp. 84–85, respectively.

corporate advertisements or subscriptions. Like other periodicals from the same publisher, *Sepia* mostly sold on newsstands.[26]

It is difficult now to locate early issues of *Sepia* magazine. The Good Publishing Company, which had produced it, folded in the early 1980s. North Texas State University did not begin acquiring issues of the magazine until 1961. As for those published in the 1950s, all I could find was a two-year run of *Sepia* prototypes: *Negro Achievements* and *Sepia Record,* a transitional form that developed into *Sepia.* The Center for American History at the University of Texas at Austin owns issues dated from 1951 through 1953. My study was based on articles from these and from 1954 issues of *Sepia Record* at Fisk University in Nashville.[27]

Negro Achievements, the predecessor to *Sepia Record,* was born in the closing months of World War II. Horace J. Blackwell, an African American entrepreneur and Texas Negro Baseball League officer, created *Negro Achievements* as a showcase for amateur writers of autobiographical stories, typically imbued with religious convictions. The magazine employed a true-confessions formula. Shorter features included African American church and social news from the south-central United States.[28]

When Blackwell died in December, 1949, his assistant Adelle Conner Jackson, also black, sought investors to take on the indebted publishing firm. For months, she encountered discouraging responses. Finally, she persuaded a white businessman to assume the company's debts. He agreed to this only if he could have full ownership and direction. Within one year, George Levitan, the new publisher, hired a young white couple to edit the magazines. In the meantime, he retained several black women from the original staff and brought in college instructors to teach them journalism skills.[29]

---

[26] Brandenstein, "Prominent Roles of Black Womanhood in *Sepia Record,* 1952–1954" (M.A. thesis, University of Texas at Austin, 1989), 77–78, 87, 96.

[27] The African-American Museum of Life and Culture in Dallas has acquired a collection of *Sepia* photographs obtained from the files of the Good Publishing Company, and museum staff hope to have them catalogued by 1995. I have located no library in or near Texas which has a full run of the magazine from the years 1953 through 1961.

[28] Brandenstein, "Prominent Roles of Black Womanhood," 76–80.

[29] Ibid., 80–86.

Seth and Anne Kantor, the new editors, came to the Fort Worth company from Dell Publishing's Modern Magazine Division in New York. The Kantors' strategy was to reshape Levitan's magazines to appeal to young urban blacks and to broaden their market beyond the South. The couple engineered the change of *Negro Achievements* to *Sepia Record* in 1953, emphasizing graphics with a bright, open layout in the new format.[30]

Following trends in celebrity fan magazines and black newspapers such as the Chicago *Defender, Sepia Record* carried an increasing quotient of personality feature stories. Confessional stories were moved to another of Levitan's magazines, *Bronze Thrills. Sepia Record,* taking cues from *Ebony* and *Jet,* began carrying profiles of African American entertainers, sports celebrities, and pioneers in business and the professions. Levitan named his operation the Good Publishing Company and contracted with an established distribution firm in Chicago to expand magazine sales nationally.[31]

My research on portrayals of black womanhood spans issues from 1952, when the magazine was still under the title *Negro Achievements,* through 1954, following the changes in the name and format. I sought out feature stories about individuals or families, since these predominated in *Sepia Record*'s content. The study analyzed articles focused on an identified woman or women in text and pictures and consisting of two or more pages. Graphic elements, such as photographs and headlines, as well as the copy were noted carefully. I read the interplay of images and text for evidence of gesture, activity, expressive attitude, dress, and relationships—all potential clues to gender and social roles.

If *Sepia Record* accurately represented a range of African American perspectives on women's roles, then it was a wider range than those promoted in general-circulation magazines in the early 1950s. This magazine's sparse coverage of women in full-time mothering and homemaking scenarios allowed for, but downplayed the likelihood of that sole option for black women.[32]

More central to the imagery of women was work, paid or voluntary, *outside* the home. The work that warranted a particular woman's

[30]   Ibid., 67, 86–87.
[31]   Ibid., 86–89, 92.
[32]   Ibid., 111.

inclusion in the magazine generally was exceptional, for white women or for blacks of either gender. Most women were not entertainers or professional athletes, but most African American women who made the news in the 1950s *were*. In this latter aspect, *Sepia Record* followed the standard magazine formulas of the time. Like other black magazines, it emphasized stories on African American professionals, countering their low visibility in mainstream media.[33]

Generally, stories about particular women (or families of women) focused on one or several of the following roles:

1) Career woman as mother and/or wife;
2) Unmarried, childless career woman;
3) Race and gender "pioneer";
4) Career woman as civic or social organizer.[34]

Some articles, when describing a woman's multiple roles, emphasized one far more than another. Whatever the emphasis, African American women overall were shown to have varied choices and to live multifaceted lives.[35]

Stressing the theme of the black "superwoman," an October 1953 issue of *Sepia Record* carried a story titled, "Concert Singer and Housewife." The subheading said, "Everybody told pretty Darwin Walton she couldn't mix a career with domestic duties—she proved them wrong." Imagery concentrated on Walton as an individual, but included a picture of her with husband Claude Walton. Near the end of the article, the writer quoted Darwin Walton: "Claude and I felt that we could have each other and still leave some area in our lives for individual expression. . . . It has worked out wonderfully." These are the words of a middle- or upper-class wife who apparently considers her work to be more a means of self-fulfillment than a financial necessity. Equally revealing was her statement that:

> Marriage and a family represent the greatest opportunities any woman can have. But this doesn't mean the cancel-

---

[33] Ibid., 110–112; Wolseley, *The Black Press, U.S.A.,* 118.
[34] This study does not include stories about institutions or social issues involving women. Such a survey certainly would turn up images from *Sepia Record* of black women in more routine jobs such as clerks, operatives, and farmworkers.
[35] Brandenstein, "Prominent Roles of Black Womanhood," 111–112.

lation of other opportunities that have to do with a career—not if a girl is willing to face life realistically![36]

At the time of her interview, Walton was fitting time with her nine-month-old daughter in between rehearsals for a ten-city concert tour. The article did not include a picture of the baby; it did contain an image of her mother posing in a bathing suit.

Walton was no exception in this magazine's coverage of female achievers. Numerous articles on career women, especially performing artists and medical professionals, included references to their successes as wives and mothers.[37]

Of course, juggling work, marriage, and/or mothering is not every woman's ideal. Even though the prevailing sentiment in American culture encouraged women to marry and have children, *Negro Achievements* and *Sepia Record* routinely provided examples of women who had chosen careers over marriage and motherhood.[38]

Gospel singer Clara Ward exemplified the single career woman as *Sepia Record* presented her. In the summer of 1953, this twenty-eight-year-old had just won awards in a national poll of jazz fans, bringing her increased media attention. Photographic imagery in this article portrayed her singing ecstatically in performance, posing with sheet music from her publishing firm and reading at home. The text emphasized her devotion to gospel music and penchant for fashionable attire. A rigorous national touring schedule reportedly fueled her $150,000 annual income. As for marriage plans, Ward said that she had not "found the 'man in her life' and that her schedule permits little time for romance." The magazine profile described a woman more committed to her vocation and religious leadings than to launching a family.[39]

Although the war years represented a watershed period for African American men to break into formerly segregated work arenas, some

[36] *Sepia Record* (Oct., 1953), 44.

[37] "Best Spook Woman in Show Business," *Sepia Record* (July, 1953), 1–4; "A Day in the Life of a Nurse," *Negro Achievements*, VI (Nov., 1952), 24–26; "Married in Harmony," *Negro Achievements*, VII (Jan., 1953), 25–27; "'Real Gone' Nellie," *Sepia Record* (Nov., 1953), 14–16; "Two Can Practice as Cheaply as One," *Negro Achievements*, VI (Aug., 1952), 28, 46.

[38] "Angel of Mercy," *Sepia* (Sept., 1954), 43–44; "No Dumb Dora," *Sepia Record* (June, 1953), 14–19; "This Teacher Doesn't Know," *Sepia Record* (July, 1953), 14–17.

[39] "Queen of Gospel Singers," *Sepia Record* (July, 1953), 42–45.

women were able to do the same. When one's race and gender made her a sufficiently rare "double minority" in a high-profile or lucrative occupation, her story landed in the pages of African American magazines. Black female pioneers in sports received special coverage when they moved into Olympic or professional ranks.[40] Issues of *Sepia Record* and *Negro Achievements* also ran articles on a Connecticut policewoman and the manager of a 500-unit luxury apartment complex.[41]

From the June, 1952 *Negro Achievements* came a story on Texas State Board of Health physician Connie Yerwood Odom of Austin. It emphasized her work in preventive medicine, especially as it benefitted Negro women and children. Also mentioned was the growing number of women attending Meharry Medical School, an African American institution from which Odom graduated. The writer specifically noted the community service activities which Odom managed to work into her schedule.[42]

If the 1950s seemed a decade of hyper-domesticity for whites, African Americans found it a time of compelling social awareness and activism. Black individuals received credit in black magazines for voluntary efforts to benefit their communities. The black press acknowledged blacks' civic achievements when daily newspapers rarely covered them.[43]

In a May, 1954 article, Blanche Calloway's former musical career came to the attention of *Sepia Record*'s readers. Most of the imagery and text described the high-energy dancer and bandleader she had been in her youth. In an update, the writer noted that Calloway recently had defeated five male candidates to become the committeewoman in her Philadelphia political ward. She was also serving on a

---

[40] See "Althea Gibson," *Ebony*, VI (Nov., 1950), 96–100; "Top Pro Ice Skater," *Ebony*, VII (Mar., 1952), 105–108; "Gal on Second Base," *Our World*, VIII, 8–11.

[41] "First Lady of the Olympics," *Negro Achievements*, VI (Oct., 1952), 37–38; "The Team with the Toni," *Sepia Record* (Aug., 1953), 32–33; "Travis Wilburn, America's Toughest Lady," *Negro Achievements*, VI (Nov., 1952), 24–25; "Pistol Packin' Ella," *Sepia Record* (Aug., 1953), 16–19; "Washington's Hotel for Society," *Negro Achievements*, VII (Jan., 1953), 12–13.

[42] "She Chose Medicine for a Career," *Negro Achievements*, VI (June, 1952), 16, 56.

[43] Wolseley, *The Black Press, U.S.A.*, 118–120. Also see "Pistol Packin' Ella," *Sepia Record* (Aug., 1953), 16–19.

citywide committee to address juvenile delinquency. She posed for the photographer at the Boys and Girls Club and at a reception honoring her community work. Award in hand, she flashed the "famous Calloway smile."[44]

Calloway was not necessarily outdoing middle-class white women in her dedication to civic efforts. Many *were* involved in lobbying and organizing. The difference was that a black woman of Calloway's notoriety received as much credit for her community activism as for her artistic achievements when covered in African American pictorial magazines such as *Sepia Record.*[45]

How do we account for the varied models of womanhood in marriage, careers and community work that *Sepia Record* presented? First, there was the precedent of most African American women having worked for wages at some time, whether married, parenting, or neither. They and their relatives were the magazine's consumers. Secondly, consider the principals in the Good Publishing Company during the early 1950s. Adelle Conner Jackson had been in the workforce all her adult life, whether single, divorced, or married. She was raising a son during her tenure at the company. Seth and Anne Kantor both worked as editors. George Levitan, the publisher, co-managed a wholesale business with his wife. These personal experiences of the management, added to the example of black wives and mothers in their employ, supported a positive model of women in the workforce. As Patricia Hill Collins has stated, African American women have survived in a society which denigrates them and their characteristics through their commitment to maintaining positive self-images. The black women at Good Publishing apparently continued that legacy of positive self-definition.[46]

As noted earlier, alluring female imagery in *Sepia Record* and *Negro Achievements* placed these magazines in step with the post-war ideol-

[44] "What Has Happened to Blanche Calloway?" *Sepia Record* (May, 1954), 20–23.

[45] Chafe, *The American Woman,* 217–218. For another example of an African American celebrity's community service, see "First Lady of the Stage," *Negro Achievements,* VI (Nov., 1952), 10–11.

[46] Brandenstein, "Prominent Roles of Black Womanhood," 1, 81–91; Patricia Hill Collins, *Black Feminist Thought: Knowledge, Consciousness, and the Politics of Empowerment* (London: HarperCollins Academic, 1990), 22–23.

ogy of women as erotic symbols. They differed from other magazines by acknowledging that women, including older women, could enjoy being sexual.[47]

That women could be portrayed as simultaneously alluring and strong, nurturing and smart, working for wages while also caring for family and community, might have posed an obvious contradiction to some white middle-class readers, and editors, in the 1950s. Yet these multiple roles and strategies had become standard for most black women (and many black men) in the century after emancipation. Their external lives involved challenging complexity, but they did not necessarily see their own *identities* as internally contradictory.[48]

In *Sepia Record*'s complex portrayals of black womanhood, we are reminded of Janice Radway's warning not to assume that patriarchy is monolithic or wholly successful. Instead, she calls it "a set of practices . . . riven by conflicts, slippages, and imperfect joinings." Indeed, *Sepia Record* testified that American womanhood was not as unidimensional in the 1950s as the white mainstream press led readers to believe. Black, brown, or beige, married or single, African American women had "a whole lot goin' on."[49]

[47] Brandenstein, "Prominent Roles of Black Womanhood," 130–132. One of the few studies of magazine coverage of older Americans indicates that elderly persons are depicted in negative tones in at least 50 percent of the samples and their sexual interest is not even mentioned as a possibility. See James D. Robinson, "Mass Media and the Elderly: A Uses and Dependency Interpretation," in *Life-Span Communication: Normative Processes,* ed. Jon F. Nussbaum (Hillsdale, N.J.: Lawrence Earlbaum Associates, 1989), 319–337.

[48] Bonnie Thornton Dill, "The Dialectics of Black Womanhood," *Signs,* IV (Spring, 1979), 548, 553; Roger Abrahams, "Negotiating Respect: Patterns of Presentation Among Black Women," *Journal of American Folklore,* LXXXVIII (Jan., 1975), 64; Collins, *Black Feminist Thought,* 94.

[49] Janice Rodway, "Identifying Ideological Seams: Mass Culture, Analytical Method and Political Practice," *Communication,* IX, 10.

Women as Literary Participants in Contemporary Events

LOU RODENBERGER*

IN 1986 TEXANS CELEBRATED the 150th birthday of Texas as an independent entity—first as a republic, then as a state. Launching the celebration, which was more commercial than spiritual, was the publication of a thousand-page tome purporting to be a novel, though some called it unassimilated history, called *Texas*. This publication, commissioned by the governor and sponsored by a state university, had been ground out by James Michener. Critic A. C. Greene says, "Ounce for ounce, [it is] possibly the dullest book ever written about Texas. . . . it has little reference value and no historical application."[1] For most of his review Greene points out the book's historical inaccuracies. Perhaps Texans might have celebrated more authentically and literarily by publicizing the first book entitled *Texas*. Published in 1833, the book was reissued in 1836, appropriately enough, the year Texas declared independence. Its author? A woman, Mary Austin Holley, "the first credible historian of Texas," according to J. P. Bryan, who edited her diary.[2] Subtitled *Observations, Historical, Geographical and Descriptive, in a Series of Letters Written During a Visit to Austin's Colony with A View to A Permanent Settlement in That Country in the Autumn of 1831*, Mary Holley's *Texas* records her keen observations during the

---

* Lou Rodenberger, who holds a doctorate from Texas A&M University, teaches American literature at McMurry University in Abilene. She is editor of *Her Work: Stories by Texas Women,* has published numerous essays on Southwestern writers, and is co-editor of a forthcoming history of Texas women writers.

[1] Dallas *Morning News,* Oct. 27, 1985.

[2] J. P. Bryan (ed.), "Mary Austin Holley: *The Texas Diary,* 1835–38," *Texas Quarterly,* VIII (Summer, 1965), 7.

first of three trips she made by boat to visit her cousin Stephen F.'s colony. Because she could write well of what she observed so carefully, we know more about living conditions, social activities, and political maneuvering in Texas colonial life.

With Holley began the literary tradition which informs and sustains women writers who have succeeded her, a tradition which has continued to record the experience of Texas for a growing and diverse audience. Before the century closed, Amelia Barr, who lived in Texas for more than a decade after the republic became a state, had written a popular novel set in Texas. *Remember the Alamo* (1888), stylistically a sentimental historical romance, nevertheless explores the realistic problems of an Anglo-Hispanic marriage during the Texas Revolution. In 1913 Amelia Barr also provided a detailed record of social life in Austin between 1856 and 1866 in her autobiography, *All the Days of My Life*. Barr's Texas experience was limited and few of her novels are set in Texas, but Mollie E. Moore Davis, who grew up in East and South Texas, wrote her novels *Under the Man-Fig* (1895) and *The Wire Cutters* (1899) from firsthand knowledge acquired through observation and experience. *The Wire Cutters* reflects the human suffering brought on by a West Central Texas water rights dispute between settlers and wealthy land speculators at the close of free range days for Texas cattlemen. It would be four years before Andy Adams's *Log of a Cowboy* (1903) was published and praised for its realistic depiction of cowboy and range life. *Under the Man-Fig* is set on the Brazos River in the region portrayed sixty years before in Mary Austin Holley's accounts. The novel is structured around the poignant early-day Texas legend of the Man-Fig Tree, where, the author says, some thought a murdered Spaniard's blood "had watered its infant roots, and passed into its great reddish-purple fruit."[3] The author's graphic portrayal with precise detail of antebellum life on the Brazos foreshadows the successful realistic fiction soon to issue from the pens of many creative women, who perceived that the Texas experience was rich material for short stories and novels.

By the 1920s women writers in Texas began to receive national attention for fiction which delivered social commentary along with

[3] M. E. M. Davis, *Under the Man-Fig* (Boston: Houghton, Mifflin and Co., 1895), 9.

realistic accounts of Texas experience. Ruth Cross's novel *The Golden Cocoon* (1924), which went through five editions in its first year of publication, reflects Cross's observations of the sterile lives of North Texas tenant farmers trying to survive on hard scrabble cotton farms. Cross's plot focuses on a resolute young woman determined to escape the hard life that has been her mother's lot. A year later, Dorothy Scarborough created an uproar in West Texas when she depicted the rolling plains around Sweetwater in her novel *The Wind* (1925) as an environment particularly unfriendly to any but the toughest of women. first published anonymously, the novel raised the ire of town promoters, but early women settlers of that area have testified to the psychological havoc constantly blowing wind and sand can create.

Although both Cross and Scarborough wrote a number of books, many women writers in this era clearly demonstrated great talent as fiction writers but produced only a few short stories or a novel or two. In the early 1920s Winifred Sanford, a Phi Beta Kappa graduate of the University of Michigan who had come to live in Wichita Falls with her attorney husband, stole time from the care of her small children to write short stories about life in the oil fields booming near Wichita Falls. H. L. Mencken published nine of Sanford's stories in the *American Mercury* between 1925 and 1931. Mencken admired her work so much that he wrote for stories when she was slow in submitting them. In 1926, she was honored by inclusion in E. J. O'Brien's *Best Short Stories* for "Windfall," which has appeared in several anthologies since. A New York agent wrote asking to represent her. She answered, "I have been writing only a few years, and since I am married and have small children, I have so far been unable to give full professional time to my typewriter. . . ."[4]

It is not surprising then to learn that when her first novel was rejected, Sanford burned the manuscript and ceased to write after publishing only thirteen short stories over a period of seven years. Her daughter concludes her biographical essay on her mother with this explanation: "New interests grew to fill her days, and she went on to other things."[5] In 1988 the late Suzanne Comer of SMU Press read the collection of Sanford's stories, privately printed in 1980 by her family,

[4] Winifred M. Sanford, *Windfall and Other Stories*, ed. Emerett Sanford Miles (Dallas: Sanford, 1980), ix.

[5] Ibid., xi.

and subsequently published a new edition of *Windfall and Other Stories*, which finally made available the first fiction by a Texas writer reflecting life in the oil fields as it really was.

A century after Mary Austin Holley's personal version of colonial life was published, several Texas women writers turned from reflection of contemporary events in their fiction to materials available in records of Texas's past history. Laura Krey's *On the Long Tide* (1940) and Karle Wilson Baker's *Star of Wilderness* (1942) romanticize colonial Texas life, but it was the life of the remarkable Harriet Potter which inspired the most realistic novel about women's lives during those chaotic times. Historians who knew the value of a good story and knew that Elithe Hamilton Kirkland had already published one good novel about early Texas life—*Divine Average* (1942)—thrust Harriet's memoirs into her protesting hands in 1953, and once she had read what this intriguing independent woman had written, Kirkland became Harriet's "aroused defender and storyteller" in *Love Is a Wild Assault*,[6] a novel published in 1959.

Scandal had haunted Harriet Potter from the days of the Texas Revolution when a charismatic Texas politician persuaded her to enter into a marriage that she believed legitimate, but for many years the union was legally questionable. In her autobiography, a manuscript she wrote at age eighty-three, Harriet explains and defends her life's choices convincingly.[7] Her account reveals the remarkable strengths of this nineteenth-century Southern woman. By the time she and her first husband, a gambler, arrive in New Orleans from Tennessee, Harriet knows that her welfare and that of her children rest on her ingenuity. She has established a successful woman's shop by the time her restless spouse gathers up his family and heads for Texas. There he abandons them, leaving them to starve in a remote Brazos Valley cabin. Harriet stands off both wild animals and starvation until rescued by a distant neighbor.

During the chaotic Runaway Scrape, when Harriet sets off on foot east with her children to find safety during the heat of the Revolution,

[6] Elithe Hamilton Kirkland, *Love Is a Wild Assault* (Garden City, N.Y.: Doubleday, 1959), 13.

[7] Elithe Kirkland narrates the story of how she discovered Harriet Potter's memoirs in the foreword of the novel. Copies of the memoir are in several university archives, including the Barker Texas History Center at the University of Texas at Austin.

the handsome and devious Col. Robert Potter befriends the attractive woman. He soon persuades her to marry him, claiming that her earlier marriage is illegal in Texas. Soon Colonel Potter leaves his young wife in a remote cabin on Caddo Lake in East Texas and spends the rest of his abbreviated life in Austin as a wheeler-dealer politician, riding home to Harriet only occasionally. Harriet lives alone much of the time, coping with Indians, childbirth, and loneliness. Her narrative appears to chronicle honestly her feistiness and her fears.

Despite the shaky legality of her marriage, and the scathing condemnation of many for her liaison with Potter—"Potter's Paramour," many called her—her tenacious protection and care of Potter's Point earned for her a reputation as "the bravest woman in Texas." When Harriet's husband was killed by a political enemy, she learned that he had left Potter's Point to a woman in Austin. Harriet spent much of the remainder of her life in court fighting for her rights.

Supplementing Harriet's memoirs with careful research into legal documents, journals, and letters, Elithe Kirkland recreates a Southern woman who discovers that she possesses the resourcefulness of that strong breed who helped settle Texas.

The journals and oral history of another independent woman tantalized the imagination of novelist Elizabeth Forsythe Hailey when she began to examine the life of her dynamic grandmother. She soon perceived that the best way to capture the essence of this individualistic woman was in fiction with words that would convey her spirit. Hailey chose to let her narrator speak for herself. Through letters she writes from childhood, Bess Steed Garner, the protagonist of Hailey's novel *A Woman of Independent Means* (1978), reveals the development of her independent turn of mind. Even the early letters of Bess Steed Garner flash glimpses of that spirit. As a college student in 1909, Bess writes her Papa: "Rest assured my education means even more to me than it does to you. I fully intend to *continue* it but since I never expect to *complete* it, why should I spend any more time at college."[8] Bess's logic and keen intelligence develop as she matures, and through her letters, Hailey traces the development of an invincible figure in Dallas civic and business life.

[8] Elizabeth Forsythe Hailey, *A Woman of Independent Means* (New York: Viking, 1978), 3.

Kirkland and Hailey's successful novels based on the lives of women who had prevailed in an earlier Texas resulted from a special kind of collaboration with their subjects, who had themselves been facile shapers of language. For West Texas novelist Jane Gilmore Rushing, it is place which inspires her works. Her choice of her native region, the rolling plains of West Texas, as the setting for her fiction about early and contemporary life in the state might also have been an automatic choice of subject. The plight of frontier women, the life of the cowboy, and the conflicts between nester and rancher have traditionally furnished materials for fiction writers who choose to write about Texas frontier life. Portrayal of the actors in the drama implicit in the colorful history of Texas all too often personifies Texas myths, which are stereotyped into concrete images of types. Rushing, however, resists such temptation. Her West Texas characters are individuals. In her novels, Rushing, with her well-defined sense of place and her understanding of rural experience, goes beyond superficial impressions of the region to depict life there honestly and compassionately. More than one critic has judged her fiction to be well-made psychological fiction. Basic to her understanding of individuals in this culture is her perception of how community life reflects the strong, inflexible religious and moral views associated with the area's fundamentalist Protestantism, views which have changed little in the last century. Free thinkers, particularly outsiders, have always risked misunderstanding and censure if they seem to challenge those views. The plight of the nonconformist dominates as theme in Rushing's novels, which present authoritatively the history and life of the region. In most of her novels, Rushing focuses on indomitable women whose strengths lie not only in their ability to prevail but also to cope with the narrow minds and harsh judgments which characterize the hardy farmers and ranchers who struggle themselves to survive in this demanding environment. In her novel *The Raincrow* (1977), a California college professor returns to the rural West Texas home of her mother to shore up the cracks in her own life. Her mother's relationship to a community which has for years considered her a sinful woman takes precedent over the professor's self-centered concerns, but she never understands her mother's loyalty to a church that has closed its doors to her and to neighbors who never visit her home. The reader, however, does comprehend how such things can be in a rural Texas community, or in hundreds of rural communities still existing apart from urban life in America.

In *Tamzen* (1972), Rushing's penetrating study of both the cattleman's and the homesteader's set of mind in frontier Texas seems to me to offer as perceptive a look backward as the works of the many male writers of cowboy life. Based on a historical dispute between free range ranchers and encroaching homesteaders over rights to Block 97, originally railroad land in West Texas, this novel reverses the traditional point of view in fiction about cowboy-nester disputes. This is Tamzen's story—a woman homesteader's story. Even more nontraditional is strong-willed Tamzen's decision to marry a cowboy, but only after she persuades him that farming has a future. When he says, "But, Tamzen, I don't even know how to plow," she counters, "Arthur, I can teach you."[9]

Rushing's strongest novel is her last, *Winds of Blame* (1983), in which she examines the tragedy, implicit even at the beginning of the novel, in a community's failure in 1916 to grapple with the problem of the abusive father. Murder and disintegration of the family result. Rushing says that she turned to community lore she had heard all of her life for the plot of this work. What she discovered was that this story "involves a kind of violence not much limited to time and space."[10] The skewed morality of this town's unspoken conspiracies reveals the chinks in the morality of most frontier towns as Americans spread westward and settled in.

Rushing, who turns usually to the stories and experiences of the traditional extended West Texas family for inspiration, conveys an authentic and powerful sense of place in her novels. Her work seeks to unravel the motivations behind the inflexibility of fundamentalist religion, the life-lies small town citizens conspire to defend, the myth versus the reality of traditional family life, and racism as those on the edge of the frontier practiced it.

Sharing Rushing's world-view evolving from her knowledge of life in both Texas and her native Tennessee, Carolyn Osborn's award-winning short story "The Grands" recently became the third publication of the prestigious Book Club of Texas. Osborn's reputation—and her talent becomes more widely recognized yearly—rests, however, upon her three collections of memorable short fiction. In 1990 "The

---

[9] Jane Gilmore Rushing, *Tamzen* (Garden City, N.Y.: Doubleday, 1972), 313.

[10] Jane Gilmore Rushing, *Winds of Blame* (Garden City, N.Y.: Doubleday, 1983), 3.

Grands" appeared in the O. Henry Awards' collection of short fiction and in 1991 the TCU Press published a third collection of her work, *Warriors and Maidens*. Her first book, *A Horse of Another Color*, was published in 1977 by the University of Illinois Press. In 1987 Shearer Publishing collected her recent stories in *The Fields of Memory*. Reviews of this work in the New York *Times*, Washington *Post*, and the book review sections of various Texas publications praised Osborn's "strong visual images" and "artistic authority," but those terms originate with critics striving for fancy labels. Osborn continues to be published not only for her ability to create "strong visual images" but also for her talent for revealing insights into human motivation through perceptive character portrayals.

Osborn's stories provide adventures, witty and entertaining, but they also insist that the reader pause and think about those adventures in retrospect. Then the impact of her meanings jolt you. Nobody understands the real modern Texas cowboy better than Osborn. In "My Brother Is A Cowboy," through the eyes of sister Celia, we learn about Kenyon the cowboy's actions, attitudes, and reactions. Probably her funniest story, this characterization of the die-hard cowboy is also one of her most perceptive. Perhaps the best story in *The Fields of Memory* is "House of the Blue Woman," in which Celia looks back at what she perceives were the realities of Kenyon's life as she clears out Kenyon's ranch house after his premature death.

In Osborn's competent prose, the major theme of contemporary writers emerges. She proves that exploring change in women's roles does not require a series of novels. In the title story of *A Horse of Another Color*, the restless woman protagonist cuts loose briefly from conventional life and morality and aims for a romantic interlude with a Texas cowboy. The cowboy is only an ignorant wrangler in charge of horse rentals on the beach where she is vacationing, but he does have "a slow crooked smile." Cavorting naked with her lover in the surf on horseback leads to near drowning, a tragicomic scene, but also opens the narrator's eyes to her self-delusion. Osborn's subjects vary widely, and her narratives occur in both rural and urban settings, but she has missed little in her sharp observation of her territory.

Osborn's themes are diverse, but it is novelist Shelby Hearon, now living in New York, who chronicles comprehensively the odyssey of the contemporary creative woman through the monumental changes in family life and women's roles which have occurred in the last quarter of a century. In the 1983 reissue of her novel *Armadillo in the Grass*, Hearon quotes from the first review of this, her first book, which describes the switch Clara Blue, the narrator, makes from housewife to sculptor as her way "of defying change and defeating loss." Hearon comments on how elated she was that "they, up there, *understood*. That it would be all right: you sit down in Texas and try to figure it out, and send your message off, and they would get it." The author admits that as she looks back, she can see after writing several more novels her artistic immaturity in this one, but she adds, "That first idea [remains] as much a part of what I write now as it did then: that it is our very mortality that presses us to give order, shape, and form to our experience."[11]

Her ordering of experience takes Hearon's readers through redefinition of self, and through changing relationships with parents, children, husbands, and lovers. The writer neither flinches nor dodges the grief that fractured relationships can bring, nor does she romanticize solutions. Her novels conclude, but are never conclusive. We understand that there are more answers to seek. Sociologist Lutie Sayre, the protagonist of Hearon's eighth novel *Group Therapy* (1984), is chastised by her lover Joe, who cannot understand Lutie's need to become involved in every life with which her own connects. She tells him, "A person can't go around by herself all time; you have to realize there's someone else out there, too. Don't the rest of you get lonesome all wrapped up in your selves?"[12] After finally talking through their disagreement, Lutie thinks as the book concludes, "how little was left of her when she had no one at all who cared. It had to do with the fact that even if you let it be true, the way Joe said, that nobody changed, you had to make provisions for the fact that they changed in *relation to you*."[13] And that, it seems, is the underlying theme that Shelby Hearon explores so straightforwardly in most of what she has written.

The writers cited here are representative of dozens of other women in Texas who are recognized outside of Texas but are not much noticed in their home state. Among them are novelists Laura Furman and Beverly Lowry and short story writers Annette Sanford, Jan Seale, Pat

[11] Shelby Hearon, *Armadillo in the Grass* (rev. ed.; Dallas: Pressworks Publishing, Inc., 1983), 12. This novel was first published by Alfred A. Knopf in 1968.
[12] Shelby Hearon, *Group Therapy* (New York: Atheneum, 1984), 271.
[13] Ibid., 272.

Ellis Taylor, Pat Carr, Harryette Mullen, Carmen Tafolla, Mary Gray Hughes, and Gail Galloway Adams. These writers represent the world from a female perspective, often reexamining myths of the past, many of which glorify masculine accomplishment and ignore feminine contributions in both frontier and modern society. With wit, irony, and insight, they probe the depths of the human heart, revealing both the dark and the shining facets of human personality. Sometimes subversive and always adventurous, these writers gift their readers with stories which force them to confront and often refute the authenticity of Southwestern experience from the point of view of the male writer. Whether drawing on historical past or personal experience, contemporary Texas women writers perceive what Virginia Woolf once called the "meaning of all this" and capture those meanings powerfully.

Women's Literature and History in Texas:

A Confluence of Traditions

SYLVIA GRIDER*

As PART OF ITS YEAR-LONG CENTENARY OBSERVATION IN 1983, the University of Texas hosted a conference entitled "The Texas Literary Tradition: Fiction, Folklore, History." In spite of this broad and ambitious title, women were conspicuously absent from most of the sessions, either as presenters or as subjects. Although a session was devoted to "The Texas-Mexican Perspective," there was no session about women's perspectives. The only presentation specifically about a woman writer was Joan Givner's on Katherine Anne Porter.[1] Later, apparently in response to widespread criticism, the publication resulting from the conference tacked on a concluding essay entitled "The Fairy Tale and the Frontier: Images of Women in Texas Fiction," by Carol Marshall.[2] If one were to judge solely from the program of this conference, one would conclude that the only woman who had any influence on the development of Texas culture, history, or literature

---

* Sylvia Grider received her Ph.D. in folklore from Indiana University and teaches folklore, anthropology, and Texas history at Texas A&M University. She is a past president of the Texas Folklore Society and is currently president of the American Folklore Society. With Lou Rodenberger, she is coediting an anthology on Texas women writers.

[1] Joan Givner, "Katherine Anne Porter: The Old Order and the New," in *The Texas Literary Tradition: Fiction, Folklore, History*, eds. Don Graham, James W. Lee, and William T. Pilkington (Austin: University of Texas, College of Liberal Arts and Texas State Historical Association, 1983), 58–68.

[2] Carol Marshall, "The Fairy Tale and the Frontier: Images of Women in Texas Fiction," in ibid., 195–206.

was Katherine Anne Porter. Such a conclusion would have come as a surprise to the Texas literary establishment, most of whom have never acknowledged Porter's stature as a writer of national and international, let alone statewide, significance.

In 1984, in partial response to the aforementioned conference, another was held in Austin on the "Texas Women's Literary Tradition." The proceedings heated up considerably when moderator Jane Marcus announced that she hoped that the conference would not crown Katherine Anne Porter "queen of Texas letters." Joan Givner replied, "Is it not fitting that she should be honored in her native state? I am not particularly happy with the title of 'queen.' I am not a monarchist, and in North America the title suggests beauty pageants more than royalty. Also, there is the unpleasant connotation of 'consort,' unless one is thinking of a beehive."[3] In general, men ignored the conference; perhaps they thought the topic was of no interest to them. The only man on the program was Don Graham, holder of the J. Frank Dobie Chair of Literature at the University of Texas, who speculated that *The Wind* by Dorothy Scarborough and *Giant* by Edna Ferber were the only two Texas novels by women to which anybody had ever paid any attention.

In 1990, at a conference devoted to "Women and Texas History," we had the opportunity to assess the role of women in the development of the unique culture that is becoming widely known as the "Texas Mystique." Women writers and the works which they have produced in and about Texas are an integral part of this broad inquiry.

This essay is subtitled "A Confluence of Traditions." The traditions in question are not the familiar ethnic ones which immediately come to mind, namely Hispanic, African American, and Anglo, but rather the academic or disciplinary traditions of literature and history. To appreciate fully the role of women in the development of Texas culture, one must eschew the artificial distinctions of academe and instead focus on the interrelationships, the "confluence," of literature and history.

As Fane Downs has pointed out in print and in private conversation, the historiography or documentation of women in Texas is in its

---

[3] Joan Givner, "Katherine Anne Porter: Queen of Texas Letters?" *Texas Libraries*, XLV (Winter, 1984), 123.

infancy, because we have only reached the monograph stage.[4] The monograph stage is crucial, of course, because we must have sufficient limited studies of specific topics before we can begin to synthesize and draw larger conclusions regarding the influence of women on the development of Texas culture and vice versa. From an interdisciplinary point of view, most of these monographs have dealt primarily with women and Texas history; a few have dealt with women and Texas folklore. Very few scholars have looked seriously at women and Texas literature. The early studies dealing with women and literature in Texas are, in general, rather obscure. By looking at some of these early literary histories, we can begin to see the broader patterns that emerge from this blending, or confluence, of scholarship.

The legacy of the Victorian Age informs much of our intellectual life today. How can we escape our nineteenth-century predecessors' penchant for taxonomy? Charles Darwin and other social scientists, especially ethnographers and anthropologists, ranged throughout the world gathering one of these and one of those to take home and display in the British Museum or in our own Smithsonian Institution. Today we call such enterprises "data bases" and record the information on our laptops and hard disks.

Following the same pattern, or tradition, as the great nineteenth-century museum collections of artifacts, published Victorian scholarship consisted primarily of multivolume anthologies and lists of related data. Sir James George Frazer's famous and controversial *Golden Bough* is typical of this type of scholarship.[5] Women were not exempt from this trend, either as subjects or compilers. Lady Alice Bertha Gomme's massive compilation, *The Traditional Games of England, Scotland, and Ireland with Tunes, Singing Rhymes, and Methods of Playing According to the Variants Extant and Recorded in Different Parts of the Kingdom*, is equally typical of this Victorian genre of scholarship or intellectual collectanea.[6]

[4] Fane Downs, "Texas Women: History at the Edges," in *Texas Through Time: Evolving Interpretations*, eds. Walter L. Buenger and Robert A. Calvert (College Station: Texas A&M University Press, 1991), 81–101.

[5] James George Frazer, *The Golden Bough: A Study in Magic and Religion* (3rd ed., 12 vols.; London: Macmillan and Co., 1912–1917).

[6] Alice Bertha Gomme, *The Traditional Games of England, Scotland, and Ireland with Tunes, Singing Rhymes, and Methods of Playing According to the Variants Extant and Recorded in Different Parts of the Kingdom* (2 vols.; London: David Nutt, 1894).

The first known descriptions of Texas women writers are to be found in these nineteenth-century lists and unanalyzed compilations of data, the predecessors of our current incipient monograph phase. Although there may be others, the earliest literary history written by and acknowledging Texas women writers that we have located so far is Ida Raymond's *Southland Writers: Biographical and Critical Sketches of Living Female Writers of the South. With Extracts from Their Writings*, published in 1870.[7] At that time Texas was still regarded geographically, culturally, and politically as part of the South, especially since Texas had been a state in the Confederacy and was occupied by Federal troops during Reconstruction. The South versus West debate did not emerge until later.[8] *Southland Writers* is essentially a biographical dictionary containing brief entries on otherwise little-known Texas women such as Miss Julia Bacon, a poet from Beaumont, as well as some of the better-known women writers of the day, among them Mollie E. Moore, the author of *The Wire Cutters* (1899), a Texas range novel which preceded Andy Adams's famous *Log of a Cowboy* by four years.[9]

By 1885 we have the first known specifically Texas literary history and it is, significantly, compiled by a woman: *Gems from a Texas Quarry; or Literary Offerings by and Selections from Leading Writers and Prominent Characters of Texas. Being a Texas Contribution to the World's Industrial Exposition at New Orleans, 1884–45*, edited by Ella Hutchins Steuart.[10] *Gems* anthologizes the work of both men and women writers, including a number of women whose names are obscure or unknown today but who were well-known and popular writers in their day, especially in newspapers.

A fascinating and ephemeral source of literary history concerning Texas women writers, and perhaps the first piece devoted exclusively

[7]   Ida Raymond, *Southland Writers: Biographical and Critical Sketches of Living Female Writers of the South. With Extracts from their Writing* (Philadelphia: Claxton, Remsen & Haffelfinger, 1870).

[8]   See, for example, Frank Vandiver, *The Southwest: South or West?* (College Station: Texas A&M University Press, 1975).

[9]   Mollie E. Moore, *The Wire Cutters* (Boston: Houghton Mifflin, 1899); Andy Adams, *Log of a Cowboy* (New York: Houghton Mifflin, 1903).

[10]   Ella Hutchins Steuart, *Gems from a Texas Quarry; or Literary Offerings by and Selections from Leading Writers and Prominent Characters of Texas: Being a Texas Contribution to the World's Industrial Exposition at New Orleans, 1884–85* (New Orleans: J. S. Rivers, 1885).

to that topic, appeared nearly a century ago in the Galveston *Daily News*.[11] Entitled "Women Writers of Texas," this two-part article by Bride Taylor, vice president of the Texas Women's Press Association, consisted of brief biographical sketches of seventy-seven women authors, starting with Mary Austin Holley and concluding with a sketch of the modest Taylor herself. Taylor always signed her articles by her initials alone, which the enlightened editors thought slighted her in the context of the article she had written. As a result, they added the sketch of Taylor to her article. Fifty-nine other women were listed by name only. Taylor stated her rationale in the introduction to the first installment of the article:

> The idea of collecting such facts about the women writers of Texas as it was possible to obtain was suggested by the lack of any complete account of them or their works. It has frequently happened that specially pleasing productions appearing in journals outside the state have after a time—and often quite by accident—been discovered to be from the pens of Texas women. Such being the case, it seemed likely that more good work than anyone suspected might be coming to light in the papers of the state itself, and a desire grew in the mind of the writer of this article to let the world in general and our own people in particular know what honorable claim to literary credit Texas possesses. Those to whom the idea was submitted agreed that the number of women in Texas who devoted themselves in a more or less desultory way to the pursuit of the literary art might be considerable. No one—least of all the writer herself—suspected that the number would, upon investigation, assume the astonishing proportions which the following list reveals.

She concluded the piece with a caveat:

[11] Bride N. Taylor, "Women Writers of Texas," Galveston *Daily News*, June 18 and 25, 1893. The only generally available copy of this invaluable article is on microfilm in the Eugene C. Barker Texas History Center at the University of Texas at Austin. The republication of Taylor's article in a journal or elsewhere is a worthwhile topic currently under discussion.

The facts of this article have been, as far as possible, gathered from the authors themselves. When this could not be done, friends authorized to speak for them gave the necessary information. And in a few cases, as where death or a difficulty of finding the persons by mail offered an obstacle, such previously published accounts as were accessible were consulted. Doubtless some inaccuracies will be discovered. Where this happens, any corrections offered by those in a position to give authentic information will be most gratefully received.

In 1896 Elizabeth Brooks published her biographical dictionary, *Prominent Women of Texas*, which contains a chapter on prominent authors.[12] As with earlier reference works of this type and period, *Prominent Women* is useful to scholars today primarily because of the information it provides about obscure and otherwise unknown authors.

Writers and Writings of Texas, edited by Davis Foute Eagleton, an English professor at Austin College in Sherman, appeared in 1913.[13] He echoed Taylor in his foreword:

We have a large body of 'home,'—yes, and 'homely' writings,—why not investigate and enjoy them? True, we have not, in our literature, reached the philosophic, the critical,—the crucial—period. But that spirit is born late in life and matures slowly. The age of unselfish enjoyment comes first. Why should the beauty, the youthful verve of our literature be ignored in our sloth and apathy, when there is so much to enjoy? This Manual makes no claim of a critical character,—simply a collection, a foundation, a collation on the part of an enthusiastic sympathizer of some good work, not all, that the genius of Texas has produced. . . .

Interspersed among the men, Eagleton provided biographical sketches of nine women authors, with representative excerpts from their works. A supplement listed the names of 131 Texas women writers

[12] Elizabeth Brooks, *Prominent Women of Texas* (Akron, Oh.: Werner Co., 1896).
[13] Davis Foute Eagleton, *Writers and Writings of Texas* (New York: Broadway Publishing Co., 1913).

with a notation of genre, such as poetry, or the titles of their significant publications.

The next significant work after Taylor and Brooks devoted exclusively to women was Annie Pickrell's famous *Pioneer Women in Texas* in 1929.[14] Although not a literary history, the biographical anthology format of this book underscores the tenacity of this genre of writing in Texas.

Pioneer Women in Texas marks a turning point for biographical reference works. By 1929 styles and tastes in American scholarship were turning away from the Victorian compendium model as scholars became more interested in specific topics. Furthermore, spurred in part by the catalyst of the 1936 Centennial, Texans began to seek recognition and legitimacy in national literary circles.[15] Subsequent literary anthologies focused on Texas as a distinct region and the literary genres being produced here rather than on the biography or gender of the authors. Among these later genre-oriented anthologies is the 1934 study, *A Century with Texas Poets and Poetry*, by Vaida Stewart Montgomery.[16]

The dominant trend in Texas literary history during the 1930s was to identify Texas literature as part of the larger field of Southwestern literature. J. Frank Dobie's celebrated squabble with the regents of the University of Texas over whether or not Texas had produced any literature worthy of the name fueled this identification of Texas with the greater Southwest. His uncopyrighted and idiosyncratic *Guide to the Life and Literature of the Southwest*, which was originally the syllabus and reading list for his course of the same name at UT, is the touchstone for all subsequent research regarding Texas literature.[17] This shift in focus away from the biographical and toward the regional also brought Texas women scholars and literary critics to the forefront with the topical bibliographic guides of Mabel Major of Texas Christian University, Florence Barns of Mary Hardin-Baylor College, and

---

[14] Annie Doom Pickrell, *Pioneer Women in Texas* (Austin: E. L. Steck Co., 1929).

[15] Kenneth B. Ragsdale, *The Year America Discovered Texas: Centennial '36* (College Station: Texas A&M University Press, 1987).

[16] Vaida Stewart Montgomery, *A Century with Texas Poets and Poetry* (Dallas: The Kaleidograph Press, 1934).

[17] J. Frank Dobie, *A Guide to the Life and Literature of the Southwest* (1942; reprint, Dallas: Southern Methodist University Press, 1952).

Sister Agatha of Incarnate Word College. Leonidas Payne's *A Survey of Texas Literature* (1928) contains some critical and bibliographical material as well as biographical information on Texas authors, including a number of women.[18]

One of Mabel Major's most significant contributions to the scholarship of Texas regional literature is the 1938 *Southwest Heritage: A Literary History with Bibliography*, which she coedited and which is described in the preface as "the first attempt to give an orderly account of it (i.e. the literature of the Southwest), to indicate the trends and relations of the writings and writers."[19] The book is broken into three chronological sections and each section is further divided into topics, including myth, historical writing, and "belles lettres." Significant authors, regardless of gender, are discussed within each category.

For many years the topical and bibliographic work of Dobie, Payne, Major, Sister Agatha, and others set the trend for Texas literary histories. Some more recent examples are *Southwestern American Literature: A Bibliography* (1980), edited by John Q. Anderson, Edwin W. Gaston, and James W. Lee; and Richard W. Etulain's *A Bibliographical Guide to the Study of Western American Literature* (1982).[20] None of these recent works classifies authors by gender.

Scholarship on Texas women writers finally is beginning to move into the monograph stage. Essays pertaining specifically to Texas women writers and their works are appearing more and more frequently. Carol Marshall's "The Fairy Tale and the Frontier," cited above, is one early example. More recent is Celia Morris's "Requiem for a Texas Lady," the token piece by a woman in *Range Wars: Heated Debates, Sober Reflections, and Other Assessments of Texas Writing* (1989),

---

[18] Mabel Major and T. M. Pearce, *Southwest Heritage: A Literary History with Bibliography* (rev. ed.; Albuquerque: University of New Mexico Press, 1972). See also Mabel Major and Rebecca W. Smith, *The Southwest in Literature: An Anthology for High Schools* (New York: Macmillan Co., 1929); Florence Barns, *Texas Writers of Today* (Dallas: Tardy, 1935); Sister Agatha [Sheehan], *Texas Prose Writings: A Reader's Digest* (Dallas: Banks Upshaw, 1936); Leonidas Payne, *A Survey of Texas Literature* (New York: Rand McNally, 1928).

[19] Major and Pearce, *Southwest Heritage*, 5–6.

[20] John Q. Anderson, Edwin W. Gaston, and James W. Lee (eds.), *Southwestern American Literature: A Bibliography* (Chicago: Swallow Press, 1980); Richard W. Etulain, *A Bibliographical Guide to the Study of Western American Literature* (Lincoln: University of Nebraska Press, 1982).

edited by Craig Clifford and William T. Pilkington.[21] In 1990 Texas A&M University Press brought out a handsome collection of essays in a landmark volume entitled *Katherine Anne Porter and Texas: An Uneasy Relationship* and the University of North Texas Press published *The Texas Legacy of Katherine Anne Porter* the following year.[22] Lou Rodenberger and I are editing a reference work tentatively titled *Texas Women Writers: A Literary History*, which is scheduled for publication by Southern Methodist University Press.

As researchers learn more about contemporary Texas women writers and their predecessors, they soon will have sufficient data to assess the integral role women have had in the development of Texas culture.

[21] Celia Morris, "Requiem for a Texas Lady," in *Range Wars: Heated Debates, Sober Reflections, and Other Assessments of Texas Writing*, eds. Craig Clifford and William T. Pilkington (Dallas: Southern Methodist University Press, 1989), 87–116.

[22] Clinton Machann and William Bedford Clark, *Katherine Anne Porter and Texas: An Uneasy Relationship* (College Station: Texas A&M University Press, 1990); James T. F. Tanner, *The Texas Legacy of Katherine Anne Porter* (Denton: University of North Texas Press, 1991).

Where Do We Go from Here?

A (Very Personal) Response to
"Women and Texas History: A Conference"

Elizabeth York Enstam*

FOR PARTICIPANTS, "Women and Texas History: A Conference" achieved exactly what its planners intended: the papers delivered during that October weekend indicated the range and variety of current research in Texas women's history, opening provocative and exciting prospects for a wider understanding not only of women's lives in Texas, but also of Texans as a people and a culture. The sessions informed us of what other scholars are doing, suggested further areas of inquiry, and stimulated additional ideas for projects already under way. The many fine presentations are evidence that a whole new set of questions about the state's past is being defined and investigated.

With so much interest and energy focused on the history of women in Texas, it is perhaps time to consider possible future directions for research and writing, indeed to ponder the development of a field of Texas women's history. As in any area of history, we must continue to dig out the basic facts. Beginning with information about specific individuals, we need more of what Elizabeth Fox-Genovese called old-fashioned, "soft," descriptive social history. The personal, subjective, anecdotal accounts of unique events and unique experiences in the lives of Texas women add more than mere "human

* Elizabeth York Enstam's research interests include community, urban, and women's history. She holds a Ph.D. from Duke University and has published in *Frontiers, History News,* and *Educational Technology.* She is currently completing a book entitled *Women and the Creation of Urban Life: Dallas, Texas, 1843–1920.*

177

interest" to the writing of history: the life of every woman speaks in some way to the larger questions of Texas's past.

The stories of individuals, however, are only the beginning. Such sources as city directories, census reports, the manuscript census, and reports from state and federal government agencies provide the "hard" data which enable us to evaluate the individual's achievements, to see how unique or typical she was for her generation. We need, that is, to see each woman within the context of "her people," and also to know how women of her group compared or contrasted with those of other groups. When we view several groups together, we will understand more about the experience of Texas women as a population: how many worked in paid occupations, and what did they do to earn money? How many were in the professions? When did Texas women enter the professions and under what circumstances? What were their marital status, the number of their children, and the types of households (nuclear, extended, augmented, reconstituted) in which they lived? When did women who worked only in the home gain access to basic services (gas and electricity, water and sewer lines); when were they able to afford appliances? What did they do about child care and medical needs?

When we have analyzed the available statistical information for specific ethnic and racial groups, we can begin to construct a profile of Texas women, one which can accommodate diversity of background and lifestyle and at the same time identify shared experiences and characteristics. We may also be able to speak to such larger questions as whether race or class has been the determining factor in the shaping of Texas as a society.

In addition to individuals and the context of their lives, we need to know more about women's work within the society, in neighborhoods and local communities as well as cities, towns, and the state as a whole. Before 1920 women's participation in public life almost always occurred through voluntary associations. How did the local women's organizations work in Texas and how did they cooperate with men's organizations, with other women's clubs or societies, and with state and national organizations? What were their purposes and goals, their origins and structure, their memberships and accomplishments? How did their projects reflect the needs and values of their community, of their generation? Studies such as Elizabeth Hayes Turner's investigation of women's organizations in Galveston can help us see the profound importance of the functioning of women's societies and clubs within Texas communities.[1]

Close examination of the associations and clubs can correct many errors and misconceptions about various aspects of women's roles in public life. Too many facile conclusions have been drawn, for example, about women's participation in politics since the Nineteenth Amendment became law in 1920, and few if any systematic studies exist of the women who have worked in Texas government for the past seventy years. We may find here a core of central values, as well as diverse goals and strategies: how have the political activities of African American women been similar to or different from those of Anglas or Tejanas? How have women in Texas sought "the American dream," defined "justice," perceived "equality"?

Despite the intentions of politicians and (usually) male writers to retain the *Lone* Star mystique, Texans have always shared a culture with people of other places. For this reason (among others), the history of women here needs to be compared with that of women elsewhere. Were the lives of German, Czech, and Italian women immigrants in Texas similar to or different from those of Germans, Czechs, and Italians of other frontiers and other states? Were the lives of black women in Texas comparable to those of black women in other Southern states, or were they more like those of African Americans in other Western states? How have Native American women in Texas compared with Native Americans elsewhere?

Such information would enable us to evaluate Glenda Riley's belief that for women one frontier was much like another.[2] If Riley's statement does hold for women's work in Texas, how does it fare within a particular ethnic context? How have Hispanic cultural forms affected the basic experiences of home life, family relationships, and day-to-day work? How have Native Americans in Texas adapted their separate cultures into urban living? The experience and accomplishments of Texas women, in short, must be compared and contrasted,

---

[1] Elizabeth Hayes Turner, "Women, Religion, and Reform in Galveston, 1880–1920," in *Urban Texas: Politics and Development*, eds. Char Miller and Heywood T. Sanders (College Station: Texas A&M University Press, 1990), 75–95.

[2] Glenda Riley, *The Female Frontier: A Comparative View of Women on the Prairie and the Plains* (Lawrence: University of Kansas Press, 1988).

if only briefly, with those of women elsewhere, on other frontiers and in the growing cities, in the changing labor force, and within the political climate not only of this state, but of other states and the nation as a whole.

During the past twenty to twenty-five years, the field of women's history has produced a number of major interpretations, among them the definition of "separate spheres," the existence of a separate women's culture, and the spread of the "cult of true womanhood." How and to what degree can—or should—those interpretations be applied to women in Texas? Until we make these comparisons and test such interpretations against several kinds of data, we cannot know how unusual or typical women in Texas have been.

Perhaps most important in this regard, historians of Texas women need to join the exploration of the concept of gender. Within every society, certain specific tasks must be accomplished, and every society has produced its own cultural definitions of the roles, duties, and ideals needed from and appropriate to both sexes. Gender involves, for women and men alike, not merely specific tasks and "roles," but also a mystique, a set of assumptions, images, rules of propriety, indeed identities for the individuals who perform certain tasks or live in a certain way *because* they are women or men. However it assigns necessary work, no society survives, or even is a society, without the work and contributions of *both* sexes. The implications of these simple facts are obvious: without the experience of women, we do not have the history of Texas.

It follows, then, that we must seek to redefine what it means to be Texan. The mystique of Texas has been, by definition, white-Anglo-male. Insofar as women have participated in that mystique, they have had to identify with and absorb the male experience and point of view. Has that happened more often and/or more thoroughly in Texas than in other areas of the United States? To what extent have women known that they were living by male values and male standards?

Beginning a study is relatively easy: research, even into one's own origins, has an objective aspect, whatever the emotional drives which inspire it. But Elizabeth Fox-Genovese made some observations which seem to present us with a challenge—perhaps even with a kind of scholarly mandate. Awareness of diversity is healthy, she recognized, yet current trends in scholarship emphasize differences, thereby separating us from each other, distracting attention from our similarities, and hampering the search for a central focus in American history. For a quite basic reason, she urged scholars of women's history to explore not only particular pasts, but also shared experience. As she wrote in the *American Scholar*, each individual finds identity essentially in relationship to the group, indeed to the entire society.[3]

With its numerous ethnic groups, Texas is an especially promising field in which to search for women's shared experience. For obvious reasons, no single model is possible: as individuals the women of Texas differ from each other in race, ethnic background, and class. They differ, too, in the most basic of life experiences from the men of their respective groups, even while sharing many aspects of men's lives. For those of us who research, study, and write the history of women in Texas, the fact of women's differences and diversity raises a question which we cannot, and perhaps should not, avoid: in terms of personal identity and historical experience, what has it meant to women to be African American, Tejana, Angla, Native American—and Texan?

One approach to the diversity of Texas women is that taken by Ann Patton Malone.[4] In her cross-cultural study Malone has acknowledged similarities, examined differences, and sought points of contact between and among racial and ethnic groups for the frontier period. Studies of particular local areas could investigate the points at which cultures have clashed, as well as identify the times when they have cooperated and shared. Additional inquiries might ask whether black and Hispanic women have recognized common experiences with women of other groups; whether moments of genuine communication have occurred between the women of different cultures; whether men of either or both groups shared those times. Have Texas women sought to create consensus and compassion? If not, why not? In what ways have they failed? In what ways have they succeeded?

The recognition of our common experiences as women first and members of a particular group second carries certain personal risks. In order to find our shared values and experiences, we all must dare a

---

[3] Elizabeth Fox-Genovese, "Between Individualism and Fragmentation: American Culture and the New Literary Studies Race and Gender," *American Quarterly*, XLII (Mar., 1990).

[4] Ann Patton Malone, *Women on the Texas Frontier: A Cross-Cultural Perspective*, Southwestern Studies No. 70 (El Paso: Texas Western Press, 1983).

certain amount of self-revelation, accept the fact that we will very likely blunder against the etiquette and sensitivities of another culture and in doing so offend and be offended. Yet, without taking some chances, we can never learn, each and all of us, to claim the traditions of Kiowa and Caddo, Tejana and German, Czech, Italian, Greek, Angla. For in a very real sense, all these belong to us as *Texans*. As we work to understand historical uniqueness and differences, to define specific identities within a particular group, we surely will also find opportunities to seek a larger, basic experience that reaches beyond race, class, and ethnicity; what Fox-Genovese called the central focus within our diversity.

And what do we do with all these exciting papers and articles once we have researched and written them? Periodic conferences can allow us to share our findings, inspire additional questions for investigation, and develop a genuine field of Texas women's history. But except for copies which are exchanged upon request, conference presentations are limited in circulation and availability. Could Texas support its own journal for women's history? Or might Texas scholars participate in the publication of a regional journal in partnership with historians of women's history in other states? Does this create a threat of "ghettoization" for Texas women's history?

The production of significant amounts of research in Texas women's history leads inevitably to a larger issue, one which must, sooner or later, affect the profession as a whole: at some point—and not only in Texas—knowledge of women's lives and experience must be integrated into historical studies in general, into urban history, labor history, and church history, into political, economic, and even military history. As Fane Downs has written in a bibliographic article, Texas women's history must be "mainstreamed."[5] On many, perhaps most, occasions women and men have worked together, men in formal and publicly accepted tasks, women usually in more or less supportive areas "behind the scenes," but no less significant or essential. For a genuine understanding of Texas, the two must be combined into the whole, complete history which they compose.

[5] Fane Downs, "Texas Women: History at the Edges," in *Texas Through Time: Evolving Interpretations*, eds. Walter L. Buenger and Robert A. Calvert (College Station: Texas A&M University Press, 1991), 81–101.